Growing Up
Smart and Happy

Other books by Julius Segal:

SLEEP (with Gay Gaer Luce)
INSOMNIA (with Gay Gaer Luce)
A CHILD'S JOURNEY (with Herbert Yahraes)

Growing Up Smart & Happy

৶ৎ JULIUS SEGAL
ZELDA SEGAL

McGraw-Hill Book Company
New York   St. Louis   San Francisco   Hamburg   Mexico   Toronto

1 2 3 4 5 6 7 8 9 D O C D O C 8 7 6 5

ISBN 0-07-056057-9

LIBRARY OF CONGRESS CATALOGING IN PUBLICATION DATA
Segal, Julius, 1924–
Growing up smart and happy.
1. Child rearing.   2. Academic achievement.   3. Child
development.   I. Segal, Zelda.   II. Title.
HQ769.S395   1985   649'.1   84–5683
ISBN 0–07–056057–9

Book design by Victoria Wong

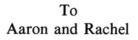

To
Aaron and Rachel

‿᠊ᢅ Contents

❧ Preface

"What do I want for my children? I want they should be happy—
a success in life." Those words were spoken often by our parents
and many of their contemporaries as they surveyed the futures of
their young. In equating well-being with success, they were anticipating by many decades today's insights by experts in human development. They somehow knew inwardly that happiness and fulfillment
often depend on competence and achievement of the potential that
lies within.

The focus of parents today appears to be strikingly similar to
that of our own mothers and fathers. In recent years we have talked
to numerous parents, and they have asked us hundreds of questions
about their children. A surprising number have shown an abiding
concern with the intellectual development of the young—how children acquire knowledge, and how they use it to achieve success
and contentment.

What is intelligence? Can it change over time? How can I foster
my child's creativity? What effects does marital discord have on a
child's school performance? How do I know for sure if my child
is a slow learner? Is it harmful to put kids under constant pressure
to work hard and achieve? Such questions mirror a widely shared
yearning to help our children grow up smart, independent, satisfied
adults.

The reader will find these questions and many more like them
posed in the pages of this book. The answers given are based on
the results of painstaking work by researchers studying the ways
a child's mind develops, and on our own first-hand experience in
helping children and their families. Such information is typically

reported in textbooks and technical journals and read primarily by students and professionals—so it remains well hidden from public view. We have attempted here to make that information understandable and meaningful. The book grew out of the conviction that parents, teachers, doctors, and all those who deal with children would profit from having distilled for them what is known about the forces affecting children's intellectual development.

Helping our children grow up smart and happy, however, requires not only concrete information but a reservoir of inspiration and insight as well. Facts alone often do not yield the insights we so often need in rearing our young. Interspersed throughout the book, therefore, are relevant observations and suggestions arising from actual experience as well as from research data. The sources for these items vary—among them poets, philosophers, child-care experts, case history files, writers, and children themselves. Such material is intended as a valuable counterpoint to the questions and answers forming the backbone of this book.

A carefully prepared index appears at the end of the book. Readers will find it useful in identifying those pages that address questions of particular interest.

Our intent is to convey important outcomes and implications of broad areas of research rather than to identify the specific findings of individual studies. The material in this book, therefore, is often based on a synthesis of findings by a number of investigators. The major sources used are listed at the close.

Tom Quinn and Elsa Dixler, our editors, provided direction and guidance in rich measure, all of it with great wisdom and patience throughout the years of the book's development.

The task of producing this book could not have been completed without the financial support provided by Patricia van A. Kind, and by the William T. Grant Foundation—whose president, Robert J. Haggerty, M.D., was a source of generous encouragement and assistance.

Julius Segal
Zelda Segal

Bethesda, Md.

Growing Up
Smart and Happy

CHAPTER ONE

❧ Opening Bell: Three Guiding Themes

Marcia is a bright and eager eight-year-old who absorbs information like a sponge. She is a marvelous student, motivated to do her best in every task she undertakes. At home she is a joy to live with—cooperative, self-reliant, and kind. For her the world is a warm and exciting place, and each day is an adventure in learning.

Robert is a ten-year-old whose life seems to have reached a dead end. At school he is described as a "lost cause"—remote and disinterested, rarely undertaking his assignments or participating in class. Nothing his parents try to do helps motivate him, and his repeated failures only seem to deepen his growing sense of despair.

How did these children get that way? What determines the way a child's mind develops? What leads one child to be bright and another dull? Why is it that some children learn readily while others do so only with great difficulty? What causes one child to be focused on practical goals and achievement, another to be mired in self-depreciation and defeat?

This book is filled with detailed information on such issues. It will show that a child's intellectual development is the product of many forces—genetic inheritance, prenatal experiences, infantile attachments, parental approaches, familial dynamics, school environment, social pressures—the influences, in short, of both nature and nurture. The fabric of the child's mind contains many strands—and the chapters ahead will help sort them out.

The book will be most profitable, however, if the reader keeps in mind from the outset the three overriding themes embedded in its pages. These themes guided us in our work, and form an essential

1

backdrop for everything that follows. Indeed they became for us increasingly strong credos as we sifted through the mountains of material from which the book took shape.

FIRST: CHILDREN NEED THEIR CHILDHOOD

No one reading this book will be left in doubt about the importance of intellectual achievement in the life of the child. This emphasis, however, in no way weakens our conviction that children do best when they are allowed to experience the milestones of their development at the pace that nature intended. The chances of our young to flower intellectually and to achieve well-being are reduced when they are hurried and harried—when our zest for tangible evidence of success leads us to forget how important it is, in Rousseau's words, to "leave childhood ripen in children."

Consider these three cases from our own experience as psychologists:

- Nancy, a charming first-grader with average intelligence, is a bundle of nerves. She is being pushed mercilessly to learn the family's home computer. Her parents have read that most girls do not match their masculine peers in math—and they want to make sure, as her mother puts it, "that Nancy can qualify for the best college when the time comes."
- Bobby, an unusually bright fifth-grader, is failing miserably. He is chronically tired and anxious, drained by his demanding schedule of school assignments, library visits, cello lessons, and soccer practice. "We don't want him to miss a thing," says his father, who remains blind to the boy's stress and frustration.
- Marcia is a high school freshman whose teacher once described her as a "budding genius." That was the signal for her parents to insist that she skip a grade and plan to enter college a year earlier than usual. She seems lost and forlorn—pushed mercilessly to forget her interests in drama, her friends, and the boy on whom, her parents insist, she is "wasting her time." Marcia's rare non-homework hours are taken up by a tutor who is coaching her—three years in advance—to scale the heights of the Scholastic Aptitude Tests.

Such cases are not unique. Many children today are victims of an unfortunate trend to erase the precious distinctions of yesteryear between childhood and adulthood. "Once parents struggled to preserve children's innocence," writes Marie Winn in her book, *Children without Childhood,* "to keep childhood a carefree golden age. The new era operates on the belief that children must be exposed early to adult experiences in order to survive."

The results are likely to be quite different from what is intended. "Children without childhood are tragic," wisely observed the Yiddish writer Mendele Mocher Sefarim. For numerous youngsters—as the cases just cited demonstrate—a hurry-up childhood may spell not only a loss in well-being, but an erosion of the capacities to handle the stresses they will encounter in the years ahead.

Many ambitious and competitive parents seem intent on rearing a generation of "superbabies"—young geniuses whose brain power is pushed to the limit from the moment they leave the womb. Instead of happily playing with their toddlers, today's mothers and fathers grimly spend their often limited parenting time priming them for their future academic careers.

"I want to make sure my child gets into the very best nursery school," a neighbor explained to us. And indeed many such schools now have entrance requirements that, in their own way, are as stringent as those of elite, Ivy League universities. Another young mother is anxiously tutoring her four-year-old in vocabulary because "next year it's make-or-break time for getting into our neighborhood's private kindergarten."

The frantic push to bypass childhood has even begun to deface the summers of our young. For today's children, school vacation no longer seems a time for freedom and privacy, for the lazy daydreams that so richly nourished us as children. Instead it is a time for action—for computer camps, tennis "clinics," or stepped-up sessions with the child's very own vocational counselor. The summer agendas for tiny tots on our street are awesome. They include foreign language lessons, scrupulously programmed museum tours, remedial reading classes, and tutoring in long division.

It is true enough, as Chapter 3 will show, that even very young babies are more receptive to learning than we had ever imagined. But in attempting to prematurely advance the child's intellectual skills, we are bucking an inexorable tide—the built-in biological timetable of human development. The flowering of children's capacities depends on the growth of the brain and nervous system. There are wide individual differences in the pace of that growth, and parents can only frustrate and confuse children by trying to force it.

Psychologist David Elkind, in his book called *The Hurried Child,* reports that a sizable number of youngsters are in the care of clinical psychologists today because they were pushed relentlessly to learn things at too early an age. Such children, Elkind believes, are victims of a "shrinking childhood," and the stresses they endure often emerge in the guise of physical symptoms. The once four-year-old hellion is now a four-year-old with a headache, and pediatricians now encounter many seven- and eight-year-olds with the classic symptoms of adult depression—low mood, apathy, self-derogation, and even suicidal fantasies.

This book, despite its emphasis on intellectual prowess and accomplishment, should not be read as a charter for dispensing with the growing-up process of children. Youngsters need opportunities to play as well as work, to dream as well as do. They need unstructured and unprogrammed time in which to try out new skills—to make mistakes without being criticized, to learn on their own terms and at their own speed. Indeed children are most likely to become successful adults if they are left with their childhood intact.

SECOND: CHILDREN NEED SOMEONE WHO REALLY CARES

Uvaldo Palomares was his name—a thoroughly deprived child in a large and desperately poor migrant worker family. He ricocheted from one impoverished school to another, leaving behind a record of chronic failure. Eventually he was considered for placement in a class for the mentally retarded.

Then, during his third year of repeating the second grade, he was on the playground one day playing marbles with a group of children. A teacher had apparently been watching him as he won all the marbles from his playmates. After the game was over, she moved in and sat down beside him. "You know," she said, "any kid who is smart enough to play marbles as well as you do is smart enough to learn to read." And so she began to teach him, convincing him all the while that he could "make it."

Uvaldo's feelings about himself changed. He remembers vividly the enormous exhilaration he felt at having a teacher who was convinced he could learn, and determined that he would succeed. She had taken hold of him—and she was not about to let go until he realized her expectations. Uvaldo is now a successful California psychologist, saved from a lifetime of wasted potential by an adult who really cared.

The story of Uvaldo is a reminder of the transforming power

of even a single committed adult in the life of a child. Today's emphasis on the mechanics of learning—on programmed instruction, computer technology, and electronic brains—should not cause us to forget that it is still human beings who hold the key to unleashing our children's potential.

The theme is dramatically evident in the lives of children, much like Uvaldo, described by University of Minnesota psychologist Norman Garmezy as "invincible." These are children who somehow succeed in life despite enormous roadblocks in their path. They do not break down despite early years filled with an avalanche of stress and trauma. Somehow they thrive—even though their parents may be mentally ill, they live in poverty, and they suffer profound bereavement and pain. They do well in school, assume roles of leadership, flower and succeed when they might well be expected to wither and fail. Here are the stories of two such children:

- Danny was born in poverty and raised in violence. At five he was abandoned by his chronically depressed mother, and for many years afterward subjected to the alcoholic rages of an uncaring father. In the foster home that finally took Danny in, he was abused relentlessly, and more than once his "punishments" led to the hospital emergency room.
- Fred is a child of status and wealth whose parents fought viciously throughout his young life. No day passed without screams, curses, and beatings—until one Sunday morning he watched in frozen horror as his father's life ended with the blasts of a revolver smoking in his mother's hand. Soon afterward Fred became the ward of an uncle whose strange friends—gamblers, racketeers, prostitutes—passed through his young life in an endless procession.

By all the usual standards, these children should have become psychological casualties, emotionally scarred for life by the trauma they suffered. But remarkably, the opposite is true. Danny is a well-adjusted young man, now living with a benevolent aunt committed to his welfare. He is enjoying the rewards of academic success, and zestfully is planning a career in computer programming. Fred, now sharing a house with friends, is about to begin his studies at Yale. Inspired by the proddings and praise of a math teacher who virtually became his surrogate parent, Fred is the recent winner of a nationwide talent hunt for "scientists of the future."

Such resilient children appear to gather strength from charismatic figures who "turn them on" to life's possibilities. Sometimes, but not always by any means, it is a mother or father who fills the role. Studies show, for example, that the emotional scars caused by one psychotic parent can be prevented if the child finds a strong ally in the other parent who is stable and healthy. Most often, however, children are likely to draw strength from a more distant member of the extended family, or from someone altogether outside it.

A child's inspirational figure can be an uncle, or an aunt like Danny's. She resolutely held him responsible for meeting high standards of school performance and personal behavior—but at the same time, she put no limits on her encouragement and love for him. The person can be a playmate's parent, a physician, coach, clergyman—anyone who communicates a sense of protection and devotion, and thereby becomes the child's psychological anchor in a sea of stress.

In the lives of many children—like Uvaldo and Fred—it is a teacher who manages to turn the tide from self-loathing and defeat to self-confidence and victory. University of California sociologist Jane Mercer has found many cases among Southern California Chicanos who, as a result, have bucked the tide and succeeded. "Almost inevitably when you begin to talk to them about their early life," Mercer observes, "they will mention that there was a teacher at some point who convinced them they were competent even though the system was saying 'no.' "

Strengthened by the presence of someone who really cares, children grow up believing they can influence the course of their lives. They operate with what psychologists call an "internal locus of control," meaning the conviction that success depends on factors inside themselves—their own abilities and efforts—and not on outside factors such as luck or "the breaks." As a result they tend to gladly accept responsibility for their own fate. Fortified by the belief that life can be mastered and controlled, they see themselves not as victims but as victors, confident about their ability to succeed no matter what crises might come their way.

"All children," says Cornell psychologist Urie Bronfenbrenner, "need someone around who is crazy about them." Such love is unconditional. It does not depend on the child's IQ score, verbal fluency, memory, temperament, or attractiveness—and it does not wax and wane in response to the child's day-to-day behavior.

When we were children, it was relatively easy to find such charismatic figures within the large extended family or the closely knit neighborhood that surrounded us. Today it is more difficult to find similar resources—now called "social supports" by mental health professionals. But in our often impersonal society, these psychological lifelines are, if anything, more important than ever for our children. Renowned psychoanalyst Erik Erikson believes that strong identity figures give the child a chance to absorb "something which most individuals who survive stress and remain sane take for granted most of the time." It is a feeling of optimism and trust, the assumption that "somebody is there," without which no one can endure—much less succeed.

THIRD: IT IS NEVER TOO LATE FOR CHILDREN TO CHANGE

The boy, now a senior in secondary school, has been given a doctor's certificate stating that a "nervous breakdown" forces him to leave school. As a young child, he spoke late. He has no friends, and his teachers regard him as a problem: "mentally slow, unsociable, and adrift in his foolish dreams." The father is ashamed not only of his son's poor adjustment to school but of his lack of athletic ability as well. The boy's parents simply regard him as "different." Why else would he have such odd mannerisms, make up his own religion, and constantly chant hymns to himself?

This case history is of a young child growing up into a life not of maladjustment and suffering but of triumph and achievement. His name: Albert Einstein.

Thirty years ago, we psychologists believed that such case histories were an oddity—that a child's personality was laid down early in life, and that after the first few years, the chances for significant change were slim. Today we know better. The life histories of thousands of children now prove that the drama of human development can take unexpectedly happy turns until the very end.

Findings from numerous studies now reveal the magnificent capacity of our young to recover from early problems and setbacks. Even youngsters who seem certain to be headed for trouble can ultimately emerge as wholesome and productive adults. In one project, Garmezy followed up children who, judged by both their heredity and early background, seemed virtually certain to develop serious mental illness such as schizophrenia. It turned out, however, that only about 10 percent broke down, while the large majority grew up without encountering major difficulties.

Other projects, tracking children into their adult lives, show similarly that it is next-to-impossible to predict from the way children behave in the opening years how they will turn out as adolescents or adults. Unforeseen events and relationships will in many cases produce striking changes in the patterns of behavior that give so many parents early cause for concern. Difficult children—stubborn, aggressive, unmotivated—often change course and suddenly blossom into mature and competent adolescents. Nonachievers become achievers, "budding delinquents" become responsible citizens, and selfish and uncaring kids become scrupulous in their concern for others. Even children who show signs of malignant behavior disorders may turn out to be perfectly normal.

One of the most startling about-faces in personality has been observed among young adults who seemed badly maladjusted even as adolescents. In a study at Berkeley by psychologist Jean Walker Macfarlane, nearly 170 boys and girls were observed from shortly after birth until they were eighteen years old, and then observed again at the age of thirty. Macfarlane found that even the most troubled adolescent—a failure in school, unsuccessful in social contacts, unpopular, and despondent—may turn into a happy, successful, well-liked, and highly respected adult. Indeed about half the subjects were living far richer and more productive lives as adults than could ever have been predicted from their adolescent personalities.

One man, for example, held back several times in elementary school, had not graduated from high school until he was almost nineteen. His IQ over the years had lagged well behind the average for his age. He had shown little interest in studies, school activities, or people. His school recommended against his trying to go to college. The research staff itself saw him as a chronic misfit, a "sideliner." But twelve years later he had become a talented environmental designer, a good father, an active worker in community affairs. Similarly, an adolescent described as a "listless oddball" had become a successful architect and model husband. And a girl who was expelled from school at sixteen and a boy expelled at fifteen—for failing grades and misbehavior—later developed into "wise, steady, understanding parents."

What triggers such dramatic changes?

Some children are just naturally "late bloomers." It seems to their parents to take them an eternity to become motivated and find themselves. Moreover, early troubles may actually be a spur to later achievement. Many children who endure difficulties and confusion are strengthened as a result by gaining greater insight and becoming more "seasoned." Indeed experts in child development have concluded that for some children, learning to handle a certain amount of stress early in life may be essential preparation for success in coping with later conflicts and crises.

Harvard psychologist Jerome Kagan likens the developing personality of a child to sand on a beach. Every day another wave comes up and moves it again. "There is much more change than we once thought," says Kagan, "and the child is much more resilient."

Today's studies of invincible children are causing, in the words of Penn State University psychologist Richard Lerner, "a revolution in our idea of the child." The image of weakness and fragility is giving way to one of strength and adaptability. For us the result should be renewed confidence and optimism about the destinies of our young. Too many parents live in fear that every stressful crisis in their child's life will result in psychological disaster. Such anxieties are unwarranted—and in fact might only increase the child's sense of vulnerability. "We need an emphasis on triumph, not tragedy," says Jesse Jackson, "on resiliency, not relinquishment."

This book will call attention to the many roadblocks that can impede our children's capacity to achieve their potential. In fact as the very next chapter makes clear, when babies leave their home in the womb, they may have already been exposed to an environment that can slow up their early development. But the message of long-range, follow-up research is clear: It pays to be patient—to be optimistic about our children's potential and to convey that optimism. Youngsters have a marvelous capacity to recover even from serious problems and setbacks. Our own confidence in them is likely to be contagious—and help smooth their journey to a successful life.

CHAPTER TWO

৩ Intellectual Development in the Womb

Little controversy remains about when the forces of heredity begin to wield their power over a child's destiny. At the instant of conception, flesh takes shape from flesh, and the genetic material transmitted by mother and father forms a blueprint of the future. Into those microscopic genes there is programmed not only the child's ultimate physical characteristics—eye and hair color, body build, skin pigmentation, facial features—but also personality trends and the range of the child's intellectual potential.

But what about the other half of the human development equation? When does environment begin to exert *its* influence on the child's traits and capacities?

Most people think of environmental forces as operating at home, at school, on the playground—anywhere that children interact with people and things in the world about them. Early experiences with mother and father, family dynamics, the influences of friends, the quality of teachers and schools—these are the factors that usually come to mind.

All these are important, of course—but they are in fact late entries in the environmental ledger of a child's life. The environment, like heredity, begins to exert its influence much earlier, at the very start of life's odyssey, when the speck of matter that will one day become a child is just beginning to unfurl in the womb.

Over the approximately 280 days of prenatal development, the initial squirming bit of flesh undergoes a remarkable series of changes. During the first eight weeks—between the instant of fertilization and the moment that a recognizable embryonic human being is formed—the infant-to-be increases nearly 2 million percent in

10

size. Alterations in the size, shape, and type of body cells take place with remarkable speed; their number increases from 1 to 26 billion during the nine months of gestation. Body structures and systems increase in bulk and complexity.

All the while, the central nervous system—the machine that will ultimately fire the child's intellectual capacities—is taking root. During each minute in the womb, the brain of the infant-to-be gains tens of thousands of new cells. As early as seven weeks after conception, some sections of the developing brain can already be discerned, and the nerves that feed electrical impulses from the brain to various parts of the body are in place and beginning to work. The budding arms of the fetus will now move in response to tapping on the sac that protects it. By the time the fetus is twenty weeks old, the nervous system is mature enough to make the developing baby sensitive to touch, pain, and changes in temperature. Surprisingly, the brain waves of a thirty-week-old fetus look the same just prior to being born as they do in the real world. The brain is clearly already "turned on" long before normal delivery.

The message from research on prenatal life is clear: Starting at the very instant of conception, the development of a child's intellectual powers can be affected by the quality of environment in the womb. Good prenatal health care and the avoidance of such pollutants as alcohol, drugs, or cigarette smoke are not just casual choices for expectant mothers. The tiny developing brain can be damaged or nurtured, the child's ability to learn threatened or enhanced, much earlier than many of us had ever imagined. Indeed it is now more apparent than ever that the quality of an entire life may be shaped significantly by the degree to which a child-in-the-making is valued and protected during its remarkable sojourn in the womb.

The pages that follow offer convincing evidence that the period between conception and birth is more than an inconsequential overture to a child's life. When newborns are cast adrift from mother's body and emerge into the real world, they leave behind an environment that has exerted enormous impact on the future power and potential of their minds. How smart a child actually grows up to be may be influenced at the very opening of life, in the dark and private classroom of the womb.

Our new knowledge about the importance of the prenatal environment places an awesome responsibility on prospective parents.

But it also gives them a special opportunity to take positive steps—before their babies are even born—to see that they get the best possible start in life. Unlike their mothers and grandmothers before them, pregnant women today know—or should know—that they have the power to avoid many potential developmental problems in their unborn babies if they think very carefully about what they take into their bodies. The old adage "you are eating for two" must now be expanded to include such activities as drinking and smoking as well.

This new awareness means that pregnant women may have to make some sacrifices for their baby's sake by giving up their cigarettes, evening cocktails, or other indulgences. But that seems a small price to pay for the peace of mind that comes from knowing that mothers are ensuring the birth of healthy human beings—babies who are receptive to learning, and capable of richly fulfilling the promises encoded in their genes.

Can the unborn child actually learn in the womb?

Not if you mean absorbing the dictionary or Shakespeare by having father read them aloud, or learning to like classical music by hearing it played constantly. But in their warm, moist world, even young fetuses are capable of some surprisingly accomplished responses to outside stimulation.

At twenty weeks, the fetus already begins to make the sucking responses that will sustain life later at mother's breast, and the grasping reflex of early infancy is already in place. The heartbeat changes when the mother is exposed to loud noise such as a ringing telephone or music, and when she is keyed up, hers isn't the only heart that pounds faster. Deep inside the womb, the new baby is beginning to exercise all of its complex machinery for absorbing information from the outside world.

As the normal time for birth approaches, a real person has emerged. A mind, however primitive in form, *is* present . . . the infant we encounter at the moment of birth is distinct from all others, with a brain already different from others.

Mortimer G. Rosen
"The Secret Brain: Learning Before Birth"

Do babies have any thoughts before birth?

There is no way of knowing, of course, what the mental life of a developing fetus might be, but there is evidence that they do already dream. Even very premature infants spend an enormous amount of time in a state known as rapid-eye-movement (REM) sleep—a period of brain activity associated with vivid dreaming in children and adults.

When we dream, our brain re-processes previous experiences—often the events in our lives the day before. While no fetus or newborn can dream as adults do, in complicated and elaborate scenarios, surely the fetus does already have some sensations to re-experience. These might include, for example, the sounds it hears, or changes in position when mother moves about. The result could well be those primitive REM periods in which the fetus is flooded with diffuse sensations that are the first raw material for mental activity and thought.

Keep in mind that the brain develops through activity. It needs stimulation for growth. Today some researchers believe that the purpose of REM sleep before birth is to provide the "exercise" the young nervous system needs for it to mature and grow. Later, of course, experiences in the outside world will furnish that exercise in abundance. In the relatively monotonous and protected world inside, however, the first stirrings of REM activity in the brain may serve as a precious substitute.

Is the fetus pretty well protected from the hazards of the outside world?

Only from mechanical ones—from being shaken up, for example, or from loud sounds or intensive light. For these, the liquid environment of the uterus provides an effective buffer and cushion.

But the developing fetus is afforded little protection from the dangers that reach it through its physical connections with mother. The alcohol the mother drinks, the coffee she sips, the cigarette smoke she inhales, the viruses in her bloodstream, even the chemicals released by emotional stress can all pose serious threats.

That is because mother and child are actually not separated. True enough, the mother's placenta does prevent mother's blood from thoroughly mixing with the infant's. But it is by no means a barrier, and the baby's body, therefore, is not isolated from the world outside. Moreover, neither is the rapidly developing brain, which can be easily damaged if hostile forces attack it. The nine-month prenatal experience turns out to be one of the most sensitive periods in the child's intellectual development.

ﾟ₰§   At few if any other times in the life span are hereditary potentials so influenced by environmental conditions as they are during the prenatal period.

Elizabeth Hurlock
Child Development

Could something as remote as cigarette smoking by the expectant mother actually affect the unborn child's future intellectual powers?

There are indications that it could. One research team studied 17,000 children born to women who had smoked ten or more cigarettes a day throughout pregnancy. They found an apparent slow-down in the youngsters' intellectual development. When these children were tested in the primary grades—at age seven and again at eleven—they were three- to five-months behind expected levels in reading, mathematics, and overall scholastic ability. Researchers have also found a possible link between heavy maternal smoking and the learning problems of hyperactive children.

The exact long-term effects of heavy smoking by the mother on the child's intellectual development are still unclear—but scientists do know that smoking during pregnancy can cause physical harm to the growing fetus and its rapidly developing brain. And when the body and brain are threatened, normal mental development is likely to be threatened as well.

ﾟ₰§   Cigarette smoking during pregnancy has a significant and adverse effect upon the well-being of the fetus, the health of the newborn baby, and the future development of the infant and child.

U.S. Surgeon General
Smoking and Health

What kinds of physical damage can be caused by pregnant women who smoke?

For one thing, the babies of heavy smokers grow much more slowly while in the uterus. At three to five months of age, babies born to smokers are, on the average, 13 ounces lighter and 1 centimeter shorter than babies born to nonsmokers. This lag in weight and height has persisted in some children even when they were well into the primary grades.

Moreover, bacterial infections in the amniotic fluid surrounding the fetus are more frequent among women who smoke. During the final weeks of pregnancy, infected fluid may enter the lungs of the fetus, causing pneumonia and premature birth. Smoking has been implicated, too, in problems of blood compatibility, leading to malformation of the fetal heart and other organs; such problems occur 80 percent more frequently among expectant mothers who smoke than among those who do not.

Even more tragic, many children will not survive their mother's nicotine pleasures. Evidence has begun to accumulate that heavy smoking is a significant cause of fatal birth defects. Investigators in a nationwide American study of more than 50,000 pregnancies estimate that over 10 percent of all infant deaths can be accounted for by mothers' smoking during their pregnancies. Mothers who smoke half a pack or more per day double the risk of early miscarriage, and significantly increase the risk of premature delivery as well.

It seems clear enough that smoking during pregnancy can adversely affect the health of future babies—and, therefore, their mental capacities.

How can puffing on a cigarette by a mother possibly affect the unborn child?

Very easily: The carbon monoxide in the inhaled cigarette smoke disrupts the maternal oxygen delivery system. Carbon monoxide passes freely across the placenta and is quickly absorbed into the fetus's blood, thereby reducing the amount of oxygen available. Moreover, smoking constricts the blood vessels and arteries in the uterus, decreasing the flow of blood and further depriving the fetus of the oxygen and nutrients essential for healthy development.

Does it make a difference how much the woman smokes?

Apparently so—especially after the fourth month of pregnancy. For example, women who smoke most heavily after that time tend to have babies who, on the average, weigh the least at birth.

What happens if a woman gives up cigarettes only after learning that she's pregnant?

At least one study has suggested that it helps. When women quit smoking just after the first month of pregnancy, the risks of bleeding complications, low-birth-weight babies, and infant deaths were about the same as for women who had never smoked.

But keep in mind that picking up cigarettes right after the child is born threatens to reestablish the new arrival's problem. The milk of breastfeeding mothers who smoke contains lower levels of vitamin C than the milk of mothers who don't. Children raised by parents who smoke have a higher incidence of respiratory problems—bronchitis, pneumonia—and are more likely to have their tonsils and adenoids removed.

Developing fetuses and newborns just don't have a "no smoking" area to which they can escape. The safest course surely is to drop the habit altogether on behalf of your child.

Do the strictures that apply to smoking also apply to drinking?

If anything, even more so.

The National Institute on Alcohol Abuse and Alcoholism points to heavy drinking by pregnant women as the third leading cause of mental retardation—and one that is completely preventable. Moreover, the more the mother drinks, the greater the risk to her unborn child.

≈ᢤ   Our mothers' wombs the houses be
Where we are dressed for this short comedy.
Orlando Gibbons
On the Life of Man

What is the likely outcome if a mother goes on a rare drinking binge?

Potentially disastrous. The maximum level of alcohol in the blood at any one time may be more crucial in causing fetal defects than the total amount of alcohol consumed during pregnancy. That is true, for example, in the early stages of pregnancy when the baby is being formed. Now a new study suggests that even an isolated heavy drinking episode by a woman in the last three months of pregnancy can damage the brain of the unborn baby more than small daily doses of alcohol.

The alcohol level in the bloodstream of the fetus is identical to that in its mother's, and so any body systems under rapid development at the time of heavy alcohol use are likely to be affected. However, since the precise timing of specific developmental stages in the womb cannot be predicted, neither can the specific effects of high blood levels of alcohol at any particular time. A heavy bout of drinking is a game of Russian roulette, with the baby's body and brain as stakes.

What actually happens when mothers-to-be drink? Is it as if the unborn child is guzzling a few, too?

Exactly. Alcohol freely crosses the placenta from mother to child. The fetal liver, like the adult's, metabolizes the alcohol—that is, breaks it down into chemical components that the body can handle. But that tiny liver is not completely developed; it can handle the alcohol at only about half the rate that the adult's liver can. The upshot is that alcohol remains in the fetal system longer than in the mother's. So if the mother is drunk, the fetus is drunk, too—and will remain that way for a longer period of time.

Knowledge of the threat posed by alcohol is by no means new. As early as 1800, there were reports of abnormalities in the growth of children of alcoholic mothers. Even then there were expressions of concern that the heavy consumption of gin among English women—referred to as "mother's ruin"—was the cause of dwarfism in their offspring.

In the past few years, however, the occasion for concern has heightened. A new and ugly diagnostic category has entered the lexicon of medical personnel who attend the delivery of newborns: *the fetal alcohol syndrome,* or FAS. It is a pattern of physical and mental abnormalities afflicting from a third to a half of all infants born to mothers who drink substantially throughout their pregnancy.

Babies born with FAS are shorter and lighter in weight than normal babies. They have abnormally small heads, facial irregularities, joint and limb abnormalities, heart defects, and poor coordination due to damage suffered by the central nervous system. Serious problems in breathing and in brain development are common. These children are almost always mentally retarded, and victims also of a number of behavioral problems such as hyperactivity, nervousness, poor attention span, and sleep disturbances. Moreover, the defects appear to be lasting: Deficiencies in height, weight, head size, and intelligence of children with FAS are still apparent at seven years of age.

⮑ Agony . . . is given in strange ways to children.

Flannery O'Connor

Does the amount of drinking influence whether FAS will develop?

The risk increases with the amount of alcohol consumed. Certain FAS symptoms are found in 11 percent of the infants born to women who take between two and four drinks a day. Having six drinks a day raises the risk considerably, and drinking above this level puts the risk at 50 percent.

Other factors can, of course, also play an important role. The mother's blood alcohol levels—at any level of drinking—are known to be variable, depending on her genetic predisposition. New evidence indicates that fetal resistance to alcohol and its damaging effects is also determined genetically—although the mechanisms of such resistance have yet to be identified. Despite inherited variations in susceptibility, it is abundantly clear that babies can be made to be born with the ravages of alcoholism—and that the choice is the mother's.

Doesn't it matter at all whether the baby's father drinks?

For years it was assumed that even if a man drinks heavily, it would not interfere with his ability to sire healthy offspring. Now this assumption has been called into question. Evidence from animal studies hints that heavy doses of alcohol in the male can lead to spontaneous abortions, and perhaps to birth defects as well, presumably by damaging the genes in the sperm.

Researchers have conducted a preliminary study of men who drink heavily. They followed fifty-two men who were taking at least four drinks a night six weeks prior to conception. The offspring of these men included a number of spontaneous abortions and infants with birth defects. The investigators did not, however, rule out other factors that might have led to the results. The data so far, in other words, are not thoroughly convincing. But still, a prudent man would think twice about drinking heavily in anticipation of fatherhood.

How important is the mother's diet?

Doctors have long assumed that pregnancy places extra demands on the mother's body—but they believed that the nutritional needs of the infant would somehow get first priority, even if it were at the mother's expense. Now we know otherwise: The development of the fetus and the growth and intellectual maturation of the newborn depend to some degree on maternal diet.

In one survey covering ten states, researchers found that the infants and young children of mothers undernourished during pregnancy were well below average on such measures as birth weight, height, estimated brain weight, and head circumference. Other investigators have linked malnutrition during the mother's pregnancy to weaknesses in the development of the baby's central nervous system and brain. Such impairments cannot help but diminish the child's later ability to learn. And in fact, reading disabilities and other learning disorders have been found at an atypically high rate among children whose mothers were malnourished during pregnancy. Mother's food, it seems, may literally be baby's "food for thought" later on.

◄§ Inadequate nutrition results in stunting, reduced resistance to infectious disease, apathy, and general behavioral unresponsiveness.

In a fundamental sense, it occupies a central position in the multitude of factors affecting the child's development and functional capacity.

Herbert G. Birch
American Journal of Public Health

Can certain foods be harmful?

There is no apparent reason why mothers-to-be should totally inhibit their yearning for pickles, or pizza, or strawberries, or whatever triggers their appetite. But scientists do suspect that one food substance—caffeine—may be harmful. Coffee, especially in abundance, is suspect, and so, for that matter are tea, cola, and even cold remedies that contain caffeine.

Like actual drugs, caffeine crosses the placenta and reaches the fetus. A recent concern of the federal Public Health Service is the possible link between caffeine and physical malformations or delayed bone development at birth. The concern grew out of research conducted by the Food and Drug Administration (FDA), which found that caffeine in large doses did cause developmental problems in rat fetuses.

The FDA is trying to find out if caffeine causes the same problems in humans. Right now the evidence is inconclusive—but the FDA has been sufficiently concerned about a possible danger to issue a warning to pregnant women either to avoid caffeine-containing products altogether or to use them sparingly until the riddle is solved. As this book went to press, the issue was being reevaluated through further studies of rats whose drinking water contains caffeine.

A prudent and protective mother-to-be will want to put caffeine on her list of unnecessary substances which she should avoid.

Jere E. Goyan
Former Commissioner
U.S. Food and Drug Administration

What about prescribed and over-the-counter drugs? Are they as risky as alcohol for the expectant mother?

There is no room for doubt. Their effects can be devastating, as the world learned nearly two decades ago when the sedative *thalidomide*, given to pregnant women, produced a host of babies doomed to deformity. The birth of thousands of legless or armless newborns revealed that even a routine sedative can harm the fetus.

Today we know that a wide range of drugs can cause problems. Even such a seemingly harmless drug as *tetracycline*, an antibiotic commonly prescribed for colds and flu, appears to produce abnormalities of the baby's bones and teeth. Drugs used for the treatment of thyroid problems in pregnant mothers can result in goiter and other thyroid problems in the newborn child. Adrenal steroids can lead to a malformed palate, anticoagulants to fetal hemorrhage, and barbiturates to cataracts of the eyes. In addition to those drugs that are known to cause problems, many others may do so without our awareness. It is often very difficult to trace the cause of a birth defect after the fact. The thalidomide case was, after all, unusual; a large number of babies were born with similar deformities, and so it was relatively easy to find the link.

All this does not mean, of course, that if you ever took a drug during your pregnancy, your offspring would be harmed. A drug that may affect one fetus may not faze another. Countless babies whose mothers had taken all kinds of drugs have been born perfectly normal. What it does mean, however, is that with every drug you take—from aspirin to prescription medications—you are increasing the risk of damage to your unborn baby.

And keep in mind that drugs taken at the beginning of pregnancy can sometimes do the most harm because that is precisely when the baby's brain and vital organs are being formed.

"I will not permit my pregnant patients to take anything, not even vitamins," says one leading gynecologist in New York. "No drugs—unless the severity of symptoms very definitely indicates that a drug is essential and nothing else will do." Unfortunately, however, pregnant women generally continue to take more drugs than women who are not pregnant—and the variety of such drugs is increasing.

⋘ In man as in animals, the physical and mental structure can be deeply affected only while the processes of anatomical and physiological organization are actively going on; the biological system becomes increasingly resistant to change after it has completed its organization.

Réné Dubos
So Human an Animal

Can something even as mild as aspirin really harm the fetus?

Yes, it is possible. Regular users of large doses of aspirin appear more likely to suffer hemorrhages either before or just after giving birth; they also seem to experience more complicated deliveries and stillbirths compared to women who do not take aspirin. There is some evidence also that large and continuous doses of aspirin throughout pregnancy might result in low-birth-weight babies, and in an increased risk of fetal brain damage.

While it is true enough that such effects are uncommon, the fact remains that aspirin—like other drugs—is able to cross that porous placenta barrier, and thus muddy the chemical environment of the baby. A cautious decision would be to curtail aspirin use during pregnancy.

What is likely to happen to babies who are born to mothers addicted to hard drugs?

Such babies are born as drug addicts themselves. Women who have become users of heroin or morphine, for example, produce babies whose first requirement in life is a program of drug withdrawal. They come into the world with all the symptoms of a junkie suddenly removed from drugs: fever, trembling, convulsions, difficulty in breathing, vomiting. Some infants actually die during withdrawal. In these cases, it is the mother who has been the "pusher."

The severity of the infant's plight depends on the period of the mother's addiction, the size of her doses, and how soon before delivery she last took the drug. If the mother has stopped taking the drug several months before birth, the infant probably will not be born addicted.

Little is yet known about long-term effects. But some investigators do believe that the baby's severe reaction to mother's drugs can threaten the mother-infant attachment process, which is so important for normal development.

A newborn normally begins to form that special loving relationship with the mother by cuddling, gazing, and growing alert when held by her. But such normal responses are lacking in babies who are born addicted. On a widely used test of newborn behavior, the Brazelton Neonatal Behavior Assessment Scale, addicted newborns differed from normal arrivals in their responsiveness, degree of stimulation, irritability, and excitability. They weren't able to cuddle and respond to their mothers the way babies normally do. As a result, it was harder for the mothers to get to know their infants and to interact lovingly with them.

What is the verdict on marijuana?

The verdict is not entirely in, but investigators have already found that white blood cells taken from regular users of marijuana were less effective in fighting viruses in a test tube than were similar cells taken from nonusers. When the evidence is complete, marijuana is likely to be added to the list of noxious substances that can thwart a child's healthy intellectual development in the womb.

Is it wise to avoid x-rays while pregnant?

Some doctors advise their pregnant patients to avoid all exposure to x-rays, even for routine purposes such as dental treatment. Most authorities, however, believe that only the pelvic area needs to be protected. In either case, it is the amount of x-ray irradiation that is important. Large amounts—for example, the doses given to treat tumors—may readily injure the fetus or cause abortions, but small amounts are not likely to be harmful. Nevertheless, the wise expectant mother would not unnecessarily expose herself to x-rays.

What if an expectant mother is careful about what she does but not about what she thinks? Can a mother's thoughts cause defects in the unborn child?

No, although many people used to believe that they could. One popular folk theory held, for example, that if mother had a nasty thought at the instant of conception, the child would be born perverted in some way.

There is no direct physical connection between mother's brain and the baby—no nerve endings in the umbilical cord, for example. A pregnant woman's thoughts, therefore, cannot be transmitted to the fetus. But when mother's thoughts lead to emotional distress, that's another story.

Do you mean that if a mother becomes emotionally upset during pregnancy, that can affect her child's intelligence?

Babies born to mothers who are upset or anxious during much of their pregnancy appear more likely to be hyperactive, irritable, anxious, and underweight. They also tend to be more troublesome, given to irregular eating, excessive bowel movements, gas pains, sleep disturbances, and crying. Such problems can make them slower in acquiring skills than more contented children, and can affect their ability to learn, remember, and reason. And that's what intelligence is all about. Overall, they simply seem less bright than they actually are.

Over twenty-five years ago, researchers had already found that the movements of the fetus inside mother's belly increased significantly when she was experiencing emotional stress. While there are many exceptions, of course, "colicky" mothers run an increased risk of producing babies with colic—and such babies tend to find it difficult to engage in the learning process. The longer the mother is upset, the greater the potential impact on her child.

All of us can feel how our bodies change when we experience emotion. We blush, sweat, tremble, suffer shortness of breath and heart palpitations. Few of us, however, can imagine what powerful chemical changes take place underneath our skins at such times. Such emotions as fear, anxiety, anger, and depression activate the body's *autonomic nervous system*—that part of our nervous system not under voluntary control. Potent chemicals start moving into the bloodstream, and the adrenal glands begin secreting hormones that "rev up" the body to meet this stress.

This cauldron of chemical activity alters the components in the mother's blood—and, via the placenta, affects the blood chemistry of the fetus as well.

꿏 Prolonged maternal emotional stress during pregnancy—whether from marital difficulties, negative attitudes toward having a child, or catastrophic life events—may have enduring consequences for the child.

> Paul H. Mussen, John J. Conger
> and Jerome Kagan
> *Essentials of Child Development
> and Personality*

Is the connection between the mother's physical well-being and the baby's development just as strong as the emotional tie?

Even stronger. Indeed during pregnancy, the physical health of the mother is probably the most important factor in safeguarding the child's future potential.

The importance of steering clear of German measles, for example, turns out to be even more critical than many had assumed. If mother contracts the illness, the result for the fetus can be not only physical problems such as cataracts, heart abnormalities, or deafness, but also seriously retarded intellectual development. The disease does not have to be severe; even mild cases may produce tragic consequences. A number of cases of birth defects have been reported in babies whose mothers did not even know they had German measles.

Fortunately for today's parents, German measles can easily be prevented. Many doctors routinely administer a simple blood test to the pregnant woman or a woman considering pregnancy to see if her body has built up immunities against the disease. If she has, the chances are good that she will not contract the illness even if she is exposed to it. Women who are not immune and who are not yet pregnant can be innoculated against German measles; they should then wait at least two or three months before trying to conceive.

Don't make the tragic mistake a number of women have made by assuming you are immune because you *think* you had German measles once. You may have had something else with similar symptoms. Check it out. The stakes are just too high.

≈§ You are the bows from which your children as living arrows are sent forth.

Kahlil Gibran

Are there other maternal illnesses in the same league as German measles?

There are, but fortunately they are less common. One, for example, is *toxoplasmosis,* which has two suspected causes, both of which can easily be avoided: eating uncooked red meat and exposure to cat feces. It may seem farfetched, but pregnant women can protect their unborn children from hearing loss, eye problems, or even mental retardation by having their husbands change the litter box until after their child is born.

Syphilis, while less common today than in the past, still poses a strong threat to the child's developing mind. So does *toxemia,* a blood disorder characterized by high blood pressure, excessive fluid retention, and anemia. Scientists are now also exploring a possible link between birth defects and a number of viruses and infections from influenza to chicken pox. Some studies, for example, suggest that mothers who had the flu or other mild viral infections early in their pregnancy seem to be more likely to produce a child with learning difficulties. In the last months, a virus may lead to premature birth, putting the child at greater risk to learning problems.

All this does not mean that pregnancy is a nine-month obstacle course sure to trip up mother and child somewhere along the line. What it does mean is that prospective mothers should give their health top priority. It is a sign of your *own* intelligence if you make sure to have a checkup before you become pregnant, and then to get medical care as soon as you get sick. It is important also, of course, to be immunized against as many diseases as possible well before your future baby begins to take shape.

꿍 Few of us would accept old beliefs that if a pregnant woman listens to classical music throughout the course of her pregnancy she will have a child who appreciates fine music; or if she reads the Bible assiduously her child will exhibit high ethical standards; or that the presence on her newborn infant of a birthmark shaped like the head of a dog might be attributable to the mother being frightened by a dog in early pregnancy. However, it is now recognized that the prenatal organism is vulnerable to a variety of factors that influence the course of its development.

E. Mavis Hetherington and Ross D. Parke
Child Psychology: A Contemporary Viewpoint

What does research show about the effects on the baby of mother's age at pregnancy?

The statistical evidence suggests that babies born to mothers who are under twenty and over thirty are more vulnerable to physical and mental problems. It may be that among some very young women, the reproductive organs have not yet fully developed—and that among some older ones, these organs have already deteriorated to some degree. Keep in mind, however, that if mother exercises the kinds of prenatal care suggested throughout this chapter, the chances of running into problems are relatively small even if she happens to be unusually young or old to be having a child.

What about the process of birth itself? Can a child's potential be affected during delivery?

From the time the first contractions begin and the new baby's head begins to squeeze its way into the world, the tiny brain is vulnerable. Nevertheless, the vast majority of babies somehow manage to wriggle and squirm into the world—or even to be pulled into it by forceps—as healthy and normal human beings. But just as you can help see that your baby develops normally during pregnancy, you can help ensure that the end of the prenatal sojourn is a safe one. One step is for parents to enroll in a natural childbirth course. Mothers are then better prepared to experience the labor and delivery process with little or no help from drugs.

What effects do drugs taken just prior to delivery have on the baby?

They can slow the progress of labor. This increases the chances that the obstetrician will have to use a forceps, thereby raising the risk of injury to the baby.

Moreover, some anesthetics and drugs can slow mother's breathing, which diminishes the vital supply of oxygen to the baby. A heavy dosing of the mother with drugs may also overload the fetal bloodstream sufficiently to hamper the child's breathing. At birth, the brain of the baby vitally needs enough oxygen for it to function properly. Without that oxygen—the condition is called *anoxia*— some brain cells may actually die. Reading disorders, affecting some 10 percent of normally intelligent school-age children in the United States, have been linked to anoxia. Brief periods of asphyxiation at birth can produce significant mental impairment.

A sedative or pain reliever may not seem as if it can have much effect on a 135-pound woman, but it can on her 6-pound baby.

Not only does the baby get a proportionately larger dose, but it also takes a lot longer for the baby's body to be rid of the chemicals—several days, while mother's body may have it flushed out in several hours. Drugged babies will often be less alert and groggier at birth, unable to breathe or suck as readily. And they are more likely to have abnormal brain waves than nonsedated babies.

In general, such babies tend to perform less well on tests of perception, motor skills, and attentiveness than nondrugged babies. Newborns delivered from mothers who had been given a sedating drug within 90 minutes of delivery gazed less at pictures than babies delivered of mothers who had not been similarly drugged. Moreover, the closer to the time of delivery the drugs are administered, the less attentive the infant is likely to be. One study even suggests that children whose systems were slightly depressed by drugs at birth may not be as attentive as other children when they are one year old.

Keep in mind, too, that the drugs you take during labor can have a palpable effect on your initial relationship with your baby. Those precious and intimate bonds that help nourish the newborn's psyche are less likely to take shape when mother is still in a chemically induced haze.

We now have thousands of pain relievers that can make labor and delivery more comfortable. Unfortunately, not one of them is completely safe for the about-to-be-born child. What's more, with most of them, the more pain relief you get the greater the risk to the infant. In a sense you play a sort of trade-off game: mother's comfort for baby's safety.

Ronald E. Gots and Barbara A. Gots
Caring for Your Unborn Child

Are some kinds of pre-delivery drugs safer than others?

Yes, but none is altogether without risk. There are many types of drugs now available to women in labor, and some do seem to present fewer hazards to the baby than others. For example, an *epidural* anesthetic—a "spinal"—is generally considered to be the safest of the commonly used local anesthetics used during delivery since it does not appear to cross the placenta.

There may be a point in labor when the mother simply needs

or wants a drug. Check out the safety factors with your doctor beforehand, and remember: The less you take, the better.

Are drugs the only risks during delivery?

Unfortunately not. A number of natural complications can occur as well, posing the threat of neurological damage and arrested intellectual development. Difficulties can arise, for example, if the placenta separates prematurely from the uterus, or if it grows in the lower portion of the uterus, blocking the passageway through which the newborn must pass. A similar hazard occurs, too, if the umbilical cord precedes the baby through the uterine opening.

Do such complications occur frequently?

Happily, they are the exceptions rather than the rule. The vast majority of labors and births proceed normally. And even when complications do occur, most babies—90 percent of them—are born without damage or developmental problems.

Moreover, not *all* pregnant women who are exposed to the various other hazards described in this chapter will produce children with lagging intelligence. The large majority of babies born to mothers who smoke, drink, or become ill, for example, will escape unscathed. The difference may lie in the child's inborn physical constitution, which is inherited at conception. Some children, in other words, are genetically more vulnerable to damage than others from the very moment they begin to form.

One day your doctor may be able to give you a simple test to determine whether your unborn child is likely to be affected by the alcohol or drugs you consume, or the viruses you contract. For now, however, the science of prenatal birth defects is not sophisticated enough to pick out which fetuses are vulnerable. So all mothers should take prudent precautions in behalf of their progeny.

Suppose a new baby has been affected somehow. Are the problems irreversible?

By no means. This book will make abundantly clear that children have an amazing capacity to overcome obstacles and limitations, and this resilience is apparent from the very beginning.

Naturally, children who suffer massive brain damage at birth are not likely to graduate *cum laude,* and those with fetal alcohol syndrome can hardly be expected to keep pace with their sober peers in the nursery. Nevertheless, an amazing number of babies do bounce back over time. For example, if the degree of oxygen deprivation suffered by a newborn during delivery is only mild, the baby's difficulties—evidenced by lower IQ scores—tend to disappear later on. By the time such children are seven or eight, their IQs are usually equal to those of other children, especially if they have been raised in an enriching, supportive environment. That's usually the key: the kind of world the newborn inhabits.

A group of Hawaiian children impaired at birth were studied over a number of years. Some of the babies went on to live in highly unstable and oppressive environments with mothers who themselves were intellectually unstimulating. Others lived in a more stable and enriched setting. As time went on, the IQs of the latter group were not that much lower—only five to seven points—than those of children who had not been similarly impaired during their fetal life. By the age of ten, the beneficial impact of family environment had erased that of early damage. The effects of many early complications, in other words, can eventually be reversed if the baby's later experiences are good ones.

Despite the hopeful outlook, caring and loving parents-to-be should not ignore the dangers known to threaten the intellectual development of children before they even enter their new world.

CHAPTER THREE

∽§ The Infant: Ready and Able to Learn

"One great booming, buzzing confusion." A few decades ago, that is how psychologist William James described the world of the newborn. Most parents would assume that he was right. The infant emerges from the mother's womb looking totally disorganized and incompetent. Shriveled, cross-eyed, potbellied, and bow-legged, its head grotesquely oversized for the torso beneath it, the newborn seems altogether vulnerable. Psychologist Robert I. Watson acknowledged that "even a fond mother may experience a sense of shock at the first sight of the tiny, wizened, red creature that is her offspring."

Today we know that the infant's appearance is utterly deceiving. From careful laboratory studies of thousands of newborns, it is apparent that these are not the weak, passive, defenseless creatures we long assumed them to be. Instead they are much more advanced than we had ever dreamed. Armed with a nine-month preparatory experience in the womb, they arrive with an amazing array of capacities, talents, and skills already in place. And, although completely unfamiliar with their new world, they are able to respond in a remarkably organized and effective way to the barrage of stimulation from the environment.

The newborn brain has only a fourth of its eventual weight, but its total machinery is in place. Tightly packed together, all the nerve cells that a human being will ever have in life are there at birth. Newborns, therefore, are already highly responsive to stimulation through all senses. They can see, hear, and smell, and they are sensitive to pain, touch, and change in position. Moreover, they are capable of a surprising repertoire of activities: They can suck,

31

cry, squirm, cough, turn their heads, lift their chins, grasp objects placed in their palms.

Infants begin early to make amazingly fine discriminations. They can learn to distinguish between two notes on the musical scale, between colors, or between odors such as alcohol, garlic, and licorice. Indeed soon after birth, their sense of smell actually begins to play an important role in their social interactions. A baby only a few days old can smell the difference between mother's milk and the milk of another woman. The taste preferences of infants are equally pronounced. Offer new babies sugar water, and they will start sucking enthusiastically even though, a moment earlier, they may have brusquely rejected plain, unsweetened water. Given sweet fluids, infants suck more slowly and swallow more, as if to prolong the pleasurable experience; it takes only a few drops of sugar water on the tongue to make their hearts beat faster.

Most new parents are quick to recognize the outward physical growth of the infant. The baby's birth weight doubles in the first three months and triples in one year. By the end of the first year, the baby's height typically increases by almost 50 percent. But there are inward changes as well. Indeed much of the newborn's progress in the early months of life reflects the maturation of the nervous system. The fibers of the nervous system grow and form additional connections to other fibers, and some of them develop protective sheaths that make them faster and more efficient messengers of information to and from the brain. The brain itself grows in size and weight. Its growth spurt during the first three months will never again be matched in life.

Thus by the time they are three months old, infants have developed the capacity to remember an event—to store experience "in their heads." And while we take it for granted, it is actually quite dazzling that in only twelve months, this supposedly incompetent creature will begin to perform the incredibly complex tasks of speaking words and of taking steps without help. From the very first, the raw material is in place for everything the child will eventually learn, do, and become.

Do all babies start reacting to the outside world right away?

Normally yes. They are born with a predictable repertoire of reflexes, or instinctive responses to outside stimulation. For example, if the sole of the foot is gently pricked with a pin, infants quickly draw the foot away—a reflex that enables them to escape from pain. If a bright light is flashed, they protect themselves by closing their eyelids. And if you tickle the side of the mouth, they will immediately turn toward your finger and start sucking, as if it were a source of food. Some of the infant's reflexes are permanent while others fade and disappear within a few months. But at birth they are so universal that they are used as a standard test to establish that the new arrival has a healthy nervous system.

✑§ *Some of the New Baby's Reflexes*

Tap upper lips . . . . .lips protrude
Tap bridge of nose . . . . .eyes close tightly
Shine bright light . . . . .eyelids close
Clap hands . . . . .eyelids close
Put fingers in hand . . . . .hand closes
Press the ball of foot . . . . .toes flex
Scratch sole from toe to heel . . . . .big toe bends up, small toes
                                        spread
Prick sole with pin . . . . .knee and foot flex
Tickle corner of mouth . . . . .head turns toward tickled area
Put finger in mouth . . . . .sucking begins
Hold baby in air, stomach down . .head lifts, legs extend
                                        Adapted from:
                                        Paul H. Mussen, John J. Conger,
                                        Jerome Kagan
                                        Child Development and Personality

How well can the newborn actually see?

Amazingly well—and better with each passing day. The eyes of a newborn are identical in structure to those of an adult, although its various parts—the retina, for example, and the nerves that run from the eye to the brain and back—are still developing. Even babies a few hours old follow a moving object with their eyes, and at two weeks they can already tell the difference between two small squares, one gray and the other striped.

The world around the infant evidently appears more interesting all the time. Newborns spend about 5 percent of their waking time actively looking at their surroundings, but by two-and-one-half months, the percentage goes up to a third.

Can the infant focus on objects at any distance?

Not at first. Focusing depends on the muscles that control the lens of the eye, and at birth these are still somewhat weak. Until about two months of age, the newborn's visual focus is fixed at about 8 inches from the face. The eye muscles cannot yet make the adjustments necessary to zero in on objects at other distances. Soon, however, the visual machinery begins to mature, and by four months the infant can put objects near and far clearly in view.

Amazingly enough, the newborn's first focusing distance of 8 inches works out perfectly. That's just about the distance necessary for the baby to see the face of mother or father clearly when cradled in their arms. Nature has somehow arranged to eliminate any fuzziness around the countenance of the infant's first teachers.

How well can infants tell different colors apart?

After only a few weeks they can discriminate not only between two colors such as red and green but also among the various hues of a color. The baby's perception of color is surprisingly similar to the adult's. Infants will gaze for longer periods at the colors that adults prefer—for example, blue and red—than they will at colors such as yellow and orange that adults like least. Like an adult, too, the infant prefers clear colors to muddy ones.

Do newborns show other preferences in what they choose to look at?

Moving objects capture their interest from the moment of birth. Five-day-olds will actually stop sucking on a nipple, seemingly enthralled, when a light begins to cross their field of vision. At one week, babies would rather gaze at patterned surfaces than at plain ones, and as early as two months after birth, they can perceive differences in brightness of as little as 10 percent. The brighter the light, the longer it will capture their attention. At the same time, they seem to enjoy looking at three-dimensional objects more than at flat ones, curves more than straight lines, and circles more than squares.

Miraculously, at ten hours after birth, an infant will choose to look at the human face rather than at almost any other shape, and over the first few months, the preference becomes even stronger. Evidently the human face embodies many of the characteristics that new babies find attractive—the oval shape, the high black-and-white contrast of the eyes, and constant movement. Even more remarkable, the young infant is able to differentiate between various faces hovering over the crib or peering into the carriage.

     During the first six months, the baby has the rudiments of a love language available. . . . There is the language of the embrace, the language of the eyes, the language of the smile, vocal communications of pleasure and distress. It is the essential vocabulary of love before we can speak of love.

Selma Fraiberg
Every Child's Birthright

Is the newborn's hearing equally well developed?

Surprisingly so. An infant is sensitive not only to the loudness of a sound but to its pitch, duration, and location. In fact babies respond to some sounds while still in the womb. When a loud, high-pitched tone is sounded close to the stomach of a woman in her ninth month of pregnancy, the heart rate of the fetus increases.

Apparently the quality of the sounds infants hear can affect their behavior. In one study, babies sucked nipples that caused various sounds to occur. High-pitched sounds produced a startle response; the infants froze, and their heart rate rose. Low-pitched, continuous sounds seemed comforting; the heart rate slowed, the eyes remained open, and motor activity increased. As many new parents recognize, sounds that infants find comforting can even stop their crying.

What about the sound of voices and of language?

Newborns seem to be naturally tuned in to human speech. They like the sound of voices most of all. At one month, a baby can distinguish between sounds as similar as "pah" and "bah," and at four months, between most of the basic sounds of speech. They tend to synchronize their body movements precisely to the sound patterns of speech even in the first days of life, resulting in what has been described as the "language dance." It seems clear that babies are responsive to quite subtle differences in the sounds of words spoken to them.

Can an infant differentiate among the voices of different people around them?

Surprisingly well. As early as the third day, the newborn appears able to tell the mother's voice from others. The heart rate increases when her voice is heard. In general, the human voice seems to have a unique capacity to evoke responses in the infant. Babies listening even to a tape recording of another newborn crying become restless and often cry themselves. But a strange-sounding cry simulated by computer causes no such reaction.

⋄ Demonstrating a baby to a second-time mother the other day, I asked her to tell me what it meant to her when her two-day-old baby responded. I had demonstrated the baby's ability to fixate on and follow my face, getting more alert as he did so. The mother said, "I didn't know he could see—I mean important things like my face." When the baby turned his head toward her voice in preference to mine, she immediately and automatically reached for him, saying lovingly as she took him, "You know *me* already." Finally I helped the baby come into an alert state and stuck my tongue out at him. He opened his eyes wider and began to match my tongue's movements by sticking out his own. His mother chortled, "My God, he knows more already than I do!" I laughed in agreement and asked, "What will that mean to you?" Quickly, she said, "It means I'll treat him like a HE instead of an IT!"

T. Berry Brazelton
Children Today, July–August 1981

Can parents increase the extent to which their babies vocalize?

By the fifth week of life, hearing another voice—especially mother's—leads babies to use their voice more. Throughout infancy, the stimulation they receive from hearing other voices can evidently make a difference. For example, babies reared in homes where parents play vocal games with them will use their own voices more and with more variety than will those raised in homes where vocal exchanges are rare. Three-month-old infants who are touched and smiled at after each sound will also tend to vocalize more. By the end of the first year, however, children are stimulated to produce sounds just by hearing themselves.

Does it matter whether or not parents use baby talk?

Yes. Virtually every study on the subject suggests that baby talk is not helpful. Talking normally and intelligently to the baby seems to be more beneficial. Mothers of children with high verbal skills typically have had a great deal of verbal interaction with their babies, praised them with words as well as hugs, and have used a normal vocabulary much of the time from early infancy. They have explained things to them and have spoken to them affectionately just as they might to an older child.

One ingenious mother solved the problem of intellectual stimulation for her baby *and* herself by occasionally reading the newspaper aloud to the baby while she offered the bottle. Whatever the technique, there is good evidence that the baby's level of language development at thirty months is related to the amount and quality of earlier communication from the adults surrounding them.

✎§ *Helping a Baby Develop Language*
- Listen carefully to what your baby is trying to say—and respond accordingly.
- Reward your baby for using real words instead of grunts, noises, or gestures.
- Talk to your baby a lot—and use sentences that are brief, simple, and to the point.
- When your baby is attracted to an object or activity, use their actual names.
- Use questions that lead to more than one-word answers: "What is Daddy doing?" instead of just "Who is that?"

Is it possible to tell from the timing of the first sounds of babies how soon they will actually speak?

No. Early cooing seems to start independently of other factors—and even of the child's awareness of making the sound. In fact deaf children born to deaf parents vocalize as much in the beginning as do normal children even though neither baby nor parent can hear the cooing sounds. Only later are babies able to babble in response to sounds in a way that lets us know that they are "processing" what they hear.

Children first learn those words that have some practical meaning—that is, objects that they know about and can act on like "sock" or "cup," rather than "tree" or "building." No one is absolutely certain, however, of all the inner forces and environmental factors that pave the way for the beginnings of speech.

One explanation is that, at about a year, children are able to remember the words that they wish to use. They now *want* to name things correctly. Moreover, in the middle of the second year, they realize for the first time that words actually represent real things in the world, and they shift from simply perceiving objects to an awareness of their symbolic meaning. When shown a picture of four objects, the fourteen-month-old will look at the pattern and symmetry of the picture—but the eighteen-month-old will already wonder what the picture means. For the first time the child is now aware that the picture represents something real. Because they can now think in symbols, babies at this age can even substitute one object for another—for example, by using a toy stove instead of a bed in which to put a doll to sleep.

Are there any sex differences as far as speech development is concerned?

Girls begin babbling earlier than boys. Although scientists don't know exactly why, there are several theories why this is so. One of them is that girls and boys come into the world with some fundamental differences in their central nervous system. Female infants seem in general to be more oral than males. They do more searching with their mouths and move their mouths more often in a rhythmic pattern during sleep. They are also more responsive than boys in their sucking to a sweetened formula. On the average, girls form words earlier than boys, and they seem to have greater facility with language throughout life.

On the other hand, it may be environmental differences that are at work. Studies show that mothers spend more time talking to their infant daughters than they do to their infant sons. Investigators have found, for example, that middle-class mothers tend to play more vocal games such as imitation games with their three-month-old daughters than with their sons.

    The additional time spent babbling to girl babies, and encouraging their vocalizing in response, tips the developmental scales in favor of girls becoming more verbal and word-oriented than boys. If mothers treated boy babies to more "conversation" in infancy, perhaps Johnny would be able to read better later in life.

Letty Cottin Pogrebin
*Growing Up Free: Raising
Your Child in the 80s*

Will early walkers also be early talkers?

Not necessarily. Parents of children who are quick to walk tend to assume that their children will also be advanced in language. But that is not necessarily the case. Just because one area of activity develops early does not mean that others will. Parents who don't accept such developmental differences could end up putting undue pressure on their children to perform feats they are still nowhere ready to display.

Nor is there any evidence that children who walk or sit early are smarter than children whose motor skills develop more slowly. There is no close relation, in other words, between the skills that emerge at six to twelve months—sitting and standing, for example—and those that typically appear at two to three years, such as speaking two-word sentences, imitating others, or playing cooperatively. These sets of abilities have different bases—and there is no reason to conclude that speed in one is related to speed in another.

Besides, remember that there is enormous room for growth and change during the first few years of life. A child who starts out a little slow in some areas—say, in language development—can move ahead briskly with the right stimulation and support.

If there is any lesson to be learned from the wealth of research on the opening months of human life, it is that all the so-called "norms" of child development can be misleading. They describe only averages, telling nothing about the vast range of variations among perfectly normal youngsters. Some children begin to walk at ten months, others not until a year and a half. Some utter their first word as early as eight or nine months after birth, while others do not do so until they are well over two years old. It is pointless to worry over where a particular child fits along the continuum.

☙ A baby is no clock and there is no timetable that can tell exactly when to expect a baby to reach a new landmark in life.
Jerome S. Bruner
New School for Social Research

Can talking to children improve their overall intellectual development?

Research findings on the subject suggest it can. The average intellectual performance of middle-class children, for example, turns out to be higher than the average for working-class children—and the difference is attributable to the fact that middle-class mothers talk more during play, and they elaborate more when answering the children's questions.

Then is talking to babies the most important way of stimulating their intellect?

Not at all. It is vital to stimulate all of the baby's senses, which are ready from the moment of birth to be played upon by the world. Parents can help by placing bright, intriguing objects around the room or over the crib, by playing music, by taking their babies to various places and showing them things—in short, by giving them a chance to use their powerful senses to explore their exciting new world.

And you don't need to buy a lot of expensive toys. Brightly patterned pillows and clanging pots and pans can be just as much fun to explore. The most important thing is that you spend time with your child. Parents are their baby's favorite and most important "toy." Infants learn by the way you hold them, by what you say to them, by the games you play with them, by your appearance, your voice.

Keep in mind that every time a baby responds to a stimulus, the brain stores the experience—which can be used later on for still more learning. There is mounting evidence that mental stimulation can improve the child's intellectual abilities. Indeed mental activity seems to help various parts of the brain develop. Exercising the brain as the child would any other muscle in the body—by using it—may actually help it grow properly and function better.

ᴥ§ Hints for Teaching Infants
- Start with something familiar to your baby such as looking at or holding a familiar object. Infants learn best when the activity is related to something they already know or do well.
- Encourage infants to do something new by offering them a reward such as a smile or a loving jiggle after they perform the new feat. But make sure the reward is offered immediately after the infant responds. Even waiting a few seconds can make it impossible for the baby to associate your smile of delight with the previous action. And unless they make the connection, they don't realize you expect them to repeat the action.
- Choose rewards that infants can clearly associate with the behaviors you want to encourage. You can stimulate babies to babble more if you smile in response to their every sound. But if you always do the same thing even when they're silent, they won't catch on to the learning game.
- Try to match the learning game to your individual infant. Remember that every baby is an individual with unique skills, moods, likes, and dislikes.
- Most important: make sure that you and your baby have a good time and enjoy the hours you spend learning together.

Adapted from: Robert B. McCall
*Infants: The New Knowledge
from Birth to Three*

Are you saying that babies' brains grow with their use?

That's what the evidence suggests—although it comes only from animal studies, of course. Scientists found that rat pups raised in an environment full of toys, exercise wheels, and other diversions made fewer errors on problem-solving tests than their litter mates who were raised in a sterile, isolated environment. And the researchers were surprised to discover that the cerebral cortex—the part of the brain that controls thinking—had actually grown heavier and begun to show changes in the chemical activity associated with thinking and memory. The nerve cells of their brains also developed more offshoots interconnecting with other cells.

We cannot study the brains of infants as they grow, of course, but a similar pattern is suggested by the findings of researchers comparing infants who are stimulated with those who are not. Young babies who are frequently stroked and held lose their primitive reflexes more quickly and enjoy greater gains in weight and more rapid increases in the body's glandular functions than do infants who are less frequently handled. Children in "enriched" and interesting environments—with more touching, handling, and opportunities for movement and visual stimulation—learn as much as 45 days earlier to grasp objects and are better able to pay attention for longer periods than other children. A stimulating environment may well have its profound effect on the intellectual capacities of babies by actually influencing the brain's rate of growth.

Interestingly enough, a significant finding in the research on stimulated rats was that the part of the brain actually involved in their activity grew faster in proportion to the rest of the brain. For example, the part of the brain called upon in vision remains underdeveloped in animals raised in total darkness. These animals don't get the opportunity to exercise the visual part of the brain, and the brain cells there do not grow and develop new branches that connect with other brain cells. But scientists have been able to reverse the pattern—causing the visual portions of the brain to grow simply by providing the previously deprived animals with a visually stimulating environment.

What happens when there is a complete lack of stimulation?

It is through stimulation that the baby's senses get their exercise and the growing brain gets the chance to store experiences needed later on to cope with the world. In extreme cases, if provided little or no stimulation, babies may turn inward and fail to thrive altogether.

The classic example of this sort of child has been seen in poorly run institutions, where infants are all but ignored. Initially they make the same demands as any other babies. They cry when they're hungry or when they need help, and they smile when someone happens to pay attention to them. But when they are left to languish in their cribs, their cries unheeded, they become less and less demanding and attentive. Soon their occasional smiles and whimpers fade. They may play feebly with their fingers or clothes, but their eyes have a vacant look. They no longer respond when someone comes into the room; they may only be mildly curious or anxious for a moment, then turn away. They have lost that vital drive for contact with the world because the world has shown no interest in them. Such children often lose weight and stop growing mentally and physically.

Can babies be overstimulated as well?

Definitely so. Most baby skills emerge only with maturation, and parents who press their children to display a particular behavior before they have reached the appropriate biological stage of development may be causing them considerable distress.

It is noteworthy that infants are quick to develop techniques for dealing with such unpleasant parental "pressure." Some, of course, simply fuss or cry. Others try to push away the offending stimulus—the intrusive rattle, toy, face, or finger. Still others withdraw, turning inward to avoid the relentless bombardment of their senses, and some simply tune out altogether and even drop off to sleep.

Harvard pediatrician T. Berry Brazelton described his remarkable experience with a newborn boy who had simply had enough of the world's encroachments on his tiny body. He was brought into the examination room for tests of his heart function and brain waves, which required rubber bands to be placed around his scalp like a headband, and around his wrists as well. Both were so tight that they caused swelling of his flesh on either side of the bands. After screaming for a few seconds, the infant quieted abruptly, keeping his arms and legs pulled up in a fetal position and remaining motionless throughout the rest of the testing. He seemed fully asleep—so much so that a series of bright lights and sharp noises barely disturbed him. Even his brain waves showed the typical rhythmic pattern of sleep. But when the stimulation ended and the tightly constricting bands were removed, he immediately roused and cried lustily for fifteen minutes. Why hadn't he cried throughout the ordeal? "This apparent sleep," says Brazelton, "seemed to be a more successful way of shutting out disturbing stimuli."

Brazelton believes that the marvelous ability of infants to handle such upsetting situations shows how well equipped they are at birth to withstand unwelcome intrusions from the outside. Evidently they are able to tune into and out of the world about them at will.

Does this mean that an enriched environment won't always help advance the baby's development?

Correct. In fact it can sometimes inhibit development if there is too much stimulation too early. An enriched environment will accelerate mental and physical skills only if the child is biologically ready. Presenting stimulation can be very frustrating and discouraging for the baby who is still unprepared to handle it. Imagine the confusion of one-year-olds who, although not yet ready to scribble, are expected to use a crayon. These children may well grow so tired of the crayon that by the time they are able to use it properly, they no longer want to. The trick, as psychologist J. McVicker Hunt explains it, is to find the right match—the right degree of stimulation for each individual child at a particular period of development. Ideally, that stimulation should challenge babies to reach just beyond their current level, but it should not demand something the child is not yet capable of. Supplying a six-month-old with a violin to fondle is not going to influence the baby's musical skills— but the same "enrichment" at age five might make a big difference.

≼§ It may be as harmful to present enriching experiences before the child is ready to benefit from them as it is to deprive the child of these stimulations entirely.

> Paul H. Mussen, John J. Conger,
> and Jerome Kagan
> *Essentials of Child Development
> and Personality*

Are the same stimulation techniques likely to be equally useful for all babies?

Certainly not. Each child is born with a particular temperament shaped in part by heredity and in part by experience in the womb.

In detailed tests of hundreds of newborns, researchers found that babies are individualists right from the start. Observing the responses of infants to a variety of stimuli—to loud noises, for example, or to gentle rocking—they discovered that the reaction of any given baby to a given stimulus might be just the opposite of another. And whatever the response—whether a sharp rise in the heart rate or increased irritability—it appeared to be constant for that baby from the opening hours of life.

Other investigators have noted remarkable individuality as the child develops not only in physiological characteristics, but in such matters as mood and responsiveness to people, in attention span and persistence, in adaptability to new situations, and in the pacing of eating and sleeping schedules. Some infants, for example, are naturally quiet while others are fussy; some are attentive while others are easily distracted. Such differences in temperament help fix children's reception to learning—and they exist *before* parents have had a chance to make what one mother guiltily described as her "stupid blunders," and another proudly as her "wise moves." Concludes psychologist Jerome S. Bruner: "Their careers as individual people start from the very beginning."

How important is it that parents react to each baby's makeup?

Probably more important than any skill in the parents' repertoire. How children fare intellectually will depend in large measure on how the adults around them respond and adapt to each child's unique style of learning. Parents whose baby is timid by nature, for example, should not let the child hide entirely from new situations, but instead introduce each one at the baby's own pace. If they were to push too hard or too fast, they might frustrate and discourage the child, and even cause further withdrawal.

Some babies quickly become bored with even the most interesting stimulus; they need constant variation. Others pay attention to anything presented to them for a long time, and in fact are thrown off by too much input. The parents of one such girl quickly learned her style—so they would make sure to remove all but one or two toys from her field of vision, thus simplifying her world. She was lucky. Her parents recognized her unique temperament and helped her explore the world and learn about it on her own terms.

Brazelton believes that the most important thing a parent can do to help a child develop well is to establish a smooth relationship with the child. And he cautions new mothers not to assume that the experts are always right. What might be the best way to handle one baby may not be the best way to handle *your* baby. "The idealized suggestions of an authority may be entirely wrong for a particular mother and child," says Brazelton. "A mother may be better advised to chart her own course via the markers set out by her own baby." And, he reminds us, the course set by perfectly normal babies may vary greatly.

ఆక్ష్   Infants are individuals who require individual treatment if they are to develop to their maximum capability.

> Jerome Kagan, Ernest Havemann,
> and Julius Segal
> *Psychology: An Introduction*

Doesn't the baby's relationship with mother affect learning?

It does indeed. Not that mother deserves all of the credit or all of the blame for everything her children do and become. But it is with her, nevertheless, that infants usually form the first meaningful relationship. Psychologists call it *attachment,* which is the baby's impulse to form bonds with the person who is the main source of interaction, comfort, and care.

The inborn tendency to attachment seems to help children develop a sense of security without which learning becomes more difficult. With it, babies seem better able to gather the courage to explore their new and strange world. In a typical experiment, psychologists placed one-year-old babies in a room piled high with toys. When baby and mother were in the room together, the baby actively looked at the toys, approached them, and touched them. But if a stranger was present, or if the mother suddenly left the room, the baby's zest for exploratory behavior dropped off.

ఆక్ష్   A mother is not a person to lean on, but a person to make leaning unnecessary.

> Dorothy Canfield Fisher

But if the tendency to remain closely attached to mother persisted, wouldn't children become totally dependent?

True enough. To become truly self-sufficient, babies must eventually explore their environment, encounter new objects and experiences, and learn how to cope with them on their own.

Oddly enough, however, though attachment and exploration seem to be conflicting tendencies, they actually work hand in hand. Babies who enjoy a solid relationship with mother eventually feel more free to move out into the world, playing and exploring more independently—confident that Mom will be there, cheering from the sidelines and waiting for the prodigal's return. Children securely attached to their mothers as infants turn out to be more enthusiastic, persistent, and generally more competent than those who are not. It also seems to make them more receptive to parental standards. One study showed that securely attached one-year-olds were more likely than others to obey the requests and commands of their mothers nearly a year later.

What about attachment to father? Isn't that important too?

Much more than many have assumed. Parents have traditionally focused their concern on mother's role rather than father's. The late anthropologist Margaret Mead once even referred to the father as "a biological necessity, but a social accident."

Today we know better. If the father plays an active role in caring for and teaching his child, he can help create the early bonds of love and attachment that traditionally have been reserved only for mother. Newborns themselves show no consistent preference for mothers over fathers. Just who it is that holds, feeds, and stimulates the baby is less important than whether these needs are consistently met. Studies show, too, that how much and how well fathers interact with their infants can significantly affect the child's intellectual progress.

ᗡ҉ Compared to children who are reared only by their mothers, preschoolers who also have attentive fathers tend to have a more positive self-concept, to feel better about being a boy or girl, to get along better with other children and adults, and to function more effectively in achievement-related situations.

David Elkind and Irving B. Weiner
Development of the Child

How can parents foster a secure attachment with their babies?

By displaying their love—by spending a lot of time with them, and by being sensitive and responsive to their needs. Such parents will listen to the baby's cues. If a baby pushes away or closes the eyes to avoid further stimulation, the sensitive mother or father will back off and give the baby a rest. Conversely, they will respond promptly when the baby lets them know it's time for play, or for some love and attention. Such parents, in other words, know how to "read" their babies' signals.

A National Institute of Mental Health expert on infancy, Stanley Greenspan, offers a few examples. The baby who tends to be passive and lethargic may need to be ardently wooed into a human relationship. "It may be necessary to experiment until one finds the special sounds, special ways of looking, special positions of holding or cuddling this baby," says Greenspan. In contrast, active or irritable infants may require the kind of handling that helps them calm down and become comfortably relaxed and alert enough to get to know the world. For an infant who tends to look away rather than toward the parent, Greenspan suggests special ways of capturing interest—such as dangling a colorful toy in front of the infant and then slowly introducing your own face next to the toy. That would help the infant to grow accustomed to the richness of human expressions.

A great deal of stimulation and learning takes place, incidentally, when Mom or Dad is simply holding or rocking baby. In fact one of the surest ways to bring infants into an alert state is to hold them over your shoulder. That gives them a chance to look around and explore while still feeling a sense of warmth and closeness— even sensing the parent's breathing and heartbeat.

Is there a special time when bonds between parent and child develop?

The so-called "bonding" process is not a static, one-time event, but rather a dynamic and continuous one. The opportunity to build a special intimacy to help infants develop and thrive is not limited to the period immediately after birth. While it is certainly desirable for parents and their new infant to begin getting to know one another on an intimate basis soon after birth, a close and loving relationship is still possible even if this contact is delayed.

The idea of a critical period for bonding arose from research with animals. Scientists showed that there is a certain time in the young animal's life when a very special type of attachment to its parent can best occur. Such a period has never been demonstrated for human beings, however. It seems instead that there are many times during early infancy when the parent and child are especially receptive to developing a close relationship.

Can bonding occur even between adoptive parents and child?

Most certainly. The emotional rapport between the parents and their new child is more important than their biological relationship—or the fact that the parents were not available to the baby immediately after birth.

⋙ We have come a long way from the early views that infantile experiences somehow fixed personality and that thereafter it was too late to remedy the faults of omission or commission in those vital pre-school years.

Michael Rutter
Maternal Deprivation Reassessed

Is the age of the child an important factor in the ease of bonding between adoptive parents and child?

Generally speaking, the younger the child, the easier for both the youngster and parents to form an intimate, special relationship. There is, however, no special cutoff time at which it can be said that such intimacy is no longer possible. Parents who are capable of offering a deep, rich, satisfying love will have an excellent opportunity for intimacy no matter what age their adopted child.

Do premature babies start out at a disadvantage intellectually?

In general, yes. Their development of intellectual as well as motor skills is erratic. They tend to be restless and easily distracted, and so they often have a harder time than do full-term babies in coping with the demands of the world.

Babies are normally born between thirty-eight and forty-two weeks after conception—about two weeks on either side of the actual due date. By that time their vital organs are sufficiently developed to handle the stresses of adapting to the environment outside the womb. Premature babies, in contrast, are usually not as well developed physically. Even their ability to breathe and suck—crucial survival skills for newborns—are hampered. Scientists suspect that the greater vulnerability of such children to oxygen deprivation, weight loss, and infection shortly after birth may account for their delayed mental and motor performance.

What factors actually define prematurity?

The actual number of weeks in the womb is one measure scientists use. Also, since it is often difficult to pinpoint the time of conception—and hence the baby's true age—they also consider birth weight. In general, babies who weigh less than five-and-a-half pounds are regarded as premature. Those who weigh less than four pounds are considered extremely so. The lower the birth weight the slower the baby's early mental and motor development is likely to be.

That goes for babies, incidentally, who are born full-term as well. Indeed full-term babies with low birth weights may actually have more lingering developmental difficulties than premature babies. Their underweight condition is likely to stem not from leaving the womb too early but from actual problems in fetal growth. They are prone, therefore, to early lags in their intellectual development.

Why are some babies born prematurely or too small in the first place?

For various reasons—many of them described in the previous chapter. They include the mother's illness or poor nutrition during pregnancy, her addiction to drugs, alcohol, or cigarettes, and complications of pregnancy.

But these are not the only possible factors. Much more elusive genetic or biochemical forces may be at work to cheat babies out of their crucial last few weeks in mother's womb. Today physicians look carefully at the prospective mother's previous obstetrical history to assess the risk of premature delivery. In general, women who have had previous miscarriages, stillbirths, or difficult pregnancies are more likely to give birth early. And teenagers are far more likely than older women to give birth to preterm or low-birth-weight babies; no one is sure why, but poor nutrition during pregnancy and lack of good prenatal care may be the culprits.

Can doctors do anything to help premature babies develop normally?

Yes indeed. Remarkable new techniques are enabling even extremely premature babies, born before twenty-seven weeks' gestation, to survive. And even some babies weighing less than two pounds have made it through. Although such infants are at high risk for developmental problems, scientists have greatly reduced the odds that they will grow up without serious mental and physical problems. Today, 75 percent of all premature babies are reported to escape significant complications.

One promising new technique—designed to help the young baby breathe properly—has saved countless babies from the brain damage associated with loss of oxygen. Through the procedure, babies are given carefully controlled amounts of oxygen through the use of a plastic hood. The machinery helps premature babies expand their underdeveloped lungs.

Psychological techniques used in the hospital to stimulate low-birth-weight infants have also proved to be effective. In one study, researchers focused on infants whose average birth weight was under 4 pounds. These babies spent an average of six weeks in the hospital, nearly half of the time in isolettes. A special stimulation program was developed that included placing a bird mobile in the isolette; stimulation sessions—including rocking, talking, fondling, patting the babies while they were in the isolette; putting a mobile over the bassinet when the infants were removed from isolation; and having the nurses rock the infants and play with them around feeding times. After the infants were discharged, parents were encouraged to play games with them, and they were given a mobile, wall posters, toys, and books for use with their children.

A comparison group in a more conventional hospital situation received no such special attention. These infants were handled only to be fed, diapered, and examined—and no visual stimulation was offered them.

At the end of a year, the average level of mental development of the specially treated experimental group was well within the normal range—and higher than the average for the comparison group.

With or without special help, do "preemies" who have developmental problems ever catch up?

They may show slower development during the first five or so years of life—but unless they were extremely premature, the lag is likely to be only slight and their chances of catching up good. A baby who arrives one month prematurely, for example, may be a little later than otherwise in developing certain skills such as physical dexterity.

Is there anything parents can do to help their preterm babies catch up?

They can indeed—by providing them with the same kind of attentive love and stimulation they would give to a healthy, full-term baby.

Some experts believe that the developmental lags of many premature babies may be caused—or at least heightened—by their initial lack of closeness with their parents. Premature babies sometimes have a hard time letting their parents know what they need. They spend less time alert and are usually less responsive than their older counterparts. The difficulties are further compounded by their physical isolation from their parents—and the absence, therefore, of sensory stimulation. They are often locked away in incubators in intensive-care nurseries for days or weeks. Even when parents are allowed to visit, they are often so tense about hurting their fragile charges or so fearful of being hurt themselves if their baby should die, that they hold back.

The staffs of intensive care nurseries are now encouraging mothers to breastfeed their babies and to spend more time with them. And that seems to help. One study showed that preterm babies who were rocked several times a day had much better motor control and auditory responsiveness than similar babies who were not rocked. The contact, the interaction, and the stimulation evidently help.

❧ We had a three-month-old baby, who had been with us for three months, expire from a heart condition. At no time had we considered the feelings of the parents who had visited every single day, standing at the observation window. When the baby died, the mother asked to hold him. Crying, she rocked him and explained that this was the first time she had ever touched him. From that time on, all mothers of prematures are allowed to scrub and gown and to touch their baby in the incubator, regardless of the baby's condition.

A hospital report, 1965

How early in life can IQ tests begin to show anything about the child's future intellectual development?

Not before eighteen months of age. The correlation between IQ test scores given during the first years of life and later IQ scores are virtually negligible. In fact experts suggest that at this early age, the IQ of the parent is probably a better predictor of the child's intelligence than infant IQ tests specifically designed for that purpose. Too many children tested early in life are classified as being of low intelligence because their IQ scores are regarded as unchanging and permanent. It is important that infants be retested when they get older.

So if I know my child's IQ in infancy, it won't necessarily tell me how bright or clever the child will be later on?

Exactly. Even the most reputable tests of infant intelligence do not predict very well the test scores the children will achieve on standard IQ tests later on. Your child's proficiency in dealing with simple motor tasks says nothing about later intellectual ability. Agility in putting blocks together or stringing beads, for example, is no sure indication of how that child will manipulate words or ideas and show overall intellectual potency later on.

Even after age two, predictions are still chancy for any given child. True enough, IQ assessments made at that age have a fairly strong correlation with tests given a year later and even further in childhood. But although intelligence measures become more consistent with age, the variations over time for any one child can be enormous.

It is only by ages nine or ten that children's performances on IQ tests begin to help forecast how they will fare intellectually in high school and college. But then again, many parents hardly need tests to tell them. If children immerse themselves in intellectual and scholarly pursuits and achieve good grades, it doesn't take a detailed IQ test to predict that they are likely to do well in an academic environment later on.

Why are early IQ tests so unreliable?

To begin with, the actual content of IQ tests differs dramatically over time. The functions of very young infants are limited, and they can be tested, therefore, on only a small range of items that deal for the most part with their sensory and motor abilities. As the child grows older, other test items can be introduced that tap social and adaptive behaviors and, later still, items that test the child's verbal ability and abstract thinking. Little wonder that early IQ results say little about IQ scores in subsequent years, when the child is already at school.

Moreover, most psychological development occurs *after* early infancy, and if a particular characteristic is not fully developed when you test it, the likelihood is slim that the results will show what the characteristic will be like later on, when it matures. Furthermore, very young children vary widely in the rate at which they develop skills—whether sensory, motor, social, or verbal—and the upshot is that any predictions made at very young ages are based on estimates that are unreliable.

Finally, environmental influences can dramatically alter the intellectual growth of a child, and there is no telling early in life what the impact of the environment is likely to be. Individual experiences can alter the child's later performance to a remarkable degree.

  Trying to predict what a person's IQ will be at 20 on the basis of his IQ at age one or two is like trying to predict how heavy a two-week-old calf will be when he is a two-year-old without knowing whether he will be reared in a dry pasture, in an irrigated pasture, or in a feed lot.

                 J. McVicker Hunt
                 Human Intelligence

~§ An Infant IQ Test

The following sample list of items is taken from the Bayley Scale of Mental Development—an IQ test widely used for infants. The numbers in parentheses identify the age in months at which 50 percent of children pass the test items. Notice that the test items primarily measure sensory and motor development.

Blinks at shadow of hand (1.9)
Head follows vanishing spoon (3.2)
Recovers rattle (4.9)
Manipulates bell (6.5)
Fingers holes in peg board (8.9)
Stirs with spoon in imitation (9.7)
Imitates words (12.5)
Builds tower of two cubes (13.8)
Says two words (14.2)
Uses gestures to make wants known (14.6)
Imitates crayon stroke (17.8)
Places two round and two square blocks in a board (19.3)
Names two objects (21.4)
Points to five pictures (21.6)
Builds tower of six cubes (23.0)

It seems that some babies learn an activity overnight. One day they're immobile and the next they're rolling around the living room floor. How do they learn so fast?

They actually don't. What you are observing is the end result of many events leading up to that new-found ability. The central nervous system is constantly undergoing rapid development in the early weeks and months of life, and when it is ripe enough to allow a certain skill to be performed, that skill is suddenly displayed. It has been "cooking" all along, with little actions hardly noticeable even to the eager eyes of parents. The maturation of the body and nervous system, in other words, cannot be observed from day to day. But in time, the results are striking.

Does this same maturation process apply to intellectual abilities like memory?

It does indeed. As the infant's brain develops, increasingly remarkable feats of memory become possible. One-month-olds show no evidence of recognizing a frequently repeated word if a day goes by without their hearing the word spoken. But just a few months later, they can recognize such a word even if they don't hear it spoken for a few weeks. The maturing brain has made this new skill possible.

Here's another example: A five- or six-week-old baby gazing at father's face might focus only on the sharp, contrasting line separating his hair from his forehead. It is only the element of light versus dark that catches the baby's fleeting attention. By the end of the third month, however, the baby will look at father fully in the face, concentrating especially on the eyes. Now the infant has begun to store in the memory system a concept—a "fact"—that will appear again and again.

By the time babies are seven or eight months old, their memories allow them to become quite comfortable with familiar things and people. And it is about that age that the sight of a stranger may begin to scare them. They may cry, stiffen their entire body, and abandon play as someone unfamiliar approaches. That's because they have not yet built up any mental image of this stranger. They can't yet explain the discrepancy between the old and the new. Later, as they continue to store new experiences, they seem more comfortable with the idea that not everyone is supposed to look like Mom and Dad. Then their fear of strangers usually begins to subside.

The emergence and growth of such remarkable intellectual skills reflect the steady maturation of the central nervous system.

What about the ability to have a thought or an idea? How soon does that occur?

Toward the end of the first year, at about eight to nine months. At this point infants can perform an incredible feat: They are able to conclude that an object which has disappeared from view actually continues to exist. This operation of the mind—referred to as *object permanence*—opens up gigantic vistas, for it allows the infant to interpret the meaning of a strange, now-you-see-it-now-you-don't event, and to develop an explanation for its occurrence.

That new-found ability—again a function of the brain's maturation—is even more remarkable if you consider that for the first two or three months of life, babies see things only in an ephemeral way. It is as if they are in a speeding car, riding by one object after another. Once an item is out of sight, it ceases to exist for the baby. And even when babies are between three and six months old and have begun to grab at objects placed before them, they nevertheless abandon the game when what they seem to want so desperately leaves their range of vision. Why bother? It no longer exists. That is also why the old favorite game of peek-a-boo is so magical for young babies. The most important people in their world—their parents, grandparents, older siblings—mysteriously disappear and then, presto, instantly reappear right before their eyes.

Before their first birthday, however, babies can begin to understand that things exist even if they can no longer see them. Now they will actually look for a ball that has rolled beneath a chair, or a toy that has been hidden in the covers. And they get upset when mother suddenly disappears.

Indeed one of the profound experiences in the life of infants occurs when they are old enough to remember that mother was there just a while ago—and is now gone. This experience, universal for babies around the world no matter how they are raised, is called *separation anxiety*. It begins to fade as soon as the baby has matured enough—usually toward the end of the second year—to remember another revolutionary concept: Even if mother does disappear for a while, she is likely to return.

    Heaven lies about us in our infancy.
                    William Wordsworth

Does all this intellectual ferment mean that the growth of physical skills is slowing down?

Not at all. It just means that, in the second year, infants are graduating to a new mode of learning. Although they will continue to develop their sensory and motor skills, they will no longer rely primarily on them to learn and to solve problems. Instead they are entering the world of symbols and concepts. They have truly become thinking beings.

And once babies have made the giant leap from acting to thinking, they are ready to embark on an entirely new, rich course of learning. During the transition period between infancy and the so-called "terrible twos," children first become concerned with the standards set by the adults around them. A little boy who spills milk over the living room rug will suddenly become worried that Mommy will be mad at him. He is upset because he now knows for the first time that he has violated an adult norm.

Even very subtle violations of standards appear to be disturbing now. At this age, children will point to their dirty hands, a cracked or broken toy, or a missing button—and show real concern. They can tell—even from the sound of father's voice or the look in mother's eyes—that their own behavior is being judged by others.

At about this time, too, children also begin to set their own internal standards. They now begin to comprehend whether or not they can accomplish something, and so they set goals for themselves. A smile of delight crosses their faces as they triumphantly fit the last piece of the puzzle into place. Or they may frown and cry if they are unable to fit all the blocks into the right holes. At the end of the second year, children have a remarkable understanding of their conduct and their abilities—and the way these may or may not live up not only to what others expect of them, but to their own standards of doing the right thing.

Moreover, researchers have found that two-year-olds will show signs of distress over their presumed inability to do something even before they actually try. Just watching someone else perform a task that seems too difficult is enough to upset the child. This tendency to become concerned even over a *possible* failure demonstrates further that children at this age have already developed an astute awareness of themselves as separate and unique human beings. It is an understanding that will accompany them throughout life— and become a source of both the greatest joys and the most painful hurts of their existence.

How do children develop self-awareness?

Until recently most modern psychologists believed that it is learned somehow—that it accumulates gradually as children interact with others and gain more and more information through experience. But based on his recent extensive research on the second year of life, Harvard psychologist Jerome Kagan believes that self-awareness, like other mental skills, is biologically based.

True enough, during this period of early development, parents teach their children many important things—including which actions are "bad" and will be punished, and which are "good" and will be rewarded. But they cannot actually teach their children to perceive themselves as separate and distinct human beings. This awareness comes from within the children themselves—and it is the maturation of the central nervous system that makes it possible.

If the advances of infants depend so heavily on biological development, then isn't the environment less important than we thought?

Not at all. As emphasized earlier in this chapter, the baby's brain is helped to develop and grow properly when babies use their biological learning "equipment"—when they practice the skills they are ready for. The brain, in other words, is an instrument through which behavior is modified by experience.

But what if early experiences are flawed because of a poor environment?

Most children are remarkably resilient. Experts today believe that when their environment is improved, children can overcome even terribly retarding early experiences, and learn skills they never had a chance to learn before. Some dramatic evidence of the brain's ability to overcome early damaging events comes from Guatemala, where researchers studied children who were routinely kept in dark huts during their first year of life to protect them from the "evil eye." As babies, they were rarely spoken to or played with. In addition, they were sick or malnourished much of the year.

As might be expected, the children emerged from the darkened huts depressed and severely retarded. But the rest of their childhood was filled with more normal stimulation and contact—and as a result, by the time the children grew to adolescence, many of their intellectual capacities approached those of middle-class American teenagers.

Such studies challenge the widely held notion that the first two years of life invariably determine the type of person an infant will later become. Two-year-olds who are slowed down as a result of bad experiences are likely to remain so only if their environment remains unchanged. If the environment improves, so will their abilities.

By the same token, babies who are off to a good start in life can find their progress slowed considerably if they are placed in an uncaring, or unresponsive and unstimulating environment. Having completed their early schooling at home, a good deal now depends on experiences children encounter in the real-life schools that so heavily dominate the world of the young.

CHAPTER FOUR
⌇ᵹ Success in School

When we were children, the drama usually unfolded at age six. Today it often takes place earlier—in many cases not long after the child's second birthday. It is the drama of the child's departure from home into the new world of school.

The setting may be a "preschool" or "nursery school" program, a kindergarten, or a traditional first grade. It may be a privately owned institution tucked away in a well-manicured suburb, or a public facility smack in the middle of a teeming city. It all matters very little to the child about to step into the vast universe outside the home. This is the critical moment of leavetaking—of shifting from the familiar to the unfamiliar, from the known to the unknown, from attachments that are secure to a world where human ties have yet to be formed.

Now it is the school that becomes the central feature of each day—the major source of adult stimulation, leadership, and inspiration from which children must draw. Suddenly there is a new adult, the teacher, whose rules children must live by and whose acceptance they must court. There are new tasks to be accomplished, new standards to be met. Now, my dear child, you will be judged by performance, not by intention—and even by qualities for which you are hardly responsible: your intelligence, your social class, your race, your physical attractiveness.

Nowhere else will the child undergo more constant evaluation than in the classroom. Indeed many students come to view the school, with its regimen of testing and examination, as a place primarily of evaluation rather than of learning. "The school—from every last stone in the courtyard to the battlements frowning down at me from the walls—was only the stage for a trial," recalls Alfred Kazin in *A Walker in the City*. "I felt that the very atmosphere of learning that surrounded us was fake—that every lesson, every book, every approving smile was only a pretext for the constant probing and watching of me, that there was not a secret in me that would not be decimally measured into that white record book. All week long I lived for the blessed sound of the dismissal gong at three o'clock on Friday afternoon."

Few experiences of childhood will leave a more lasting imprint than the school adventure about to begin. Its outcome, studies show, depends heavily on the figure at the head of the classroom. The child's teacher may be a woman or a man, a volunteer parent in a cooperative nursery or a highly trained educator in a well organized classroom, a sparkling twenty-year-old, or a seasoned grandmother. In every case the teacher's power is awesome—for it is in the shadow of the teacher that children's perceptions of their capacities and competence take hold. Indeed the teacher's ability to shape a child's self-image is one of the best documented findings of school psychology.

All of the emotional forces necessary to exert a strong influence are in place. Already embedded in the child is the insistent urge to capture the attention of authority figures and please them; the teacher is in command, the student in a subservient role; and a potent system of rewards and punishments is in operation. Moreover, no longer can children ask their parents to intervene to protect them. Now they must deal with the environment on their own. Little wonder that the classroom is such a fertile arena for either building up or eroding the student's self-concept.

As a young teacher, the late psychologist-author Haim G. Ginott recognized his enormous influence. "I have come to a frightening conclusion," he wrote. "I am the decisive element in the classroom. It is my personal approach that creates the climate. It is my daily mood that makes the weather. As a teacher I possess tremendous power to make a child's life miserable or joyous. I can be a tool of torture or an instrument of inspiration. I can humiliate or humor, hurt or heal."

Today our kids spend more time in school than ever before— an average of five hours a day, 180 days a year. Especially with the increasing popularity of early education programs, they now start their schooling at a younger age and stay in school for longer periods. How smart and happy children grow up to be will depend in great measure on what they learn here—not only from books and blackboards, but from the minds and hearts of others. Not only about the world, but about themselves.

These days, with so many parents working, children start their "schooling" as mere toddlers in daycare centers. Will that stimulate or slow down the child's intellectual development?

It may do neither. Studies of middle-class children exposed to daycare have provided no convincing evidence one way or the other.

One important five-year study conducted at Harvard University found that daycare had no effect on the child's mental, emotional, or social development. The children seemed to develop at the same rate as those raised entirely at home by their mothers. The researchers could find no significant differences, for example, on tests of intellectual performance between the daycare and home-reared children. Indeed the daycare group actually seemed to excel in one area—the ability to imitate adult behavior—probably as a result of their greater opportunities to interact with a variety of adults.

But keep in mind that the Harvard-based center was a high quality operation. It had a very low child-to-adult ratio, making one adult primarily responsible for each child. And it encouraged intellectual skills and provided ample opportunities for children to master them. Unfortunately, parents are not always able to find or afford such quality care for their young children. But if they could, they might safely assume that their child's development will not be stunted.

But isn't the parent-child relationship damaged when the child is removed from the home at such an early age?

Not necessarily—although for many years many parents as well as professionals thought so. In fact the expectation of such damage was for a time the main argument against daycare or nursery school programs. The public was concerned about studies conducted in the 1940s and 1950s which revealed that children deprived of adult attention and affection were retarded intellectually, socially, and emotionally. But those studies were conducted mainly on orphans and other deprived children languishing in institutions, not on children from intact, loving families. In the 1960s, when researchers started examining the effects of temporary separations of young children from home rearing, they found no such universal impairments.

How do daycare children relate to their mothers, specifically?

A number of studies have found that daycare does not generally damage the precious early relationship between mother and child. Children in daycare can enjoy emotional ties with their mothers that are just as secure as those of children who spend their days at home. Given a loving relationship with their mother to begin with, they seem to know full well the deep difference between her and their teacher. Even when they have been in daycare since infancy, they still prefer Mom.

In one typical study, children between the ages of nine and thirty-one months were observed as they entered a room where there was a male stranger, their teacher, their mother, and some toys. All the children had been in daycare since they were three months old—but still, they overwhelmingly preferred the company of their mothers. In fact they spent 75 percent of the time near them—touching them, sharing their toys with them, and asking them to be held.

At the end of the session, each child was given a cookie inside a difficult-to-open container. Three-fourths of the children wanted help opening the container—and all of them turned to mother for help. The tie between child and mother was clearly dominant.

Scientists have found also that daycare children are no more likely than home-reared children to experience anxiety when they are separated from Mom. Israeli preschool children brought up in kibbutzim—cooperative settlements where mothers are absent most of the day—display the same normal pattern of separation anxiety as American children brought up by their own mothers.

◆◈ A mother is a mother still,
    The holiest thing alive.
        Samuel Taylor Coleridge

Can we assume then that children sent off to daycare or nursery school programs won't be damaged at all by early separation from their mothers?

That appears to be a safe assumption—but only when the children come from a loving home, go to a quality program, and are welcomed back home each day by an adoring parent. Parents, in other words, cannot blithely deposit their kids in just any daycare or nursery school program and expect the staff to take responsibility for nurturing all of the child's emotional needs. Children know instinctively where their most enduring links lie—and when these links become weak and uncertain, the child's development may well be adversely affected. Youngsters at all ages whose minds are layered with insecurities and anxieties are not likely to be open to learning.

After thirty years of experience in the field, I am seeing for the first time in the past decade forms of neglect in educated, middle-class parents which cannot be differentiated from our slum population. These parents may not recognize it, but their children are clearly neglected. Often both parents are working or are in school, and their young are peddled around to various neighbors, to tenement centers, or casual and haphazard child care arrangements. Or, they are dumped off at the "Y," in the kiddie park, anywhere. These children suffer some of the same problems that we used to see only in slum children.

Selma Fraiberg

Will children who have attended a preschool program have an easier time adjusting to a formal school than those who have spent most of their preschool years at home?

Not necessarily. In fact it seems that for some, adjustment may even be a little harder—especially if they have come from a nursery school that is run in a totally unstructured way.

In one study, daycare graduates did seem initially to have a jump on their home-raised peers. They sought help from teachers more frequently, and were generally more successful in getting the attention they felt they needed from adults. They seemed more curious, more likely to finish what they had started, and more competitive. They talked more, and more loudly, and tended to make their needs known. Overall, compared to home-reared children, they appeared considerably less passive.

So far so good. But by the time the daycare children were into the "serious business" of the first grade, many of them had become aggressive and downright bossy. Often they seemed frustrated—as if their needs were not being met.

A pattern of aggressiveness has also surfaced in other studies of first graders who had been in daycare. Some of these daycare graduates seem less cooperative as well. The cause may well be the change in environment—from "laissez-faire," learn-while-you-play groups to regimented classrooms. But some believe that the pattern is more closely related instead to the extended time daycare children have spent with their peers rather than with adults. As a result, they may be slower to absorb adult standards of behavior than are kids whose preschool years are spent altogether at home.

Parents who think their children ought to be more independent and assertive—even if also somewhat more aggressive—may well be happy with the outcome of the daycare experience. Others may not.

But what's the bottom line? Are daycare programs good or bad for a child's mental development?

There is no clear cut answer. There are just too many types of arrangements—and too many different types of children—to make a blanket assessment. Here is the measured view of psychologist J. Ronald Lally: "Talking about the harmful or beneficial effects of daycare is like talking about the harmful or beneficial effects of Tuesday. Daycare centers are what goes on inside them. They can be incredibly enriching experiences or they can be horrible, threatening, degrading places. We have to define ways to look at the quality of what goes on there and not talk about daycare centers as if they can be universally good or bad."

On one point, most authorities are in agreement: Full-time, nine-to-five, daycare or nursery programs for very young preschool children can hardly be in the child's best interests. That is simply too long a span of each day for preschoolers to be away from their primary sources of attachment and care.

~♂ For two years, we watched daycare children in our own preschool/
daycare center respond to the stress of eight to ten hours a day
of separation from their parents with tears, anger, withdrawal, or
profound sadness, and we found, to our dismay, that there was
nothing in our own affection and caring for these children that
would erase this sense of loss and abandonment. We came to
realize that the amount of separation—the number of hours a day
spent away from parents—is a critical factor.
           William Dreskin and Wendy Dreskin
           The Day Care Decision: What's Best for Your Child

Aren't there any guidelines to help parents decide what type of daycare is likely to be best for their child?

One of the most important items to look for is the staff-to-child ratio. How many children is each adult expected to look after? Experts may disagree over exactly what the best ratio should be, but as a general rule, the younger the child, the more adults should be available. Indeed some would argue that very young preschoolers would do better if taken care of by a babysitter in the parents' own home or in the home of a relative or neighbor who is responsible for few, if any, other children.

Staff turnover is also important. Once your child becomes attached to someone, it can be traumatic if that person leaves. And watch carefully how the adult taking care of your child interacts with kids. Is she energetic, affectionate, patient? Does she get down on the floor and talk to children at their own level? Is she imaginative and creative in her use of playthings?

Look carefully also at the facilities and at the choice of playthings and learning materials the children have. Are there enough stimulating toys or games, or is the TV tube the main form of entertainment and diversion? Is there a well-equipped and safe play area outdoors? Are the activities diverse enough to stimulate the child mentally as well as physically?

Do children have some free time for their own individual pursuits? Some observers feel that daycare or nursery "students" can feel helpless at times because they are expected to participate in an endless series of activities, regardless of their personal preferences.

Check out whether the program encourages children to play in small groups or, better yet, in pairs. Certain children may be turned off by a group composed of many children. "At a tender age children have trouble coping with large groups and can easily become discouraged working alone," says child expert Jerome S. Bruner. "But if you arrange the nursery with corners where pairs of children can play privately, you get longer, richer bouts of play. A play group is cluttered and noisy, and there is a real problem in figuring out how to get a word in edgewise. It's easier in pairs. Talk is more connected."

You should also look to the other children at the center for clues. Do they get along well with each other and with the staff? Do they seem to be enjoying what they're doing? Do you think your own child would enjoy spending time there? And would you?

Most important of all, given the choice, think about what type of arrangement would be best for *your* particular child. Some young children thrive best when left in the totally unstructured but cozy atmosphere of a neighbor's home. Others seem to love having many other children around and an agenda of things to do together with them. There is no one best type of preschool daycare program—any more than there is any one type of preschool child. It all depends on what your individual child seems to need—and, of course, what you can find and afford.

~ᶜⱝ Every child deserves to have someone around who knows what happened yesterday.

Margaret Mead

~ᶜⱝ The Boom in Baby Schools

Although the overall number of children ages 3 to 5 dropped nationally since 1970, the number enrolled in nursery schools jumped astronomically. In 1970, only 13 percent—or 454,000—of all American 3-year-olds attended preschool classes. Now 27 percent do. The comparable percentages for 4-year-olds were 28 percent in 1970 and 46 percent today.

National Center for Education Statistics

Aren't preschool programs important for stimulating the minds of children and raising their level of intellectual functioning?

That belief swept our country in the 1960s, when psychologists began to promote the idea that early learning experiences could dramatically enhance the child's cognitive powers. It was then that the famous Project Headstart was introduced to give preschool ghetto children an academic push and raise their level of performance when they eventually started their formal schooling.

Many studies have attempted to evaluate such efforts. The consensus is that enrichment programs designed to foster intellectual development can raise children's intelligence levels in the short run, but that the gains soon evaporate once the program is ended— *unless* the child continues to be stimulated in the home. The lesson for parents from all this seems clear enough: You can't depend on a preschool program to stimulate your toddler's mind unless you yourself provide an environment that is intellectually stimulating as well.

Are you saying that the child who never even gets to a preschool program is not necessarily going to be at a disadvantage?

Precisely. Educational specialists agree that the best way to stimulate the minds of preschoolers is by exposing them to an environment where they are encouraged to explore and learn. And that can certainly be accomplished at home.

Take language development, for example. The vocabulary of preschoolers grows at a phenomenal rate. Beginning in the second year, children learn an average of eight new words a day—and by the age of six, the typical child knows somewhere between 8,000 and 14,000 words. To help the process, parents need simply to be good verbal role models. Talk to your children a lot—and use proper English. Don't be afraid to use words they don't yet know; it is astonishing how quickly they can figure out their meanings. Growing up in an environment rich in language is still the best way for the child to learn language. Parents can stymie children's development of verbal skills by ignoring their questions or by answering them in monosyllables.

You can enrich the child's preschool years as effectively as any "school" by making the act of learning an enjoyable, fun-filled experience. If, for example, you want to teach children math, play Rummy or other card games with them—games that offer a chance to work with numbers. If you want to interest them in science, take leisurely walks and encourage them to observe and to question. Ask them to help you figure out how everyday things work. There are infinite opportunities each day for your child to learn and to grow intellectually in the family environment.

Family therapist instructor Roberta Holt has studied families that produce geniuses. She points out that the parents of Darwin, Freud, and Einstein did not try to pump knowledge into their children. Instead they were simply a stable and constant presence for them. They were available. "Rather than viewing their child as a vessel they had to fill, they let the child go on and fill up his own vessel." It is not likely that the creativity of these men would have been enhanced by even the most carefully crafted preschool enrichment programs.

But isn't it important for most children that they be started on the path to intellectual achievement as early as possible?

There's certainly no reason to deny children the stimulation and excitement for learning that many of them are ready for well before they take their kindergarten seats. Indeed many kindergarten programs today have come to assume a given level of knowledge on the part of new entrants. "Whether they learn at home or in a preschool, children today are expected to enter kindergarten with certain basic concepts and some facts at hand," write William and Wendy Dreskin in their comprehensive book on *The Daycare Decision.* A kindergarten readiness test, the authors point out, typically requires children to understand the concepts of loud and soft, light and heavy, big and small, less and more, as well as to be able to count, and to name body parts, colors, and shapes.

But such knowledge—and much more—can be absorbed by children casually, in the normal course of their preschool years. Certainly there is no need to incite the kind of relentless, "gotta-get-sharp-for-school" pressure that is apparent in homes where parents seem intent on raising a generation of "superbabies." Instead of happily playing with their toddlers, too many of today's mothers and fathers grimly spend their limited parenting time priming them for their future academic careers.

One father starts each day by drilling his fifteen-month-old with Russian flash cards as part of an intensive program to help prepare the baby for as many career options as possible. Teacher Masha Spiegel, at the Charles E. Smith Jewish Day School in Rockville, Maryland, reports that the lawyer-father of a five-year-old kindergarten student appeared on the first day of school to inform her of the serious problem they must now share: His daughter, he admitted sadly, was still unable to solve math equations—the kind usually solved by ninth graders—despite his persistent coaching efforts. "There's so much pressure to get into college," says one mother, "that you have to start them young and push them on toward their goal. They have to be aware of everything—the alphabet, numbers, reading. I want to fill these little sponges as much as possible."

 Everyone wants to raise the smartest kid in America rather than the best adjusted, happiest kid.

                 T. Berry Brazelton

Can children be pushed too hard?

They can indeed—and many of them are, both before they begin the primary grades and after their formal schooling is already under way. The result can be a child "turned off" from any zest for learning, or worse yet, a child beset by physical and psychological symptoms of stress. Better the child face school with a slight lag in "reading readiness" than with an acute anxiety state produced by stress.

The talents and the emotional resources of many a tender, contemplative child will not survive the junior "rat race" geared to intellectual performance. Sandy, an eight-year-old we saw recently, is typical. Her days are so crammed with learning tasks—extra language and music classes, math tutoring, a "computer readiness" program—that she has lost interest in all of them. Moreover, she is chronically exhausted—as emotionally spent as her frenetic parents. She fits teacher Spiegel's description of a new depression syndrome in children: the nonspontaneous child, whose zest for learning—and life—is buried under an avalanche of pressure to succeed.

Educator Mary Sue Miller, author of *Childstress,* advises parents to encourage children to be learners, not performers. A performer does everything possible to get high marks and please both the teacher and the parent. A learner, in contrast, is excited about the world, filled with a sense of wonder. Learners are not afraid to fail on occasion because failure is an inevitable part of the learning process. But a performer doesn't dare fail. Such children are under incredible pressure to be perfectionists, she warns. "No matter what they do, it's never good enough."

But don't schools reward performance?

Of course they do—and children need to confront that reality. But they will be better prepared to meet the challenge if, beginning from the first grade, they face their academic careers in an upbeat spirit, eager to learn and succeed rather than afraid to flounder and fail.

Keep in mind also that in the learning process—as in any human interaction—it takes two to make things work. Children's destinies as students rest not only with what they themselves bring to the classroom, but with what their teachers bring to them.

How important actually is the specific teacher a child has?

Experts agree that of all the factors that influence a child's adaptation and progress in school, none is more important than the individual relationship that forms between pupil and teacher. In the lives of many children—including those with serious learning problems or who come from miserable environments—it is a committed teacher who holds the key to intellectual development.

A classic example lies in the famous accomplishments of Anne Sullivan, teacher of Helen Keller. When Helen was nineteen months old, an illness left her blind and deaf. She was abruptly cut off from the world's sights and sounds—all of the rich stimulation of infants described in the previous chapter. Her learning stopped dead in its tracks. Her memory contained only the meager store of information already acquired in the opening months of life. She had a brain capable of processing information and learning—but it could not operate in the silent world that surrounded her. In the years that followed, her mental development was at a standstill. She knew nothing of other people except through the sense of touch. She could not communicate with them, and they could not reach her. Without the usual sensory input we take for granted for our children, she was helpless.

Helen's eventual fate is testimony to the resilience of the human spirit—but also to the role played by a teacher dedicated to making that resilience a reality. When Helen was six, she came under the care of the celebrated Anne Sullivan, who herself had once been blind. Confident and undaunted, she led her blind and deaf student through the quagmire of sensory deprivation. She taught Helen to use her sense of touch—through signals pressed into the palm of her hand—to acquire the knowledge ordinarily gained through the eyes and ears. Soon Helen achieved the gift of language—and eventually she graduated college *cum laude,* and became a linguist and author.

Lucky are the children blessed with teachers who never yield in their belief that their young charges can fulfill their inherent potential. They *expect* their students to "make it"—and the children are quick to get the message.

⚬ A teacher affects eternity;
he can never tell where his influence stops.
Henry Adams
The Education of Henry Adams

⚬ How can I say what a ten-year-old boy remembers of a school-teacher lost in time? She was stout, gray-haired, dimpled, schoolmarmish, almost never angry . . . and she was special, the first person who made me think I might make something of myself. She was the kind of teacher who could set fire to the imaginations of ordinary children who sat in lumps before her, and to do so was probably the chief reward she sought.

Theodore H. White
In Search of History

Do children actually do better academically when their teachers show confidence in them?

In one study, researchers gave a battery of intelligence tests to a group of grade school students and told them that the results would be fed into a computer and then communicated to their teachers. When the teachers were informed who the brightest kids in the class were, they were amazed; the majority were ordinary students. But they nevertheless accepted the outcome of the tests.

The result was a dramatic change in attitude toward these "brightest" students. It was now graced with respect and confident expectations of success. The impact on the children was remarkable. A follow-up study revealed that the average intellectual performance of these children, formerly considered totally ordinary, was now significantly higher than that of their fellow students.

The researchers then revealed the truth to their teachers. No computer had been used. The tests had never been scored. The so-called "brightest" students had been chosen at random. The transformation in the students' performance could only have resulted from the shift in the teachers' attitudes.

Attempts to duplicate this experiment have not yielded similarly dramatic results. Nevertheless, it seems that many teachers often do transmit their expectations to their young subjects, who, like the students in the experiment, then begin behaving in ways that validate those expectations. Another indication comes from studies showing that teachers tend to anticipate from their students the strengths or weaknesses of older siblings, whom the teachers also had as students. Students whose older siblings were bright do better than similar students taught by different teachers. But they do worse if their older siblings were dull.

The evidence suggests an important conclusion: Our kids tend to begin early to play the role laid out for them by the classroom directors of their life's scenario. Teachers clearly have the power to help set in motion a self-fulfilling prophecy.

How do children actually figure out what their teachers' expectations are?

They don't have to be told in so many words. Investigators have found that teachers anticipating superior performance in their students engage in more positive physical behaviors. They smile more, lean forward toward the student, make eye contact, and nod their head in approval. The teacher need not inform the student outright what the world anticipates from them. The message is there in subtle yet potent ways.

Data from both research and the observations of educators are clear enough: In our children's long journey through school, they are likely to develop from the teacher images of themselves that will serve them either well or poorly later, in the real world outside the classroom.

Can the teacher's personality actually have a negative influence on the child?

Very much so, unfortunately. Some teachers clearly increase the problems, frustrations, and difficulties of children rather than helping them overcome handicaps and capitalize on talents and interests. Poorly adjusted and poorly motivated teachers can have disastrous effects on kids.

Children tend to do best with a teacher who is relaxed, warm, and responsive to their needs and interests. Under such a teacher they are likely not only to engage in more classroom activities, but to display greater self-assurance and a healthier attitude when they fail at a task. In contrast, teachers who dominate the classroom as rigid disciplinarians, and who make no attempt to respond to the child's individual needs, tend to induce frustration and to foster negative and hostile attitudes toward both learning and figures of authority.

This does not mean that it is best for teachers to be totally passive. Children appear to thrive under *authoritative* teachers— but not authoritarian ones. Such teachers establish clear goals and standards—but they accept the child's present capacities. They set appropriate limits, but at the same time encourage individual initiative and creativity.

"Rigidly authoritarian," "hostile," "narcissistic," "preoccupied with personal problems and anxieties," "unresponsive to student needs," "indecisive and uncertain,"—these, researchers find, are among the traits of teachers likely to block your child's academic achievement and personal growth.

From the first day Mr. Gordon struck terror in his heart; and the master, quick to discern the boys who were frightened of him, seemed on that account to take a peculiar dislike to him. Philip had enjoyed his work, but now he began to look upon the hours passed in school with horror.

W. Somerset Maugham
Of Human Bondage

First the teacher doesn't think we tell the truth. She thinks we are slaves and she's the king and I think she stinks. When we do our pictures she wants us to do it over and then when we do it over she puts her stinky dirty slimy fingers on them and reks them. Then she says to do it over and if you don't she sends you to the office and then they say bend over and touch your toes and then all of a sudden you feel a pain where you don't like to. When she snaps her fingers she wants us to jump. She also thinks shes the prettiest thing on the face of the earth. She is just like a picture all painted up. She gives us sum assinments and then we hand them in and she gives you your grade then throws them in the garbage and wouldn't even give them back to us. We tell her we want them back and she sends us to the office. Therefore the teacher stinks and makes me sick to my stomach.

"What's Wrong with Art"
Essay by a twelve-year-old

Are our children's teachers of higher quality than the ones we had as children?

Many of today's teachers are marvelously prepared for their responsibilities, but sadly, the overall competence level of teachers today is still far lower than our kids deserve. In fact as this book is being written, the questionable state of American education is being graphically portrayed in a number of reports, among them by the Carnegie Foundation for the Advancement of Teaching, the National Commission on Excellence in Education, and the Twentieth Century Fund. The general conclusion is that American schools are in trouble.

Various experts point to different reasons, but the most compelling one is that the teaching profession simply is not held in high enough esteem. A recent study by the National Institute for Education concluded that the relative status of teaching among American occupations has declined over the past 30 years, and that its standing as a white-collar job is even more marginal than in the past. While an unusually large number of dedicated young people train to become teachers, it is precisely these motivated young people who are most likely to abandon the profession. Most of those who stay on as teachers, the study finds, are looking only for job security and favorable working hours.

How motivated are today's teachers? How committed are they to their work? Two surveys, made twenty years apart, provide a disappointing answer. In 1961, 50 percent of teachers said they would certainly become teachers again if they could start all over. In 1981, only 21 percent gave the same positive response. The National Institute for Education study reaches a worrisome conclusion: The quality of those entering the teaching profession is falling fast and will continue to fall unless somehow the teaching profession is accorded a status comparable to other human service occupations.

Here is the somber prediction of education researchers Philip C. Schlechty and Victor S. Vance: "If radical reform in the teaching occupation does not occur over the next decade, the public schools of the twenty-first century will probably be as bad as . . . critics now say they are. Indeed, without such reform, these are the good old days, and the teachers we now have are the best we will ever have."

◀ゟ A Century of "Progress"

Brutalizing is the only adjective for the public schools of that district around 1908 and '09. . . . Teaching requirements were easy: graduation from high school and two years at Teacher Training School. Few teachers had the true vocation of their work. They taught because it was one of the few jobs open to them;

because it was better paying than factory work; because they had a long summer vacation. . . . They got a pension when they retired. They taught because no one wanted to marry them. . . . These barren women spent their fury on other women's children in a twisted authoritative manner.

Betty Smith
A Tree Grows in Brooklyn

 formula [In 1983] we found that education disproportionately attracts persons from the lower ranges of academic ability. . . . The result is that it is increasingly the case that those who enter teaching and those who stay tend to be disproportionately drawn from among those college graduates whose academic attributes and personal circumstances make them the least likely candidates for employment in other fields.

Victor S. Vance and Philip C. Schlechty
*The Structure of the Teaching Occupation
and the Characteristics of Teachers*

What can ordinary parents do to improve the quality of their children's schools?

We can become our children's advocates in the community. We can voice our concern about the attitudes of our local school board members, about the policies the principal of the local school will follow, and about the quality of the school's teachers. In the view of Kenneth Keniston, chairman of the Carnegie Council on Children, "We need to become more adept at taking political action through community service councils and community health agencies . . . by encouraging organizations that are concerned with children, such as the local and national PTA or the Junior League, to keep pushing political issues that touch children. Writing letters to Congress, supporting lobbying efforts, and preparing tough questions for campaigning political candidates about their views on children should be as much a part of childrearing as changing diapers or drying tears."

In the light of the teacher's awesome power, we must help see to it that the schools to which we entrust our children are staffed by men and women likely to help rather than to hurt their charges. Feelings of competence and well-being among our young are too precious to be squandered in the classroom.

Is it true that at first the child perceives the teacher as a mother substitute?

Understandably so. Consider the fact that the teacher is usually the first adult outside the family with a major role in the child's hour-by-hour, day-by-day activities. She is likely to be a woman, and she is often a psychological—and, sometimes, even physical—replica of the mother reluctantly left behind at home. Especially if they are both members of the same social class, her appearance, attitudes, and actions are similar to mother's. The young child looks to the teacher as a source of support away from home and senses quickly that she will reward "good" behavior and punish "bad."

So it is not surprising that beginning students tend to perceive their first teacher in the same way that they do their mother—and that they maintain this projection throughout the first year of school. Studies show that if the child has seen the mother as nurturing and supportive, the teacher shares the benefit of this positive attitude. But if the mother is seen as rejecting and disapproving, the teacher has a prejudice to overcome before she even begins to interact with the child.

When children first go off to school, is it better to have a male or female teacher?

At first probably a female—especially for children who saw their own mothers as benign and nurturing. In any case, women generally arouse less fear than men in children.

But as children move on in school, children of both sexes ought to have more exposure to male teachers than they typically do. Boys in particular are likely to be better off. Many of them tend to think of school activities as more appropriate for girls simply because most of the teachers are women. Some psychologists have suggested that this tendency may account for the fact that boys generally find it harder to master spelling and reading in the early school years, and that they tend to develop more behavior problems. It could be that boys who are strongly affected by sex-role stereotypes begin to feel inhibited about academic achievement and shun school work in general if they view it as a "sissy" activity.

Male teachers can also provide real-life evidence that some vocations, like teaching, need not be limited to one sex, as they might have seemed to be in the past. This knowledge can be of value to both boys and girls as they develop their childhood fantasies about "what I want to be when I grow up."

Over the course of their school careers, children should have contact with teachers of both sexes—especially so because many children today are growing up in single-parent households where one or another role model is absent.

Do teachers tend to treat boys and girls differently?

Although many of the traditional sex-role stereotypes seem to be fading in our culture, sex typing is still strong—and teachers contribute their share to the process. In various ways, often through open praise, they encourage boys to be aggressive, strong, independent, self-reliant—everything boys "should" be. Girls in the classroom, on the other hand, win points primarily for their attractiveness and appearance, and for being nurturant to others. Girls, incidentally, are judged by their teachers to be considerably more altruistic than boys—despite the fact that their actual classroom behavior shows no significant difference.

The sex typing process starts early. Even in kindergarten, teachers usually encourage boys to play a dominant role in the classroom and girls to take a back seat. They anticipate that boys will be noisy and "troublemakers," but that girls will be docile and quiet. When they assign chores, they ask boys to stack books and move furniture—and girls to serve cookies and fruit juice. The schools, it seems clear, are a potent force in building the kind of hard-to-break sexual stereotypes that can become troublesome later on in life in the relationship between the sexes.

Do children tend to model themselves after their teachers?

They do indeed. Some, of course, consciously emulate the teachers they admire. But there is evidence also that the process is often more subtle—that young children unwittingly absorb some of the personality traits displayed by their teachers. In one study, for example, first-graders taught by teachers judged to be "impulsive" tended to become more impulsive and hasty in their own responses. In contrast, those taught by more reflective teachers became more careful and deliberate in their responses.

Some authors have suggested that the tempo of teachers might be tailored advantageously to the needs of students. They point out, for example, that the trouble some boys have in learning to read is attributable in part to their greater impulsivity. So if an extremely active and impulsive boy were placed with a very reflective teacher, it might promote a more reflective attitude in the boy— and enhance his reading progress.

By the same token, students may instinctively model negative attitudes as well. An intolerant and impulsive teacher is likely to encourage similar behavior in students. And teachers who show little interest in their jobs or their students are likely to find that their students also become bored—as bereft of motivation as the models before them.

⋙ No teacher can teach in a moral vacuum. It doesn't matter how high you score on the test or how many degrees you have or how much tenure you have if you come to school as late as you can, leave as early as you can, make as much as you can, and then sit on your can.

Jesse Jackson

Overall, what is it about a school that seems to make the most difference?

The psychological climate—the way it is run and the relationships it fosters.

An extensive study of schools in London found that physical factors—the size of the school, the age of the buildings, or the space available—do not seem to matter much. What does matter are the ways the students are dealt with in the school. They accomplish more and display fewer behavior problems when they are given positions of responsibility and opportunities to help run the school, when they are rewarded and praised for their work, and when staff members are available for consultation and help. Students also do better when their teachers emphasize their successes and good potential rather than focus on their shortcomings. Even the way staff members get along with one another can affect the outcome for students. Dissension in the ranks often means a deterioration of student performance and behavior.

Which is preferable, a large or a small school?

Large schools may appear to offer the student greater choices, especially of extracurricular activities, but most studies suggest that students in small schools actually end up participating in a greater variety of programs—among them, student government, music, student newspapers, and science fairs. Because smaller schools have a more limited pool of students from which to draw, there is more pressure on students to participate in order to keep the activity going. As a result, students also view their participation as more important.

The consequences of such involvement are good: boosted self-confidence, new skills, a feeling of being needed, a chance to "prove yourself" and "make good." Probably as a result, marginal students in small schools are less likely to drop out than are their peers—with similar backgrounds and abilities—in larger schools.

Does it matter where a child sits in the classroom?

In the typical classroom, with seats arranged in rows, researchers have found what they describe as the "action zone." That is, children sitting in the first row participate more in classroom activities than those in the rear, and those in the central portion of the room more than those on the edges. The pattern seems to persist all through school—from the elementary grades through college.

The data do not in themselves provide an answer to the cause-and-effect question: Do students sit closer to the action because they are interested, or do they take an interest because they happen to be sitting in the ideal place? Nevertheless, there does seem to be a greater psychological distance between students and teachers—and less involvement in the affairs of the classroom—when the student is either far to the rear or the side.

How critical is the number of students in the classroom?

There have been surprisingly few studies of this important issue, but what evidence there is suggests what you might expect: Smaller classes are preferable—and for obvious reasons. Children beginning school in a crowded classroom may get discouraged if they have to wait too long for their turn—to talk, paint, build, or spell. Many simply "turn off" if they must sit around while others in the class are actively doing things, and they become frustrated over not being able to establish their identity in the group. At any grade level, participation and discussion tend to decrease when the classroom is overcrowded. Teachers don't have the time to offer individual instruction tailored to each child's needs and strengths, and to help elicit the child's participation. They have to rely more heavily on a strict regimen, on rules and restraints, to maintain order and control.

But classroom size is hardly the major factor affecting the classroom environment and the way the students function. A great deal depends on the personality of the teacher—whether interacting with ten children or thirty.

  There were dozens of teachers before Thornley, some good, some indifferent, some incompetent, some probably insane. . . . Thornley alone, among the events and personalities of my adolescent years, refuses to petrify. . . . He is not a fossil artifact of memory, but—though he is now dead—an active influence on me. . . . What a gift that small man, Thornley of the attentive smile, gave me.

Liane Ellison Norman
Writers for Life

Do children do better when the class is run in an "open," informal style rather than in the traditionally structured and organized way?

Firm evidence is hard to come by, but it seems that in a number of ways they do. In a so-called open classroom, children are not organized in the usual rows of desks, with everyone working at the same tasks simultaneously. Instead, they are arranged in various groups doing different things—whether sprawled on the floor with a world map, reading, playing word games, taking notes from a history book. The teacher—and sometimes a teacher's aide as well—visit and work with each group in turn.

Children in such informal classrooms do not appear to learn more as measured by achievement tests, but their answers to questions seem to be more creative and less routine. They appear to be more motivated and to engage in more social interactions and more imaginative play. They express their feelings more freely—and they seem also to be more independent, volunteering to participate more often in classroom activities.

Keep in mind, though, that not every child does equally well in any given environment. The open classroom may stimulate and motivate the extroverted child, but it may thwart the academic development of the insecure and withdrawn child who needs a more formal setting, with someone "in control," in order to relax enough to learn.

This much seems clear: For most children, neither a totally free environment nor one in which the teacher rules with an iron, authoritarian hand is best. A classroom that is altogether without structure produces students who appear listless, inefficient in their work, disorganized, and quarrelsome. And those laboring in a classroom dictatorship end up either passive or aggressive, and unable to work toward a goal. Producing the best results is an environment in which the children feel that they are participants in a democratic process. Classmates are free to arrange some of their work in groups—but the teacher is always there as a frame of reference, making judgments and giving directions that are fair and objective.

Many teachers today combine both the formal and informal approaches, using a structured setting to teach basic skills, and a looser style for other elements of the curriculum such as geography, art, and creative writing—subjects that are more likely to elicit the child's own innovations and creativity.

ᴥᴥ The art of teaching is like being a good hostess. You keep breaking up your big party into small clumps; everybody is busy and everybody is doing things. No one is left on the fringes.
James L. Hymes, Jr.
"Three to Six: Your Child Starts School"

Is it wise to group students in classrooms according to their presumed ability levels?

The rationale behind such a so-called "track" approach is obvious enough: Children supposedly will show more progress when grouped with others of similar ability, and teachers can do better if they don't have to concentrate on students with widely disparate needs.

But studies of rigid tracking show a reduction of interaction among students on different tracks, and sometimes strong antagonisms among them. Moreover, too frequently, little is expected of students in the lower tracks, and inexperienced teachers are assigned to them. The result is that the "bottom" kids often develop their own subculture within the school.

One solution lies in finding ways to reward children on the basis of their own relative improvement rather than on an absolute scale. And recognition should be offered for achievement in "nonacademic" pursuits such as drama, woodworking, or sports as well as in formal classroom subjects.

Isn't the current view that school is a place primarily for learning basics—the "three Rs"—and not for pursuing individual, extracurricular interests?

Both are critical. Schools must help prepare our young for the real, nuts-and-bolts world of work. But they must also attend to the development by children of a positive self-concept—and that can often depend on school experiences outside the formal classroom.

A research team in London is reconstructing the lives of a group of young women born into abusive and shattered families, and placed in foster care when they were under five. As expected, many of them grew up to be troubled and troublesome adults, with emotional disturbances, criminal records, and meager chances for a stable relationship of their own. But a sizable number with exactly similar backgrounds show no such problems. Indeed these women are now leading normal and satisfying lives.

Accounting for their success, the researchers find, were confidence-building experiences in school—and not necessarily in the classroom, but rather in activities such as sports, drama, and arts and crafts. These experiences were critical because they left in their wake pleasant feelings of success and accomplishment—feelings that nourished in the children a sense of competence and self-confidence in handling the rough times ahead. The girls began to see themselves not as victims but as victors. They grew confident about their ability to plan their future, no matter what crises might come their way. And, indeed, they managed to steer their lives in constructive directions. Eventually most of them chose supportive and caring husbands, and are now enjoying stable family lives far removed from the miserable ones they knew as children.

Studies such as this graphically demonstrate how important it is to go beyond the so-called basics—to open up for children a world of experiences that will make them self-confident and ready to take on the challenges they inevitably will meet.

Can the schools really help in strengthening the child's personality?

They surely can—but with the current exclusive emphasis on achievement and performance rather than personality growth and development, many schools are not doing so. Keniston believes that we are creating in our children the "computer terminals of tomorrow." He is convinced we are victims of a growing emphasis of the child as brain. We are nurturing, in his view, "a breed of children whose value and progress are judged almost exclusively by their capacity to do well on tests of IQ, reading level or school achievement."

Virtually forgotten, Keniston believes, is that "children like adults are whole people, full of fantasies, imagination, artistic capacities, physical grace, social relationships, cooperation, initiative, industry, love and joy."

No responsible psychologist or educator would ever suggest that schools should forsake their goal of preparing our kids with the essentials needed to learn and achieve. But, as Cornell child psychologist Urie Bronfenbrenner has pointed out, American education seems peculiarly one-sided in its emphasis on drilling subject matter rather than teaching the human skills it takes to live as a productive and contented member of society. Our emphasis, in short, has been too much on the child's gray matter and too little on matters of the heart and soul.

Does scholastic success in early childhood necessarily mean success later on?

In general, yes—but there are exceptions. Some children who earn the highest grades in elementary school can run into roadblocks later on. Even more often, children who perform abominably at age ten become outstanding achievers by the time they are twenty. And many children who seem to be on the verge of being defeated both scholastically and emotionally end up turning their lives around altogether. At play are not only intelligence, but also motivation—the subjects of the next two chapters.

CHAPTER FIVE
❧ Intelligence and Creativity

Few topics have caused more controversy among professionals and more misunderstanding among laypersons than intelligence. Three quarters of a century ago, when the French psychologist Alfred Binet began to develop the very first IQ test, he could hardly have guessed what emotionally charged issues and confusion his efforts would leave in their wake.

Binet's goal was immediate and practical. The public schools in Paris were overcrowded, and there were many children who appeared mentally retarded and unable to handle their schooling. The city leaders decided they needed a more accurate technique to identify these students so they could be removed from regular public school classes. They commissioned Binet to construct a test that would provide a fair and valid gauge of a child's ability to profit from academic instruction. Binet built his test with this goal in mind, and the result was an admirable accomplishment.

Binet did not begin with any theories of intelligence. He knew that some children did better than others on different kinds of tasks. He assumed that children differed in the capacities they were born with and that these capacities could be measured through the tasks that made up his test. His purpose was simple enough: to obtain scores by which children could be ranked along a range from very smart to very dull.

Today's IQ tests retain much of the flavor and even some of the content of Binet's original product, but their uses have been extended beyond anyone's expectation. Few children now grow up without taking such a test—children in kindergarten already being evaluated against their peers, third-graders having their learning problems analyzed, adolescents dreaming of college careers.

There is little doubt that intelligence tests are here to stay. Just as Binet intended, they offer a useful way of sorting out children according to broad levels of intellectual ability. Moreover, they can be used to spot strengths and weaknesses among the various aptitudes of any one child.

The problem lies not in the tests themselves but in the perversion of the test results by uninformed users. Too often the IQ test score is used unfairly to label a child—or even whole cultures and races. And parents continue to be confused about the meaning and relevance of their children's IQ. In the view of Paul Mussen, John Conger, and Jerome Kagan, authors of one of the leading textbooks on child development: "Typical American parents are anxious about their child's IQ, and attribute more value and mystique to a high IQ score than to almost any individual characteristic possessed by the child."

Parents and teachers alike are uncertain about whether a child's intelligence level is inherited, how much it is affected by early environment, how accurately it can be measured, whether it can be modified by experience and thus vary over time, and what it portends about the child's personality, emotional adjustment, or future achievement. And there is still confusion over the degree to which IQ test scores can ever actually define that elusive and mysterious trait we call creativity. Many mothers and fathers continue to look vainly to the intelligence test to tell them whether their child will, perhaps, grow up to be a Shakespeare or an Einstein. And what of those children who clearly do not score anywhere near the top on an IQ test? What can be expected of them?

The mountains of research evidence accumulated on the subject of intelligence convey one message above all: Regardless of the numbers spewed out by IQ tests, each child remains a unique individual with a wellspring of capacities that can flourish over time. Each has precious talents and skills that IQ tests can help identify— but that only life experience can bring to full flower.

When you say that a child is "intelligent," what does that really mean?

The definition of the word "intelligence" has been debated for many decades. In Roget's *Thesaurus,* the terms associated with it take up three full columns. If you were to do a street corner survey, you would probably discover people defining intelligence as "the smarts," "mental ability," "quickness of thought," "shrewdness," "common sense," "braininess," "understanding," and much more.

The concept has proved so elusive that, in frustration, experts have sometimes fallen back on a completely circular definition. Over half a century ago, Harvard psychologist Edward Boring observed: "Intelligence as a measureable capacity must at the start be defined as the capacity to do well in an intelligence test." Closer to our own day, the British authority P. E. Vernon wrote that intelligence tests "measure the average efficiency with which testees cope with the kinds of problems the tester chooses to include."

Most definitions of intelligence describe one aspect or another of a person's ability, but there is still no consensus on what aspect is paramount. Virtually every possible intellectual skill has been proposed at one time or another as *the* indicator of intelligence. Various cultures have developed dramatically different views. For the ancient Greeks, intelligence was the talent for public speaking; for the Jews, a knowledge of religious law; for African tribes, the ability to hunt successfully. In our own society, psychologists have defined intelligence to include such abilities as the capacity to solve problems; learn from experience; adapt to the environment; see relationships among things and ideas; behave in a competent and effective way; and think in abstract terms.

The late David Wechsler, famous for constructing a number of the most widely used tests of intelligence bearing his name, offered a useful definition of intelligence: the capacity to understand the world and cope with its challenges. The definition came to life for us a number of years ago while having dinner with Wechsler in a Jerusalem restaurant. Our waiter had repeated problems getting things straight. First he brought soup when none was requested, then he offered us the dishes ordered by the diners at the adjoining table, next he produced trout rather than the salmon Wechsler had enthusiastically asked for, and finally he presented a bill that was off by $17. "Now *that,*" said Wechsler, "is *not* intelligence!"

In Wechsler's view, people described as intelligent know what is going on in the world around them, can learn from experience, and act successfully in any set of circumstances. Actually that's not far from the definition our parents had in mind when they described a child as smart. Smart children did more than just muddle through. They were "on top of things," "used their heads," "made the most of themselves." They met and mastered their environment.

Is intelligence a single ability or a combination of several abilities?

Many years ago, some psychologists argued that each of us has an overall level of mental ability—called the "g factor," or "general intelligence." To support their argument, they attempted to show through statistical analysis that people who show skill in one area—for example, in understanding what they read—also show skill in other areas such as perceiving spatial relationships or being able to remember what they hear.

Now, however, it is generally accepted that when we speak of intelligence, we mean not one ability but a conglomerate of abilities, which are rarely equally strong in any one child. The famous American psychologist L. L. Thurstone proposed over a half-century ago that intelligence is composed of seven "primary mental abilities," which today are still viewed as major elements of the intelligence package. These are the ability to perceive spatial relationships, manipulate numbers, be fluent with words, comprehend verbal material, memorize, reason logically, and perceive and identify objects quickly.

In one way or another, Thurstone's seven factors—and more—are embedded in the items of most intelligence tests our children take. No longer do we think of intelligence as comprised of some mysterious, underlying "g factor." Indeed the work of a University of Southern California team headed by J. P. Guilford led to the conclusion that intelligence is made up of as many as 120 abilities as varied as storing and retrieving information, making sound judgments, seeing the implications in events, making logical decisions, and perceiving similarities and differences. While it takes a certain amount of intellectual strength to do any of these, it is clear that intelligence is a mosaic composed of many different factors.

🍃 Intelligence . . . is not a single, scalable thing like height.
> Stephen Jay Gould
> *The Mismeasure of Man*

Do most children vary in their level of ability from one intelligence factor to another?

They do indeed, sometimes very widely. Just as children have different kinds of body structure, habits, and personalities, they display different kinds of intellectual skills. Some children are terrific at handling language or ideas, others at juggling numbers, others at logical reasoning, and still others at manipulating concrete objects. These are quite different skills—which is one of the reasons why kids grow up to become writers, or accountants, or lawyers, or architects.

If intelligence is made up of so many different factors, how come a child who is given an intelligence test ends up with a single IQ score?

As definitive as it may seem, the IQ—or intelligence quotient—defines only in a general way the range within which the child is functioning intellectually. The score is actually made up of many different subtest scores—and it can be terribly misleading, therefore, to assume that two children are similar in their intellectual capacities just because their overall IQ scores are the same. Each of them may have achieved that score via a totally different pattern of strengths and weaknesses.

Consider, for example, the widely used Wechsler Intelligence Scale for Children. It contains subtests with such names as Vocabulary, Digit Span, Similarities, Information, Block Design, Mazes, Comprehension, Arithmetic, and more. The patterns of individual subtest scores made by two children—let's call them Mary and Joan—may bear no resemblance to each other, yet these scores may still add up to the same overall score. Mary, for example, may have done well on items requiring intense concentration and reasoning, but poorly on items that put a premium on numerical ability and the recall of information. Joan's pattern, on the other hand, may be just the opposite. From their identical scores on the Wechsler scale, you would never know that Mary and Joan have quite diverse talents and skills.

This should come as no surprise to observant parents and teachers. One child may be great at solving math problems but awful at putting words together, and another may be terrific at memorizing historical or geographical facts but awful at reasoning logically. Experienced psychologists who administer IQ tests will not stop after they compute the total score of any child. Instead they will patiently analyze the scores made on various subtests in an attempt to discern an underlying pattern.

⌐Ϛ Being intelligent is a little like being an athlete. Athletics encompass many diverse skills, including distance running, weight lifting, rowing, archery, ping-pong, and so forth. While there is a tendency for individuals who are agile, strong, and fast afoot to be good at a variety of athletic events, they do not excel at all of them. A weight lifter is not likely to be a good high jumper, an American football lineman may be quite clumsy at soccer, and sprinters may be terrible at gymnastics.

Robert B. McCall
*Infants: The New Knowledge
from Birth to Three*

Can you draw any conclusion at all then from the child's IQ score?

Only how a particular child is functioning intellectually, overall, compared to other children at the same age level. For convenience sake, the developers of IQ tests set the average IQ score at 100. A child at age five, say, who passes all the test items passed by the average five-year-old will get an IQ score of 100. The ability to pass items beyond one's age level results in a score higher than 100, and the inability to pass all the items appropriate for one's age level results in a score under 100.

The specific score for any child is meaningful only as an indication of the range of intellectual ability within which the child falls. Most intelligence tests yield scores that can be divided into seven categories. Here they are for the well known Stanford-Binet Intelligence Scale, together with the percentages of children who fall in each:

140 and above	very superior	1%
120–139	superior	11%
110–119	high average	18%
90–109	average	46%
80–89	low average	15%
70–79	borderline	6%
below 70	retarded	3%

You can see that an IQ score anywhere between 90 and 109 falls within the average range, encompassing the scores made by nearly half of all children. At the extremes, an IQ of 140 or above is made by only 1 percent of all children, and a score below 70 by only 3 percent of all children.

But keep in mind that a host of totally extraneous factors can alter the IQ test results on any given day—how the child feels, the rapport between examiner and child, noises and distractions outside the room, and much more.

Think of your performance on the "test," say, of balancing your checkbook. The accuracy and speed of your performance may reflect a lot more than your ability to manipulate numbers. Your success may depend also on the time of day, the stress you're under, or whether your dinner agreed with you. Likewise, on any given day, many things unrelated to intelligence can interfere with the children's ability to answer the questions posed by the tester. The upshot is this: A small difference between the scores of two children may be about as meaningful as a difference, say, of two or three pounds in their weight.

✎ An Early Psychologist's Caution:
Instead of attempting to describe each individual's endowment by a single index such as an intelligence quotient, it is preferable to describe him in terms of all the primary factors which are known to be significant. . . . If anyone insists on having a single index such as an IQ, it can be obtained by taking an average of all the known abilities. But such an index tends so to blur the description of each man that his mental assets and limitations are buried in a single index.

L. L. Thurstone
Theories of Intelligence

Who scores better on IQ tests, boys or girls?

There is no significant difference between them. Most intelligence tests were constructed in a way that minimizes any sex differences that might actually exist. If a test developer were to find a test item seriously favoring one sex over the other, it would either be thrown out or balanced with another item favoring the other sex.

In specific abilities, however, there are indeed some sex differences. For example, girls are better on the average at spelling, vocabulary, reading comprehension, and creative writing—at least in the early years. Boys, on the other hand, are better at perceiving depth, solving mazes, figuring out what an object would look like from a different perspective, or finding a geometric form in a complex figure. Girls are thus likely to do better if asked to write a poem or tell a story, and boys if asked to read a map or aim at a target.

Don't boys have a significant edge in math?

Only beginning at about age twelve. At age two, girls do fully as well as boys in counting. Later, in the lower grades, they can still master numerical operations and computations as readily as boys do. But by the time boys reach adolescence, they generally show greater math ability. Indeed by junior high school, most children who reveal exceptional talents in math are male.

Psychologists are still debating whether this advantage is innate or bred by experience. The argument for the latter is strong. In the past at least, it has been common in our society for girls to leave to boys the conquest of such "masculine" domains as math and science—as if it were unseemly for girls to try to do so. They have tended to abandon any aptitude or interest they might have in such traditionally "unfeminine" subjects. Even today, although it is evident that girls do as well as boys in math in the early grades, fewer females take advanced high school math courses— or go on to become physicists, engineers, or computer scientists.

Doesn't performance on an IQ test depend on the culture that the child is growing up in?

It most certainly does—which is one of the problems with IQ tests. The way children think and express themselves reflects their way of life. Kids reared in environments where only very simple language is used will not do very well on intelligence test items requiring a more extensive vocabulary—even if they do in fact have great intellectual potential. Similarly, children who have not learned basic numeric skills will not as readily be able to solve mathematical problems posed in an IQ test. And quite apart from the contents of the test, attitudes toward taking it may differ dramatically. Children living in a bleak and unstimulating environment are not likely to develop the same degree of achievement motivation to do as well on intelligence tests as children who are "turned on" by their parents and teachers to master intellectual challenges.

It is precisely because environment and culture so strongly affect children's performance on IQ tests that many of the tests currently used in the schools are being called into question. On one, children are asked "What should you do if you were sent to the store to buy a loaf of bread and the grocer said he didn't have any more?" As Kagan points out, the correct answer ("Go to another store") assumes that the child is growing up in a middle-class, urban environment with more than one grocery store within safe walking distance. Rural or ghetto children who answer "Go home" would receive no credit—even though this is a perfectly reasonable solution in their particular environment.

~§ Fact and Fiction about Racial Differences in IQ

The average IQ of American black children is about 10 points lower than that of whites. For some people, this fact has justified ugly biases and unfounded theories of racial superiority. In fact, however, there are logical reasons for the difference:

• *Motivation:* The motivation to score high on tests is often depressed among black children because of low levels of aspiration or because of greater test anxiety.

• *Racism:* The black child, faced with a white adult tester and an IQ test made up of items from the white culture, may be the victim of racism, however subtle.

• *Health care and family life:* Black children often have a poorer environment—both in the womb and during their infant years—than do white children even from the same economic class. Moreover, they come from broken homes at least three times as often as white children.

• *Unfair test items:* The IQ test bias against black kids appears especially in heavily verbal sections of the test—which use many words that are more familiar to white children than to black. Even so, the overlap in scores between black and white children give the lie to claims of racial superiority. The IQs of black children range approximately from a rare 40 to a rare 200—exactly the same as for white children. Moreover, there are over 4 million American blacks whose IQ scores are higher than the scores made by about 85 million whites.

Aren't there any IQ tests available that don't depend on a child's prior environment?

Numerous attempts have been made to devise so-called "culture-fair" tests that measure learning ability without requiring any specific earlier knowledge. Unfortunately, however, the efforts have not been successful.

Even nonverbal tests don't solve the problem. Although they do not involve language, they are still based on experience. The most widely used test of children's intelligence, for example, includes a test of the child's ability to copy a given design, using a set of patterned blocks. No words need be spoken. But still, children growing up in households where they were never exposed to a set of blocks would clearly be at a disadvantage.

One of the world's leading authorities on testing, Fordham University's Anne Anastasi, is among those who believe that no test can be fairly applied to all cultures. "The mere use of paper and pencil or the presentation of abstract tasks having no immediate practical significance," she points out, "will favor some cultural groups and handicap others." Perhaps the best we can expect is that we reduce as much as possible the built-in cultural differences in IQ tests. But it seems unlikely that we will ever totally eliminate such differences.

Does heredity figure much in a child's IQ?

Intelligence, like virtually every psychological trait, is shaped in part by genetic factors. Researchers have found that the IQs of parents and children or of brothers and sisters are more closely matched than the IQs of persons who are genetically unrelated. The IQs of children and their natural mothers, for example, are more alike than those of children and their adoptive mothers. And the more closely related two people are genetically, the greater the similarity in their IQs.

The most dramatic evidence of the genetic influence on intelligence comes from studies comparing the IQ scores of twins. The IQs of identical twins who, by definition, share the same genes, are more similar than those of nonidentical, or fraternal, twins whose genetic structure is different. Even when identical twins are separated and reared in different homes, they end up with more similar IQs than do fraternal twins growing up together.

Despite all the evidence from genetics, however, our current knowledge is not enough to say for sure how *much* of a child's intelligence is explained by heredity and how much by environment.

ᵜᔖ   We don't need intelligence to have luck, but we do need luck
to have intelligence.

Yiddish proverb

Will a child's IQ usually remain at about the same level?

The chances are surprisingly good that it will not—and often precisely because of environmental influences that can dramatically alter the child's attitudes and motivation. While it is true that the IQ becomes more stable as children grow older, it is still risky at any age to try to predict Johnny's intellectual status tomorrow from his intelligence test score today. A child may show sizable increases, or decreases, in IQ from year to year.

In one study, investigators tested children intermittently between the ages of twenty-one months and eighteen years. The IQs of almost two-thirds of the children changed fifteen or more points between their sixth and eighteenth birthdays, while the IQs of a third changed twenty or more points. During the same time span, nearly 10 percent of the children's IQs varied as much as thirty points.

ᵜᔖ   Whenever one measures a child's cognitive functioning, one is
also measuring cooperation, attention, persistence, ability to sit
still, and social responsiveness.

Sandra Scarr
American Psychologist

What causes a child's IQ to shift so much?

It can be due to many things—problems of health, emotional crises such as bereavement and divorce, shifts in motivation, or dramatic developments in the environment. Researchers find substantial fluctuations in IQ scores—both up and down—that reflect the healing and disturbing periods of children's lives.

One girl was sickly and shy as a young child, but after the age of ten, both her health and her social life flowered. She suddenly came into her own and grew interested in what was to her a whole new world of studies as well as music and sports. The changes in her life were mirrored in a dramatically improved IQ score—from well below average to well above.

In another case, a girl's IQ sank from 142 during her preschool years to 87 at age nine. Her immigrant parents, unstable and educated only through grammar school, became mired in chronic marital discord. They were divorced when the girl was seven, and she was extremely anxious around her young stepfather during the first years of her mother's remarriage. Her constant turmoil and the deterioration in her well-being were reflected in her plummeting IQ test score.

Can the environment play a more important role than heredity?

The upper limits of children's intellectual attainments are fixed by heredity, but the range over which any given child functions will depend on environmental influences. Intelligence, in other words, is not frozen at conception—like eye color or sex. Each child is born with a genetic potential for intellectual development that can either be realized or stunted through life experiences.

Indications of the role of environment come from various studies. In one project, investigators studied a group of black and interracial children from disadvantaged homes adopted by white families when the children were an average of two years old. The benefits to the children of living in more stimulating homes were clear several years later. These adopted children scored fifteen IQ points higher than comparable children who continued to be raised by their own parents in a considerably more deprived environment.

So parents can affect a child's IQ score?

In many ways—notably through their attitudes toward intellectual pursuits, and how they spend time with their children. The appetites of kids for the kinds of tasks posed in IQ tests can be whetted at the hearth, and their actual skills in performing them can be sharpened.

Studies show that parental attitudes can help determine how efficiently children deal with numbers or with words, how clearly they can perceive spatial relationships, and how much imagination they bring to the solution of problems—all of which are critical in IQ test performance. The IQ scores attained by children are strongly related also to how much encouragement they get from parents to use language and expand their vocabulary, and how many rewards they get for signs of intellectual accomplishment.

Even the emotional rapport between parents and child seems to be a factor in the child's performance. The greater the warmth and affection shown by mothers and fathers, the sharper their children's intellectual performance is likely to be. When parents display constant hostility and rejection toward their children, one of the effects appears to be lower IQ scores.

How about birth order? Do older siblings have an advantage over younger ones?

On the average, firstborns do score higher on intelligence tests than their siblings. It is easy to guess why. The more mouths to feed and bodies to clothe, the less time and energy parents usually have available per child to introduce them to activities that will stimulate them intellectually.

According to psychologists E. Mavis Hetherington and Ross D. Parke, young children are likely to benefit most from individual, one-on-one contacts with their parents. As the family grows larger, parents have less time to interact with each child alone in activities like reading and playing. Older children not only reap the benefits of living in a small family unit for a longer time, but they also often find themselves passing along their gains to younger siblings by tutoring them when parents are unavailable. This teaching role may well contribute to the senior child's advantage in intellectual development.

What about children whose early years are spent in an awful environment? Can their IQs ever be raised?

They can indeed—as shown by both follow-up studies and individual case histories. Improvements in a miserable environment, even when they occur in middle or late childhood, give children the chance to make astonishing strides in their intellectual development.

Too many parents and teachers harbor a pessimistic attitude about the potential of children to overcome early disadvantages. The data from follow-up studies present a more optimistic view.

In one famous long-term project, investigators studied a group of children who began their existence in a crowded, poorly staffed orphanage with little chance for any intellectual stimulation. Thirteen of the orphans were moved to another setting—a state home for retarded teenage girls and women. Their average IQ was only 64—in the range identified as "retarded." Their new setting was less crowded, and the older girls and women, despite being handicapped themselves, provided an affectionate and stimulating environment for the newcomers. There were learning materials available—books and toys—and the new "hosts" competed among themselves to show who could help their charges make the greatest progress.

The children—enriched by such focused attention—advanced remarkably. In less than two years, their average IQ zoomed up by an average of 28 points—to 92. They became candidates for adoption into foster homes, and later were able to complete an average of twelve years of schooling. Most went on to hold jobs and earn incomes that could never have been imagined as possible when they started their intellectually undernourished existence.

In contrast, another group of children who remained in the overcrowded and unstimulating orphanage met quite a different fate. Although they started out with higher IQs—an average of 87—the average declined by 26 points within two years. A third of them remained institutionalized, and the rest went on to what amounted to a marginal existence.

From time to time, dramatic examples surface of the human capacity to rebound intellectually after a period of severe deprivation. A psychologist in Czechoslovakia, for example, has reported the case of twin boys whose first six years were spent under what can best be described as cruel and inhuman conditions. Their retarded father and psychopathic stepmother kept them in a cellar or closet and restricted them from leaving the house. They had contact with no other children. When they were discovered as six-year-olds, the twins looked about three. Virtually unable to speak or walk, they were so retarded that it was impossible even to administer an intelligence test to them. But after being moved to a healthy environment, they began to catch up. By age eleven, their IQs had reached the average level, and their personalities and social interactions had become normal.

✎§ The Case of Genie

A decade or so ago, linguists at the University of California and psychologists at the Los Angeles Children's Hospital began following the development of a girl they called Genie, taken from her home by authorities when she was well over thirteen years old.

Genie had been immobilized and isolated from any contact with others for most of her life. From the age of twenty months, she lived the life of a brutalized captive. She was left to sit naked on her potty seat day after day, restrained by a harness. She was offered no stimulation whatsoever. If she made a noise, she was beaten by her father who addressed her only in barking sounds. At night, she was caged in a crib, often hungry after hurried feedings delivered in total silence by her brother.

When Genie first arrived in a hospital after her twelve-year ordeal, she was a malformed creature of 59 pounds. She was without the gift of speech, and like an infant, she was unable to chew and soiled herself. She spit and masturbated constantly. On two preschool tests, she scored as low as normal one-year-olds.

But soon Genie began to make dramatic progress. During her first half-year of freedom, she became toilet trained, and she learned to recognize words and to begin rudimentary speech. After six years in a normal environment, she developed a fund of language, and started to display some basic human emotions and social skills. Genie could even take a bus to school. Her IQ—measured with tests devised for deaf children and requiring no verbal instructions—went from 38 in 1971 to 65 in 1974, and 74 in 1977. Surprisingly, on some of the nonverbal subtests of the Wechsler Intelligence Scale, her scores reflected almost average ability.

Although Genie is quite far from a normal young adult, she did mature dramatically in a relatively short time—and the level of her intellectual capacities rebounded at least to some degree from the abyss of neglect and abuse in which it had for so long languished.

If a child's early environment is filled with positive experiences, will that protect the child from the effects of a poor environment later on?

The evidence is that it will not. Powerful enrichment programs such as Headstart, given to children in the preschool years, will lead only to a temporary benefit if the children are later mired in a disadvantaged environment. Intellectual "inoculations" do not seem to last in the face of deprivation and stress.

Do children's personalities affect their IQ?

The evidence says yes. One investigator found that children born with difficult temperaments are likely to score lowest among their peers on intelligence tests in their third year of life. These are children who are highly irregular, who withdraw or protest when exposed to new situations—whether pertaining to food, clothing, people, or places—and who, when frustrated, tend to react with tantrums.

The reason for the diminished intellectual prowess of these children could be seen in observations of them as one-year-olds interacting with their mothers. Their difficult behavior had led their mothers to stay away from them more—to look at them and play with them less. Easier children, in contrast, evoked in mothers the tendency to stay close to their babies and to interact with them—and as a result, their IQs tended to be appreciably higher.

In another study, investigators selected from a larger group those thirty-five children who showed the greatest increases in IQ between the ages of six through ten, and those thirty-five who showed the greatest decreases. They then analyzed the detailed observations that had been made of these children at home and at school during the first ten years of their lives. Those children whose IQs had increased stood out as more independent, competitive, and verbally more forthright and aggressive. They also worked harder in school, showed a strong desire to master intellectual problems, and were not likely to withdraw from difficult situations. Apparently, children who tend to take on challenging problems are more likely to show increases in IQ than children who shy away from such situations.

Are more intelligent children generally healthier than others?

In his famous study of very gifted children begun sixty years ago, Stanford psychologist Lewis M. Terman found that highly intelligent children enjoyed somewhat better health than did average children, and that they matured physically at an earlier age. But among children within the normal range of intelligence, there appears to be no strong relationship between intelligence and health.

Keep in mind, though, that IQ scores can be depressed by poor health. A child who is the victim of inadequate nutrition and repeated illnesses is likely to spend less time at school and thus suffer a gap in learning during critical periods of development. The result is a reduction in the amount of information and skills accumulated—and, therefore, in tested intelligence.

What about mental health? Are bright kids better adjusted?

The answer is no if you look only at children whose behavior falls within the normal range. However, if you compare a group of children with fairly severe mental health problems to a group whose behavior falls within normal bounds, you are likely to find that the problem children have, on the average, a somewhat lower intelligence level. The reason seems obvious. It is difficult to live up to your intellectual capacities when you're feeling overwhelmed by anxiety, depression, or anger.

Take, for example, children diagnosed as delinquent. As a group, they score about five IQ points below their peers, with chronic delinquents showing the lowest abilities. One study found that disturbed eleven-year-olds eventually lost more time from school, made poorer grades, and obtained lower IQ scores. Students with the most anxiety or aggression were still scoring poorly as fifteen-year-olds.

Famed British psychiatrist Michael Rutter, looking at all the data, concludes that psychiatric disorder is generally associated with a slightly depressed intelligence level—but that the differences involved are usually quite small.

Can you tell from the IQ score how well a child will do in school?

That's what IQ tests do best—predict future academic performance. Many studies have been made of the relationship between IQ and grades among students ranging from elementary schools to universities, and the results are consistent: the higher the IQ, the higher the grades. The correlation is highest for school subjects such as English and Reading that put a premium on verbal skills.

All this should not surprise us. IQ test items are in fact selected precisely because they are related to success in traditional school subjects. In constructing the test, those items that don't differentiate between good and poor students are dropped. High IQ scores and good grades in school depend on the same body of knowledge, and the same skills and motivations. Success in both situations relies on rich vocabularies, facility with the language, self-confidence and high motivation to succeed in intellectual tasks, and thinking about answers to questions instead of just blurting them out.

So if Johnny scores 135 on an IQ test, he probably won't have trouble with his work in school; he should be close to the top of his class. Jimmy, on the other hand, with an IQ of 95 is more likely to be an average student with report cards showing plenty of "C"s. And his potential for college is not likely to be as bright as Johnny's.

That's the way it usually works out. But not always. While a skillfully administered IQ test provides an estimate of future performance, academic progress actually depends on many factors other than the kinds of skills tapped by IQ tests. Children are human beings, not robots whose performance always clicks in tune with their abilities. Frequently the achievement of children does not match the promise of their potential. Perhaps something has gone wrong emotionally, and a behavior problem begins to sap the child's intellectual energies. Motivation may be low, or the environment might be deadening. Sometimes a specific educational disability—a reading or math problem—blocks progress.

The opposite, of course, may be true as well. Many children achieve more than you would expect based on their IQs simply because their motivations, interests, intellectual energy, and overall drive are so high.

Is IQ related to choice of occupation?

Not very much. One famous study did show that the average IQ of professionals—accountants, teachers, engineers—is around 120, while the average for truck drivers and miners is below 100. Children with high IQs generally manage to acquire more education than their peers—and so they generally end up in higher status occupations. But the study also showed that, in every occupation, the range of IQs is extremely wide—among accountants, from 95 to over 140, and among truck drivers, even wider. The child's ultimate choice of vocation clearly depends on considerably more than only IQ.

How about achievement? Do children who have high IQs tend to be the ones who succeed in life?

Those who are unusually gifted seem to do well, and those whose IQs fall below 80 or so are likely to encounter difficulties. But among children in general, there appears to be little relationship between IQ and success in the world outside the classroom. Certainly financial success depends mostly on factors other than IQ. So does success gauged by the degree of a person's sense of happiness and well-being, and the richness of an individual's interpersonal relationships. IQ tests simply do not measure many of the factors essential to the fulfillment by children of their potential.

⮩   Often it is the seemingly unimportant gift which is most useful in life. The ability to communicate confidence may at times serve a doctor better than medical skill; a passionate love of justice, discouraged as forwardness in a child, may one day contribute more to a lawyer's success than the ability to prepare a brief.
Hughes Mearns
"Every Child Has a Gift—Find It! Encourage It!"

What does it mean when a child is described as "gifted"?

The word has assumed so many different meanings that it has become a source of confusion not only to parents but to psychologists and educators as well.

Some regard gifted children simply as that percentage of youngsters who have extraordinarily high IQ scores. Period. By this criterion, the gifted are solely those 1 percent of kids with IQs that soar over 140.

But most authorities argue that there is more to giftedness than high IQ. By their estimates, as many as two and one half million children can be regarded as gifted. It is true enough that the IQs of these children are, on the average, atypically high—but whatever their actual IQ score, it is their unique abilities and talents that place them in a category apart from their peers. Their gifts range from artistic ability to mathematical wizardry, from prowess in chess or music to special skills in language or the visual arts. Still others may display an uncanny skill for writing, public speaking, or leadership. Here are some typical cases: a two-year-old who had already collected and read a library of over 100 books; an eight-year-old who achieved grand master status as a chess champion; a thirteen-year-old child whose writings were good enough to be sought by a publisher.

Do gifted children have any unique personality characteristics?

The patterns vary. Some are blatant individualists and non-conformists, others inquisitive, flexible, and open minded. Most, however, are more likely than other children to be highly motivated, competitive and conscientious, and able to tolerate highly ambiguous situations. Often, too, they can be very demanding of themselves.

Won't most gifted children ultimately be recognized for their achievements?

Unfortunately not. Some attend schools where their talents go unrecognized or, even worse, where their gifts are viewed as trouble-some—traits to be obliterated for the sake of classroom order and "normality." Teachers and peers sometimes lose patience with gifted students' vast knowledge, frustrated that they always seem to "have all the answers." Gifted children quickly learn from this attitude that they can either be themselves and risk ridicule and ostracism, or hide their abilities and feel miserable.

"It is not enough to discern a native gift," writes Hughes Mearns in his essay on encouraging giftedness. "It must be enticed out again and again. Above all, it must be protected against the annihilating effect of social condemnation. . . . The budding scholar may be discouraged by the epithet 'bookworm,' and the young humorist may be suppressed as a troublemaker."

Some gifted kids unfortunately find themselves in schools that totally ignore their gifted students, assuming erroneously that they will somehow make it on their own. In fact many gifted children may become so discouraged by everyday, routine schooling that they tune out of education altogether—and thus never really get the chance to fulfill their promise.

ও৪ Full many a flower is born to blush unseen,
And waste its sweetness on the desert air.
Thomas Grey
"Elegy Written in a Country Churchyard"

Should a gifted child be pushed ahead in school?

That's an individual matter. There is no sure rule of thumb.
But this much is sure: All gifted children need opportunities to
express their special talents—whether at school or at home.

Many gifted students, especially those who are highly motivated,
seem to thrive on acceleration and show no signs of maladjustment
as a result. Others cannot handle it. They may have the intellectual
ability to skip several grades, but the experience is emotionally terrify-
ing—especially since they may end up being frozen out of normal
social relationships. The temperament of the individual pupil needs
to be taken into account when considering acceleration.

Some gifted kids manage to flourish intellectually without being
pushed ahead in school. Although they find the classroom bland
and uninteresting, it is at the same time benign and unthreatening.
The key is that they get the extra support they crave on the home
front; talented children tend to appreciate nearly any stimulation
that goes beyond traditional schooling. A philosophy professor recalls that, as a gifted child, his parents helped him learn multiplication, algebra, and calculus while his classmates practiced adding
and subtracting. He taught himself Hebrew when he was five. In
the seventh grade, he entertained himself reading the philosophy
of Descartes and Hume. As long as he could do this extra work,
he says, he enjoyed the ordinary schools he attended.

**What about the special educational programs available for
gifted children?**

They have traditionally been inadequate. Four hundred of the
most eminent men and women of the century, exceptionally talented
as children, were questioned in adulthood about their early educational experiences. Nearly two-thirds of them remembered being
unhappy with their teachers and schools.

Special programs for gifted children have improved in recent years, but hardly enough. Unfortunately, in many areas such programs are not available. They are especially easy targets for federal and state educational budget cuts, and as a result, they are often neglected by school districts under pressure to teach basic skills to the majority of the school population.

Moreover, where special programs do exist, they often do not adequately nurture the abilities of gifted kids, whose lives are thereby cheated. In some settings, for example, "enrichment" may be equivalent to busywork, with bright students simply doing more of the same tasks required of the average pupils. Occasionally, these students are given special assignments in areas where they show unusual talent, but the slow-paced classroom situation is otherwise left unchanged. Others are exposed to cultural education—instruction in music, art, drama, dance, creative writing, or foreign languages—earlier than it is generally made available, but their academic needs still go unmet. In some acceleration programs, new material is presented so quickly that students have little time to practice or absorb it, and as a result, important topics may appear superficial and unimportant. In the view of education expert Sheila Vaughan of the University of California, "Americans have always had trouble on the question of how to handle people who are different *better,* rather than different *poorer.* "

In recent years, however, more attention and funding have been given to special education for the gifted. Many programs have been started, staffed and coordinated by dedicated experts. The new curricula are providing more of the academic challenge and support gifted children need.

&ᔕ   Most people live . . . in a very restricted circle of their potential being.

William James
The Letters of William James

What happens to gifted children whose needs are not met?

They may lose interest in school—possibly to the point of failing subjects. They may develop psychological problems or a sense of insecurity in their social relationships. Unless compensatory steps are undertaken at home and in school, gifted children may suffer from feelings of being "different," and of alienation, loneliness, and self-doubt. Says George Roeper of Detroit's Roeper School: "We hadn't realized until recently that giftedness is a kind of handicap. Bright kids need a structure and challenging environment just as much as deaf kids need an atmosphere sensitive to their personal needs."

Moreover, it is sometimes too easy to overlook the emotional needs of these precocious children. We tend to forget that they are, after all, kids. The nature of their achievements sometimes leads adults to believe that they are more mature than they may be. Actually some may feel enormous stress when pushed to focus on academics or accelerate in school when they clearly do not feel prepared to do so. Elementary school principal Joanne Yatvin believes this may make them "feel guilty about wanting to play, to make noise, to act silly—guilty about being children."

    The first thing we have to remember about gifted children is that they are children. Like other children, they grow, get measles, cry, laugh, and suffer the glories and pains of growing up. Because they are smart, people are sometimes intimidated by them and think that just because they have giant vocabularies or understand quadratic equations they have the world by the tail. Not so.

Priscilla L. Vail
The World of the Gifted Child

Is it true that gifted children tend to turn out to be emotionally maladjusted?

Contrary to popular image, gifted children do not generally grow up to be neurotic or unhappy. Terman's long-range study of fifty gifted children described earlier helped debunk many popular myths about people with high IQs. In comparison with a group of children with average intelligence, the gifted turned out to be blessed with remarkably good social adjustment, and later on to be relatively free of marital and sexual problems. Moreover, they were less prone to nervous symptoms such as headaches, tics, and stuttering.

Still, some gifted kids don't adapt—mainly because the people in their environments do them in. Insensitive classmates can make gifted children miserable by labeling them as "creeps" or "eggheads." One precocious ten-year-old, for example, became the constant butt of classroom jokes. His schoolmates taunted him, demanding that he spell difficult words for them—as if his was the talent of a freak. Rather than face humiliation at school, he eventually became the willing victim of various physical symptoms so that he could stay at home.

Sometimes gifted children react to their boredom with the rigidly structured school curriculum by becoming disruptive. Robert Rinaldi, assistant superintendent for exceptional students in the schools of Baltimore, Maryland, has observed the phenomenon. "If a child is always talking out of turn," says Rinaldi, "if he always thinks things are funny, if he's always trying to teach the class, it is not necessarily a sign that he is a troublemaker. It can also mean that he has potential that is not being tapped." Psychiatrists speculate that some young gang leaders may actually be talented individuals who, uninspired by school, channel their skills in an antisocial direction.

Gifted children may also pay a price for their unusual sensitivity to the environment around them. They go around burdened by the feeling that the world is unfair, and in trying to make things right, they put themselves under more pressure than they can handle. Parents have observed that, as adolescents, such children seem to be carrying the weight of the world on their shoulders.

ex§ Three Tips for Helping Gifted Children
- Give them something to do as well as something to think about—whether it is painting, cooking, carving, playing an instrument, athletics, carpentry. Gifted children clearly have a great capacity for absorbing information—but they need opportunities for "giving it back" as well.
- Allow them opportunities for caretaking—of smaller children, older persons, or pets. A sense of responsibility creates a bond between the child and the world—something gifted children often need badly.
- View the child's special learning pattern as a bonus, not as the main thing. Try to see gifted children in the same human terms as you would any child.

How should the parent deal with a gifted but solitary and introverted child?

Unfortunately, the pressure parents feel to have their children achieve is often matched by the need to have them meet arbitrary standards of adjustment—to "mix" to be "in" and socially popular. Moments of seclusion for the contemporary child are to be avoided, even feared. "Thou shalt socialize" appears to be the eleventh commandment of modern juvenile life. We tend to equate a spirit of contemplation with an "oddball" personality, and many parents even view the introverted child fearfully as the incipient victim of a serious psychological problem. "Catatonic" is how one parent described her shy and musically gifted ten-year-old daughter.

"A man is not idle," wrote Victor Hugo, "because he is absorbed in thought. There is a visible labour and there is an invisible labour." The same is true for the child—except that the private workings of a child's mind are often even more precious than those of the adult's. Youngsters who are rudely catapulted from their idle moments in the lazy world of fantasy and solitary thought are being blocked from more than a temporary feeling of happiness and well-being. They are being deprived of an opportunity to test the limits of their soaring interests, or to develop an identification with heroic figures, or to puzzle out a personal solution to one of life's perplexities.

These pursuits are not usually tangible, but they are as important in their own way as the hours spent learning the multiplication tables, the piano scales, or the stance that Little Leaguers must take at home plate. Being President, even for a few imaginative minutes, is as enriching an experience as memorizing the Gettysburg Address. "There are other truths," wrote Loren Eiseley, "than those contained in laboratory burners, or on the blackboards, or in test tubes."

In order to improve the mind, we ought less to learn than to contemplate.

René Descartes

Is the "gifted child" the same as a "genius"?

No. Children within the tiny group fairly described as geniuses typically do, of course, have high IQs. But to qualify for the term "genius" requires more than being a highly intelligent and gifted child. A genius operates with a fund of talent that results in extraordinary and rare accomplishments. The originality and creativity of these accomplishments are so superior that they stand out as a lasting contribution to society. Put another way, winning a contest at a science fair doesn't necessarily make Johnny another Einstein.

Is it critical to provide potential geniuses with just the right environment in order for them to realize their talents?

Some people are convinced that children born with exceptional talents will never bring them to fruition unless they are surrounded by nurturant adults who recognize and stimulate their abilities early in life. The truth is, however, that many persons who have grown to be geniuses lived their early years in what would appear to be deadening environments. Isaac Newton's father was a humble farmer who died before Isaac was born. Karl Gauss, the great mathematician, was the son of a bricklayer. Abraham Lincoln was the son of a carpenter. Martin Luther was the son of a peasant. Louis Armstrong, a true genius who originated a new art form, was actually a neglected child. His father abandoned the family, and his mother was more often "out on the town" than at home. As a young child, he was apprehended for firing blank cartridges from his stepfather's revolver and was placed in the New Orleans Colored Waifs Home for Boys—and it was there that he was taught to play an instrument.

Ideally, of course, the capacities of a genius are nurtured by the environment. But those capacities are inborn, and their release is difficult to deny. Psychologists Sandra Scarr and Richard Weinberg describe Mozart's early products this way: "When Mozart composed his first minuets at the age of five, his precocious talent reflected his father's teaching, his opportunities to get a harpsichord—and a little help from his genes."

Are kids who show signs of genius likely to be abnormal in some way?

It has long been a popular belief that those who show rare originality are likely to be psychologically abnormal. The phrase "mad genius," for example, is widely used to describe individuals who are viewed as unusually brilliant—but only at the cost of also being quite odd. The belief probably arose because many famous geniuses did in fact suffer from mental disorders. Among them are the scientist Sir Isaac Newton, artists Vincent van Gogh and Leonardo da Vinci, writers Jonathan Swift and Edgar Allan Poe, and composers Robert Schumann and Maurice Ravel.

The existence of such cases does not mean, however, that in order to be a genius, you must have some abnormality. Most people who have great and enduring talents go through life without ever suffering symptoms of mental disorder.

What is creativity?

Like the definition of intelligence, this has been the subject of considerable debate. A practical definition was developed by D. W. MacKinnon, a University of California psychologist, who emphasized the products rather than the process of creativity. He saw creative acts as having three characteristics: They result in the production of something rare and new; they help reach a specific and identifiable goal; and they are pursued to completion.

By this definition, Johnny cannot necessarily be regarded as creative, however beautifully he plays the piano, and however many hours he sits at it practicing. Just having the talent is not enough. He must put the talent to work in a productive way. Like Mozart, he must eventually produce something of merit—something specific and tangible.

Is it possible to measure the extent of a child's creativity?

Although psychologists have expended considerable effort attempting to devise tests that will measure creativity, the task has proved difficult. In such tests, children are asked, for example, to think of as many uses as possible for something ordinary like a paper clip, to devise as many problems as possible using only a fixed set of numbers, to list all the words that might be associated with an ordinary word, or to describe the underlying similarities in seemingly different things.

No one is sure, however, that such test items actually measure creativity, and it is difficult, moreover, to ascribe a valid score to the child's answers. Parents and teachers are constantly evaluating how "original" children are in approaching their work or in solving problems—that is, the extent to which they bring to their daily tasks a unique and personal "touch." But in the final analysis, such evaluations are largely subjective. It is more difficult to "score" a child on creativity than on the items of an intelligence test that tap skills in memory, numbers, or vocabulary.

Moreover, creativity doesn't necessarily end up in a tangible product right away. The child who sits daydreaming for hours may actually be giving birth to something startlingly new—but for the moment, the product is only in the child's head. It's virtually impossible to test this in any quantitative way.

How can you tell then if a child is creative?

Children may be displaying a creative streak if they are quick to arrive at innovative concepts, or to see fresh and novel connections between apparently different ideas and objects. Their kind of thinking goes well beyond that of children who simply have a wealth of knowledge—who have mastered a lot of facts and can readily solve problems or puzzles. If your child is demonstrating the capacity to perform intellectual tasks and produce information, that's one thing. But if the child is constantly adding a new dimension— taking the raw materials of life and developing a totally fresh insight or product—*that's* a sign of creative potential.

✑ The highest intellects, like the tops of mountains, are the first to catch and to reflect the dawn.
                                                                                    Thomas B. Macaulay

Can a child be creative without having an unusually high IQ?

That's true of many children. Having superior intelligence, according to MacKinnon, certainly "does not guarantee creativity." While creativity in most fields—especially the sciences—requires a certain threshold of mental ability, creative acts ultimately depend less on intelligence than on other factors. In fact in some artistic fields such as painting and sculpture, there is little overlap between creative ability and IQ.

Standard intelligence tests, after all, hardly provide a valid measure of a child's creative potential. Many children whose scores on IQ tests are just average or below emerge as creative individuals— while others even with astronomically high IQs never light up the world with fresh and creative ideas. At any given intelligence level, children may harbor varying degrees of creativity.

⌇ Helping Kids Be Creative
In his book *Psychology in Teaching, Learning, and Growth,* psychologist Don E. Hamachek suggests a number of ways that teachers can help encourage and release the creativity that, he believes, is present to some degree in all children. His suggestions might be followed equally well by parents.
- Make clear that you value creative, novel, different, innovative, and unique ways of doing things.
- Accept nonconformist thinking. Traits that characterize the creative child—adventuresomeness, uniqueness, impulsiveness— often tend to evoke negative responses in many adults.
- Teach children to ask "extending" questions—that is, questions that take them from what they know to new and different ways to think about what they know.
- Be willing to accept imperfect products. Recognize that mistakes and imperfections are typically natural consequences of learning activities that are new, different, and original.
- Most of all, children need to know that "expressing themselves in new and different ways is not only possible, but valued, so that those who want to can and those who are somewhat more hesitant may at least try."

Are creative children likely to be maladjusted or lonely?

There is little evidence that they are. Studies do show that some creative people were "lone wolves" as kids. But whether they were rejected by their peers or just wanted to spend time alone, being different from others seemed to cause them no anxiety or anguish. In fact many creative people want very much to be different and original—off the beaten track.

Sometimes, of course, creative kids may cause problems for themselves—for example, when they take on projects beyond their abilities, or try to impose meaning and order when none is possible, or express views that are radically non-conformist. Some are hostile and aggressive—not the kind of child who turns out to be "most popular in the class." But in general, creative children—especially those also high in intelligence—are also likely to be blessed with a number of very positive traits: flexibility, assertiveness, self-assurance, a sense of humor, curiosity, venturesomeness, resilience to stress, and positive and constructive ways of reacting to problems.

Should daydreaming be discouraged in a creative child?

Not unless it is becoming a chronic substitute for dealing with reality. Daydreaming can become a persistent avenue of escape—so much so that the distinction between fantasy and reality gradually becomes unclear. Instead of motivating children to do what they are capable of, daydreaming can serve as a substitute for achievement, even blocking it altogether.

The existence of such a relatively rare clinical problem does not mean, however, that normal children should be deprived of the luxury of retreating at times into their private worlds of inaction and reverie. Many of the world's great insights and creative leaps have occurred in a state of inner absorption. Indeed, daydreaming behavior, far from being pathological, is often an integral element of a truly creative process.

Are children born with creative talents, or can they be developed through training?

A child without the potential ability will not develop creative talent no matter what the circumstances. But some people born with a creative streak do not find opportunities to express it until they are well past childhood. Some of the very finest artists, composers, and writers do not really hit their stride until much later in life. It is only then that they can explore the creative gift that has been lying dormant all along. Missing until then were the training and practice that allow creativity to come to light.

Are some creative children inhibited about displaying their ideas?

Because of the achievement standards often set in schools and at home, many children probably do inhibit their fresh and novel ideas for fear of "making a mistake." Typical schoolchildren are afraid of criticism. They struggle to avoid the humiliation of not meeting the standards of performance and competence set for them.

Children who offer a creative, off-beat response are often left with a sense of failure in the face of ridicule from others. The most common reaction to such an episode is to assume a cautious stance and hold back from sharing any comment or ideas that are less than certain. Such children find comfort in knowing their silence will avoid public failure, even if this means foregoing the chance that their ideas might be applauded rather than put down.

To be creative, children must not only have a base of knowledge but be willing to use that knowledge in new ways. They must, in other words, be willing to risk setbacks, failures, or even derision for letting the world know about a strange and new idea. They must have an accepting attitude about making a mistake.

✏ Hide not your Talents, they for Use were made. What's a Sun-Dial in the shade?

> Ben Franklin
> *Poor Richard's Almanac*

Is the traditional kind of education superfluous for the creative child?

Not at all. Creative acts require a base of knowledge. They must spring from something. Creativity demands the combination of earlier ideas and products into new forms. The painter who produces a new shade of green uses already existing colors. Similarly, the creative child who composes a song cannot set it down without first having learned the rudiments of music notation.

If children are to be creative they must acquire basic information and skills. Otherwise they have nothing with which to kindle their creative potential. The motivation may be there, and as the next chapter shows, that is often critical for success in school and throughout life. But first you have to know the subject matter. Motivation to create without the raw materials to create with is likely to produce miseries rather than masterworks.

CHAPTER SIX
↭§ The Magic Flame: Motivation to Achieve

"I give up. I'm not even going to try."

Many parents have heard those words—or seen them acted out—as their children address the task of learning. They are spoken by children who are ready to throw in the towel before they have tested the limits of their resources. Such children lack the motivation to achieve—the magic, internal flame that can spell the difference not only between success and failure but between happiness and despair.

Consider the case of Robert. "When you're through with high school," the counselor said to him, "you might do well to take up a trade or find a job. Your abilities are just not the kind that suggest a college career." That was ten years ago. Today young Dr. Robert Norton, with a good medical record in medical school behind him, is about to begin his residency at a large hospital.

Was the counselor a quack? By no means. Were the tests the counselor used invalid? Again, no. They provided an accurate enough picture of the boy's potential. But neither the counselor nor Bob's parents had reckoned with the motivation factor. They failed to recognize that the young man had sighted a goal so precious that he was willing to use every element of intelligence, every ounce of energy at his disposal—and then some—to reach it.

Bob's case is admittedly extreme. Ability and achievement usually do go hand-in-hand. Yet many young people with higher IQs and aptitudes than Robert have achieved far less. The reason often lies in that magical quality our parents used to label "stick-to-itiveness." Much of a person's success in life, we were taught, depends on hard work as well as on brain power—on perspiration as well as on inspiration. Counselors have repeatedly found this truth revealed in the triumphs or defeats of children. A child's "I will," rather than IQ, often determines success or failure.

Virtually all children recognize early that achievement in school is one of life's key ingredients. They are endlessly exhorted to learn, to master, to show that they are as smart or smarter than their fellow students. But children differ radically in how prepared they are for such competition. Some are psychologically geared up for achievement; others remain psychologically limp and passive. Children can make their way through the educational maze more successfully if they are aroused to compete, if they lust for success. With sufficient motivation, many children—even those of barely average ability—pursue their goals with unswerving determination. And their levels of achievement turn out to be far higher than either their parents or teachers would have anticipated.

From studies of the impact of economics on family life, many have concluded in the past that high motivation is likely to be fostered only in middle- or upper-class families—that we should not expect equally sturdy bridges to the minds and hearts of children to be built in the homes of the poor.

Not so. The key to motivation does not lie in the material resources of the family. The parents of countless "disadvantaged" youngsters manage to provide both the stimulation and rewards necessary for stoking the child's motivational fires. The correlation between social class and competence is far from perfect, and the careers of many children, even from the most destitute homes, run counter to the trend. Many impoverished families, despite an appalling lack of material resources, have continued to nourish solid connections to the minds of the young. Intellectual stagnation is hardly a sure trait of poor children, and many such children learn early to associate achievement with joy.

By the same token, a good prognosis is hardly inevitable for the minds of well-to-do children. Many wealthy kids grow up in homes with fathers and mothers too preoccupied with choosing among available pleasures to kindle the motivational flames of their young.

Lacerating tensions often rage between parents and children over the issue of motivation. Explosive family arguments rage when school children fail to do as well as their teachers rightly expect. Problems surface at home when children who are clearly well above average in intelligence do poorly simply because they expend only minimal effort. Many stop doing school work altogether or even refuse to go to school. Parents become alarmed not only because their children are failing now but because they exhibit the kind of uncaring attitude that bodes ill for the future as well. It is such a scenario that often also triggers in parents a desperate quest for professional help—a search for ways to turn their children's potential into reality.

And yet it is often the parents themselves who are largely responsible for the child's achievement drive, or lack of it. Children grow up with a powerful urge to achieve when their early displays of competence are reinforced by undiluted affection. Even infants begin to view themselves as masterful when their unfolding skills—smiling, gurgling, sleeping through the night, crawling—evoke rapture in their caretakers. And later, the most onerous school tasks can take on a special luster for youngsters whose hints of success bring torrents of parental praise.

The origins of achievement motivation vary in subtle ways from one child to another, and no single theory, therefore, is likely to encompass all of them. Many of the roots, however, can be traced to those early and transforming relationships in which kids learn to equate their own unfolding competence with the world's approval and love.

What is it inside children that leads one to work hard to achieve, while another seems to let every opportunity pass by?

It is often impossible even for the most expert observer to tell. Children, like adults, vary considerably in the motives that underlie their behavior. Often it takes patience and a cool head to see beneath the surface.

Consider the case of Eddie. He spends all his free time studying, and wants nothing but "A"s in his school work. From outward appearances, it would seem that Eddie's consuming passion is to be a resounding success in life. But in reality, Eddie's motivation has quite different roots. His driving purpose is simply to please his parents. He knows that they expect only the best from their son—that they revel in his good grades and shower him with affection in their wake. Another child, Janet, seems equally driven to succeed. But her motive is quite different. It is power. She is convinced that the way to be admired and stay in control is to be at the very top of her class.

It is equally difficult to discern why it is that some children are totally unmotivated, and allow their school work to languish. Many may not lack ambition at all. They may want to succeed in the worst way, but they expend little effort because they live in morbid fear of failure. Other children, showing exactly the same drift-along behavior, have quite a different reason: They have made achievement the centerpiece of their struggle for independence. Their driving need is to show their parents who is really boss—in this instance, by doing precisely the opposite of what their parents would wish.

Guessing a child's actual motives is a difficult task. It often takes time and energy—and the willingness to look beyond the obvious behavior to its sources. It means listening sympathetically to what children say, and trying to puzzle out its true meaning. Otherwise we often end up dealing with appearances rather than reality.

Does achievement motivation tend to remain at about the same level over the childhood years?

Surprisingly so. There are peaks and valleys, of course, and many children don't even begin to apply their potential for many years. But in general, achievement motivation is among the more stable elements of a child's personality. Children who appear eager to master intellectual challenges in their preschool years tend to maintain a similarly positive outlook through adolescence and into adulthood.

What types of families are especially helpful in cultivating high achievement motivation in children?

Those that leave little or no doubt in the child's mind about the value of intellectual pursuits. Family members read more, for example, and they frequently discuss intellectual matters. They also talk about achieving individuals as the kinds of people they admire, holding them up as models. The parents make their own intellectual aspirations obvious, and they furnish their children with a constantly replenished store of stimulating experiences and materials. Such an environment—where self-reliance, curiosity, and exploration are encouraged—tends to fuel the achievement drive.

Is the relationship with mother especially critical in generating the zeal to achieve?

Beginning in infancy, children learn that their accomplishments are likely to bring one of the most gratifying prizes life can offer: the love of mother. Here is a sketch of the mother most likely to generate achievement motivation in her young: She rewards the developmental strides of her infant from the very opening days of life; she tends to notice and praise the baby's emerging skills—sitting up, coordinating hand and eye movements, speaking words, standing, walking; she responds to her infant's cooing and smiling by cooing and smiling in return; she delights in the child's demonstrations of emerging intellectual competence—in language, memory, or numbers—and she shows her delight without restraint.

Such a mother, in other words, makes it clear from the start that she values achievement. She sets high standards for her children, rewarding them when they perform well and admonishing them when they do not. Poet Carl Sandburg remembered how his mother "couldn't help saying nice things when we did well at anything. Whether it was school work, or learning the catechism, or hanging out sheets and shirts on a cold winter day, she would speak thanks and say I was a good boy."

The result of such maternal behavior is to strengthen the child's lifelong zeal for mastering new skills. Children favored with rich rewards for their developmental victories grow up with the powerful belief that they are causal agents—that the world can be controlled and mastered effectively through individual efforts.

A number of investigators, looking into the fact that Japanese youngsters seem to be showing an extraordinary advantage in intellectual and academic pursuits, have identified the Japanese mother as the key. In the words of University of California anthropologist George De Vos, who has been studying the Japanese for well over two decades, "She takes it upon herself to be the responsible agent, reinforcing the educational process instituted in the schools." Known as the "kyoiku-mama," which translates into "education-mama," she is so vocal and active in the Japanese PTAs that some Japanese have recommended that the organization be called the

MTA. All the while, she keeps reminding the child of her deeply warm feelings—and that her child is the most important thing in the world to her.

 ⌐♦ A man who has been the indisputable favorite of his mother keeps for life the feeling of a conqueror, that confidence of success which frequently induces real success.

Sigmund Freud

Can't mothers be overly zealous—too much in the mold of the overbearing "Jewish" mother—and end up harming her children rather than helping them?

For at least two generations, the so-called "Jewish" mother—upward striving, prone to worry, zealous for her children's welfare—has been targeted as the source of all her children's problems. Although it is true that such mothers (they can be Italian, Irish, Japanese, black) may spawn a degree of guilt and anxiety in some children, they typically serve instead as a source of psychological strength and well-being, and high motivation.

The errors of these traditional "Jewish" matriarchs lie largely in their chronic hovering—which may be difficult for some children, but which, on the other hand, does not induce the kind of anger, emptiness, and despair that so often haunt children who are denied the lifelong benefits of early affectional bonds. Note that it is the "overprotective" mothers who have produced the John F. Kennedys and Leonard Bernsteins of the world—not the Lee Harvey Oswalds.

To keep their motivations high, all children have a desperate need on the home front for a defender who will stem any erosion of their sense of competence, who will keep them from beginning to live as if the world's sometimes negative portrait of them is actually true. Children have to find in their kitchens and living rooms passionate protectors—yes, worriers—who will persistently rebuild resources so often depleted in the struggle to grow up whole.

The mother's yearning for her children's success has given many youngsters the precious capacity to disengage from a corrosive and destructive environment. Psychiatrist Gloria Powell, who grew up to be the director of the child outpatient department at the UCLA Neuropsychiatric Institute, recalls her early beginnings as one of five fatherless children of a black family living in poverty in Roxbury, Massachusetts. "Everything my mother did and said somehow got the message across that we would succeed—and that we deserved to. There was never any doubt that I would go on to college."

For Powell herself, a self-concept as "poor" or "disadvantaged" never developed. "In fact," she says, "it wasn't until I went off to college that I realized that I was poor. When I filled out the forms required to apply for financial assistance I suddenly realized that one year of tuition cost more than my mother's entire annual income."

ᮃ Mighty is the force of motherhood! It transforms all things by its vital heat.

George Eliot

If the early relationship with mother is so important in achievement motivation, where does all this leave the father?

Newborns show no consistent preference for one parent over the other. Babies grow attached to whichever parent, male or female, satisfies their needs and provides their comforts.

Mothers generally have the advantage during the opening days of life in handling, cuddling, and feeding the infant, and it is not surprising, therefore, that infants prefer their mothers during the first year. But there is no reason to suppose fathers cannot do these things equally well, and thus create an emotional bond between themselves and their children. Indeed, during the second year of life, many infants appear to show stronger preferences for the father than for mother.

As many child researchers point out, however, the rapport of the infant with the mother and father often differs in quality and evokes different kinds of interactions. Each parent has the potential for exerting a unique impact on the intellectual development of the young. As the next chapter makes clear, kids are likely to do best when they have both a loving mother *and* father to motivate them.

Do children's interactions with father actually make a difference in their attitudes toward achievement?

The evidence says yes. Differences in children's abilities and goals appear to depend, at least in part, on the characteristics of their fathers.

The research literature on the effects of fathers' absence on children's cognitive development reveals considerable differences in performance between children from intact nuclear families and fatherless families in terms of achievement scores, IQ scores, and grade-point average.

Most of the relevant studies have focused on boys. Investigators have found, for example, that among adolescent boys who have warm relationships with their fathers the motivation to succeed is stronger than among boys who do not enjoy such a relationship. The amount of time adolescent boys spend with their fathers seems to be directly related also to the degree of responsibility and leadership these boys show in school. Here are the recollections of one confident and successful teenager about the generous paternal commitment of his father. "He had a big effect on me because he was a gentle person and he was always interested in what I had to say. *Anything* was important and he was willing to sit and listen to me and talk to me. I was a person to be listened to, not a thing to keep quiet. He never said he couldn't talk to me because he was too busy. He would always stop what he was doing and help me."

One researcher found that boys scored higher on tests if they had fathers who were kind, helpful, and given to praise. Boys whose fathers were cool, aloof, and remote scored lower. A survey of 16,000 British children revealed that a paternal attitude of caring—demonstrated by attending school conferences and accompanying youngsters on outings—resulted in measurably better academic performance in children. Highly available fathers, report investigators, can serve as models of both perseverance and the motivation to excel. However, having a competent father will not facilitate a boy's intellectual development if the father is not consistently accessible to the boy or if the relationship between father and son is poor.

The data are convincing—but unfortunately, many fathers remain surprisingly remote from their kids. For countless fathers, the conflict between the "outside" world of work and the "inside" world of paternal tasks and feelings has been resolved in favor of a life altogether irrelevant to their children. The masculine role of family provider has been a signal for them to abdicate virtually any involvement in the duties and challenges of parenthood. The addiction to work appears often to provide a guilt-free rationalization for the father's lack of commitment to the responsibilities of childrearing; the task of "making a living" becomes a convenient excuse to sidestep the awesome responsibilities toward children inherent in fatherhood. Difficult and challenging as they may often be, the worlds of business, academics, or government are seen by many men as considerably more rewarding than PTA, homework, or just quiet, intimate hours with a child.

 Tips for Traveling Fathers
    Here are some steps to help fill the "father gap" faced by many children whose dads must often be away from home:
* Be aware that your trips are likely to cause some anxiety. A child who appears tense on learning of the father's imminent departure from home can be helped by being reassured that the trip is necessary, and by knowing how eagerly the father looks forward to a reunion.
* Share as much information as you can about what you are going to be doing.
* Keep in reach and in touch. Any anxieties a child builds up about an absent father's whereabouts can be allayed to some degree by hearing father's voice.
* Whenever the occasion permits, take your child with you on one of your business trips.
* Save some energy for the taxing reentry to home and family.
* Let your children know that being away was tough for you, too.
* Leave room for family vacations. You can use vacation periods to reestablish bonds that are interrupted by travel.
* Most important, don't be reticent about showing warm feelings when you are together with your kids.

Do fathers affect the achievement patterns of girls as well as boys?

Relevant studies do not often include girls along with boys, but what studies exist do show that their cognitive development and achievement motivation are affected by their fathers as well.

Unfortunately, fathers' impact on daughters is not always positive. "Fathers, even more than mothers," writes psychologist Ross D. Parke, "tend to respond to their children in sex-stereotyped ways and to encourage masculine pursuits in their sons and feminine ones in their daughters. Since intellectual achievement is still viewed by some parents—in spite of recent changes—as a masculine activity, fathers may actually undermine their daughters' intellectual advancement because they view academic success as unfeminine." Fathers are more likely to emphasize the importance of a career and occupational success for their sons than for their daughters.

But the potential for a positive influence is there. If the father-daughter relationship is structured so that the daughter is encouraged to model herself after father's intellectual pursuits and achievement drive, his influence can be potent indeed. Margaret Mead recalled: "It was my father, even more than my mother, whose career was limited by the number of her children and health, who defined for me my place in the world."

Is birth order related to the strength of the child's achievement drive?

The answer seems to be yes—at least as far as firstborns are concerned. Firstborn children tend to set higher standards of achievement for themselves than do those born later. They are also more competitive and have higher educational aspirations. Indeed a strong achievement motive appears to have inspired many firstborns to become outstanding successes in life. If you were to survey any list of prominent people—eminent scholars, people listed in *Who's Who,* even American presidents—you would find an unusually high proportion of firstborns. They include Theodore Roosevelt, Harry Truman, Martin Luther King, Winston Churchill, Margaret Mead, Muhammad Ali, Pablo Picasso, Jane Fonda.

Various explanations have been offered, all of them emphasizing—as indicated in the earlier discussion of intelligence—that parents tend to treat firstborns differently from later children. One investigator showed that mothers not only spend more time with the firstborn, but are more protective, take a greater part in the child's activities, and are more extreme in both their praise and criticism. In contrast, later children receive less attention, guidance, and direction from their parents.

Are there specific ways that parents can help start their children off on the right track as far as achievement motivation is concerned?

Evidence suggests that it is important to encourage independence early. In one significant study, mothers were asked at what ages they had demanded that their sons begin to demonstrate their independence—for example, by going to bed by themselves, staying in the house alone, entertaining themselves, choosing their own clothes, making their own friends, and earning their own spending money. All the mothers in the study had made many demands by the time their sons reached ten years. But boys who were high in achievement motivation were urged to become independent at much earlier ages than the others. They received about as many demands by age two as the boys with low achievement motivation got by age four.

Children with a zest to achieve appear also to have parents who set high standards for their young and who openly express concern for their performance. At the same time, their parents are able to express encouragement and warmth, unabashedly displaying their affection when their children do well.

How can parents teach their children that doing well in school is important?

By conveying how important it is in their own scale of values. If mothers and fathers regularly talk about the value of learning, their children are likely to get the message. But if they constantly emphasize other values, children will pick up a different message altogether.

It doesn't help youngsters, for example, to observe that their parents get more excited about sports and social events than about books and grades. Many mothers and fathers remain blissfully unaware that the values they preach so vehemently to their children are nowhere in evidence in the everyday business of living.

Take the matter of homework, for example. Researchers have been struck in recent years by the fact that Japanese children appear to be more achievement oriented and to be doing better academically than American kids. They asked Japanese and American mothers how much time someone in the family spent helping their first-graders with homework. Interestingly enough, the Japanese mothers reported an average of nearly a half hour a night, while the American mothers reported an average of only 14 minutes.

Our own parents, in giving our school work their unswerving attention, often without fully understanding its content, let us know how deeply it counted. In showering us with warmth and affection for long-division problems solved, with awe and admiration for history dates memorized and delivered in a single breath, they provided episodes that conveyed how important it was to learn. The act of our learning was overlaid with their commitment and love.

How hard should children be pushed to reach their potential?

The answer differs for each child, but this much is clear: Some parents appear to be so fearful that their children will fail that they push them much too hard. In the process they stir up so much resentment that the youngsters revolt altogether.

Children growing up in homes where parental pressure is extreme often settle for low achievement goals. In some families, the child who begins to find the going rough at school is stigmatized, labeled as a nonentity who is destined never to do anything well. Such children eventually end up feeling as if they are not *expected* to show interest in success—and so naturally they oblige.

There is no point in generating so much pressure that it creates in the child an unbearably high pitch of anxiety about failure. Not only is academic performance affected as a result, but the child's overall self-concept and adjustment suffers as well. Some children, pushed mercilessly beyond their capabilities, may become overly dependent and unsure, or unable to think rationally under pressure.

But keep in mind that the other extreme—too much parental indulgence—can also lead to low achievement motivation. Then youngsters end up feeling that they do not have to meet any tangible standards of excellence. Since everything is done for them, they need not exert themselves.

The key seems to lie in being neither too harsh and authoritarian, nor too passive and permissive. A combination of firmness and caring is usually the soundest approach.

Who has the greater influence on a child's motivation to achieve— parents or friends?

It may come as a surprise to many parents that the values and standards of the home typically take precedence for the child over those of peers.

Mothers and fathers often tend to view their child's peers as a threat. They are fearful that friends will exert an unwholesome influence, causing motivation and school performance to decay. The result can become a contest: Who will control the destiny of my children—we who gave them life and know what is best, or friends who are likely to tarnish their future?

Such confrontations are typically unwarranted. Studies show that friends do not necessarily work at cross-purposes with the positive influences of parents and teachers. Indeed, the relationship between the child's educational aspirations and the parents' is surprisingly high. The peer culture just does not disturb the child's sense of identification with parents as much as is popularly assumed.

Peer influence is likely to be significant mainly for children who grow up in homes lacking warmth or support. Such youngsters are prone to feel insecure and carry out into the world a consuming need for acceptance by others. These children have no misgivings about letting their parents down since they have little to lose in the first place. Acceptance by "the group" is all the acceptance they feel they are going to get—so they are willing to adopt its values at any cost.

In short: the weaker the family ties, the more likely a child is to be influenced by friends. Kids who grow up enveloped by warmth and encouragement are less likely than many parents fear to align themselves with peers who do not share parental values and standards of achievement.

&§ . . . I sat on the curb and watched the other boys on my block play baseball. . . . I was never asked to take part because they took it for granted I would be no good at it. They were right, of course. . . .

One of the boys once asked, "What's in those books you're always reading?"

"Stories," I answered.

"What kind?" asked somebody else without much interest. . . .

I launched full tilt into the book I was immersed in at the moment. . . . They listened bug-eyed and breathless . . . I was offering them, without being aware of doing it, a new and exciting experience. . . .

Not one of them left the stoop until I had finished, and I went

upstairs that wonderful evening not only a member of the tribe
but a figure in my own right among them.

Moss Hart
Act One: An Autobiography

Why is it that some children don't give learning tasks a try?

Often they have become convinced that their efforts are futile.
Experiences with failure cause them to question their abilities, and
they see themselves generally as incompetent and good-for-nothing.
They are victims of what University of Pennsylvania psychologist
Martin P. Seligman has termed "learned helplessness."

In laboratory experiments, many of the symptoms of learned
helplessness have been produced by giving students problems they
were told could be solved when, in reality, it was impossible to
do so. In real-life situations, children display attitudes of helplessness
as a result of failure in school assignments, say in mathematics.
They then take on a pessimistic attitude toward their overall abilities
and their prospects for the future—and end up failing in other
subjects as well.

Many children suffer at times from such a learned sense of futil-
ity. Fortunately, their pessimistic attitudes usually do not persist
because the hopes they harbor for success are eventually realized.
A child who is defeated by math, for example, can learn to feel
victorious by doing unusually well in another subject.

ఆర్ర్ Hope is eager expectation. It defines direction; it calls the soul
to take up its journey, to marshall its energies, to follow its aim.

A. Powell Davies
The Mind and Faith of A. Powell Davies

Isn't it important for parents not to accept helpless behavior? How about punishing failure in order to spark motivation?

The evidence is that it won't produce the desired results. In
one experiment, students were subjected to punishment in the form
of loud and unpleasant noise. They were told they could stop the

noise by learning how to manipulate certain control devices—but actually these devices had no effect. Later, when placed in another situation where it *would* have been possible for them to turn off the noise, the volunteers made no effort to change their predicament; they simply put up with the punishment until the experimenter called a halt to it.

Such experiments on learned helplessness suggest that attempts to change human behavior through punishment are fraught with danger. Children who are continually reprimanded or spanked—especially if the punishment is inconsistent—may very well acquire a give-up attitude. They may conclude that they have no control over when, how, or why they are punished. They may become chronically passive, even deeply depressed. The same unfortunate results may occur when elementary school teachers, unsympathetic to slow learners in their classes, constantly berate them for their "stupidity."

Then physical punishment is not a good motivator?

The evidence says it is not. Studies assessing the effects of constant physical punishment show that it can actually lead to various forms of behavior disorders, including delinquency. There is little evidence that physical punishment inhibits or eliminates undesirable behaviors, or promotes desirable ones. The predominant finding is that such punishment stimulates aggression.

University of California psychologist Norma Feschback has devoted considerable effort to the issue. "If we combine the experimental research on the subject with data on the effects of physical pain," she writes, "it would appear that physical punishment has little utility as a response suppressor and may well produce . . . negative consequences for the child's adjustment that can be more undesirable than the response being punished."

᳓ Children who have been hit grow up to hit their spouses and their children. And children who have been hit often enough . . . are likely to become violent youngsters and violent adults. . . .
Murray A. Straus
University of New Hampshire

How can teachers work with slow learners to overcome their feelings of helplessness?

The best approach is to provide them with evidence that they *do* have the ability to "make it." By structuring situations where children can succeed, teachers are able to demonstrate to them that they are more competent at more tasks than they ever realized. This new confidence in their abilities tends to generalize to other situations, and children begin to feel a growing faith in their capacity to control their own future.

Many apparently defeated youngsters manage to regain control of their lives only as a result of rewarding experiences in school. Such was the case, for example, for a surprising number of women in the study, described earlier, by child psychiatrist Michael Rutter and his colleagues at the University of London. These women—born into broken and abusive families, and placed in foster care—grew up to live normal and rewarding lives. Their positive school experiences were critical, Rutter believes, because they left in their wake pleasant feelings of success and accomplishment that nourished in the children "a sense of competence in handling the rough times ahead."

What can parents do to encourage stick-to-it-iveness?

Help your child experience the joy of attainment. Reaching, even straining, for a worthwhile goal is welcomed by those whose efforts have enabled them at times to hit the mark. And such satisfaction is learned early. The infant who successfully grabs a rattle hung almost but not quite out of reach, or the seven-year-old who hits a fastball are learning not only muscular skills. They are experiencing delight in their achievements as well.

To learn stick-to-it-iveness, a child must reap the rewards that come from perseverance. Perceptive mothers and fathers know their children's strong and weak points and can help them set goals that are neither too high nor too low. These goals should not frustrate them on the one hand, nor encourage an attitude of bland contentment on the other. Perseverance can hardly be expected from those who grow up aiming so high that they must inevitably give up trying, or so low that they can never fail.

If you allow a young child to do things independently, couldn't this lead to disheartening failure and a loss of motivation?

Sure, but not if enough attention is paid to the small successes—whether buttoning up a jacket correctly, learning the difference between red and blue, or even putting dirty clothes in the hamper. It is important to praise achievements, however minor, and to play down failures. If enough is made of their successes, children will begin to see themselves as competent and capable—as persons who can accomplish things. And youngsters who view themselves as successful at home are likely to carry a sense of confidence with them to school.

Expectation of success is a vital factor in the zest for academic achievement. When the time comes to learn to read, for example, those who have learned to enjoy doing things well at home, and who have been praised for their skills, will view reading as just another new challenge to conquer. And they will learn more readily as a result. In contrast, children exposed to constant criticism or punishment for failures at home will be anxious about new challenges and will often fall short at school.

Shouldn't children be exposed to a lot of activities early so that they can find at least a few that really turn them on?

Yes, but it is important to avoid overloading the channels. Experts in communication have long been aware of the dangers of giving people too much information on too many subjects at the same time. The results are often frustration and a lack of interest in listening and learning.

Many of us are guilty of filling our youngsters' lives with so many things that each experience loses its meaning. We run the risk of creating people who sample life rather than live it, who rarely experience the satisfaction of seeing a task through to completion. Tommy, a ten-year-old on our block, shuttles wearily between school and clarinet lessons, scout meetings, swimming classes, home, and homework. "We're giving him everything," says Tommy's mother proudly, "and money is no object at all."

The result? Our young friend is a passable clarinetist, a routine scout, a fair swimmer, a C student. He stands out in nothing and has never felt the glow that accompanies a job well done. Tommy is not likely to learn to persevere until his parents begin giving him a limited number of rewarding tasks in which he can excel—and clearing the channels so he can have a go at them.

Wouldn't it help some children to be rewarded just for trying—even if they fail?

Indeed it might. Failures can often teach a child as many valuable lessons as successes.

University of Pittsburgh psychologist Robert Perloff has questioned our traditional approach of rewarding only successes and always punishing failures. Achieving children find themselves in a garden of rewards—high grades, praise from their parents, admiration from their peers. But less successful children, even though they may have tried quite hard, do not receive any such laurels.

"Truly significant success eludes the person who does not flirt with and learn to thumb his nose at failure," says Perloff. Those who anticipate only punishment or, at best, the absence of rewards, will likely take only the safe road. They will take up tasks that have a high probability of producing a reward. After all, why stick your neck out and take a chance that your head will be chopped off? It is far more pleasant to choose a path leading to success—even if only a modest success—rather than risk failure.

The unfortunate outcome of this avoidance-of-failure strategy is that many successes may be missed altogether. Important breakthroughs may never be made by people who shun trailblazing opportunities lest they not succeed on their first attempts and thus not receive positive recognition right away. Most kids need encouragement and "stroking" before they risk failure on chancy enterprises. If they get this kind of support, their occasional failures do not feel like the end of the road.

How should a parent react when a child gets a poor grade or fails at a task?

Accept them as normal, not as disasters. Parents often respond to a failing grade, say, or a strikeout in a Little League game, as if it were a major crisis from which the child could not possibly recover. They make no effort to hide their own grief and disappointment, thereby making the child feel rejected and worthless.

Rejected often enough, children may become unwilling to compete either against themselves or anyone else. Kids need to learn that failure, like success, is only a stepping stone from which we advance to the next task.

ಆ§   Failures are the pillars of success.
                                            Hebrew proverb

Does that mean that everything along the way needs to be smooth and untroubled? What about the "school of hard knocks"—can't it teach lessons?

Yes, it can. "Hard knocks" can teach perseverance and determination, and the capacity to keep your eye on major goals without being defeated by problems encountered along the way. Too much stress, of course, can sometimes produce insensitive, driven people—or discouraged, defeated people who have come to expect failure. But learning to survive and to overcome the anxiety that goes with problems can lead to great strength and achievement. Experts in child development have concluded, in other words, that discovering how to handle a certain amount of stress early in life may be necessary preparation for coping with later crises.

Many mothers and fathers assume they are helping their young by protecting them from some of the nastier realities that they themselves encountered as children. The efforts of these parents may be misguided—for the evidence is that a childhood altogether sealed off from hard knocks is not likely to help build psychological strength and emotional resilience.

Chicago psychiatrist Roy R. Grinker, Jr., often sees young children of affluent parents who are, in his words, "handicapped in their perception of reality and their ability to deal with it." Says Grinker: "They cannot tolerate frustration." In contrast, children who cope well accept life's frustrations—and doggedly work toward their resolution. Moreover, they appear to grow more resilient in the process, as if for them, early troubles may indeed be a blessing in disguise.

It is intriguing to consider that many famous people, especially writers, actors, and artists, have come from very troubled, unhappy homes. Mark Twain and Eugene O'Neill are two such American writers. The Russian writers Anton Chekov and Leo Tolstoy were poor students, and came from quarrelsome, eccentric families. Eleanor Roosevelt also came from a "broken home." She was considered ugly and something of an embarrassment by most of the aristocratic Roosevelts.

꧁ I must make it known that I do not believe it is required of art, science, religion, philosophy or family to assure every man born into this life a secure childhood, in which the child knows only love and harmony. If such a childhood happens to come to pass for a child, excellent. If the child, as a result of such a childhood, becomes a truly pleasant or excellent adult who functions in a satisfying manner . . . again excellent. The supplying of such a childhood to a child, however, appears to be impossible. It may not even be desirable. It may just create a nonentity. . . . I think it is inevitable and in order for the human creature to be unhappy in childhood. . . . I was bitterly unhappy as a small child.

William Saroyan
The Bicycle Rider in Beverly Hills

Is it possible to teach children to work hard for goals that are off in the distance?

It's not easy—but this much seems clear: Learning to work now for pleasures that will be realized later is one of the most important lessons of childhood.

The capacity to delay gratification is virtually nonexistent in infants—as every parent knows. "Children," writes Stanford University psychologist Walter Mischel, "are not born with the ability to wait for pleasures, and unless they learn to tolerate delay, they will have a difficult time coping with frustration."

Slowly, however, with experience and maturation, children do begin to understand that not everything can go just as they wish at the moment they wish it. The ability to postpone immediate gratification for the sake of eventual rewards allows children to be motivated to work now for distant goals, to sacrifice now for the sake of later achievement. Such children learn to accept the gap that so often separates our wishes and their realization. In the psychologist's terms, they are "goal-directed"—with a sense of purpose and the capacity to put off short-term rewards for long-term benefits.

On New York's East Side and in Brooklyn tenements a half century ago, dozens of immigrant children endured years of grinding hunger, overcrowding, and deprivation. Yet, from that miserable environment, a startling number grew to be among the brightest lights on the American scene—writers, scientists, entertainers, politicians—men and women who made enduring contributions to society. It was their capacity to look beyond today's trials to tomorrow's triumphs that helped them overcome adversity.

Such children are not impervious to pain. Their ability to cope in the early years does not mean that they are free of anguish along the way. "We suffer," said one young adult who had suffered great stress as a child, "but we don't let it destroy us."

⧽ Let us, then, be up and doing,
With a heart for any fate;
Still achieving, still pursuing,
Learn to labor and to wait.
    Henry Wadsworth Longfellow

Sometimes children who have been high achievers suddenly seem to change overnight when they become teenagers. They lose interest in school and in grades. What happens?

In adolescence children begin to see themselves as separate from the family and to realize that someday soon they will be on their own, unique and separate from others. This is what psychologists call "forming an identity," and what is popularly called "finding yourself." It is a scary time, although most teenagers won't admit it. When the feeling of separateness is first sinking in, the teenager may seem like a totally different person—often criticizing and even avoiding parents, teachers, and school, and ready to take on society as a whole.

The adolescent's critical attitude actually reflects an important advance in development. The ability to view the world in ideal terms—not as it is right now but as it might one day be—flowers during adolescence, and sometimes it is the brightest kids who are the most critical. It is comforting also to realize that much of the adolescent's passionate concern and anger with the "failures" of their parents and society turns out to be more a matter of word than deed. In time, most teenage children tend once again to embrace the values they had set aside, and to recapture their motivation for doing well in school.

The Strengths of Adolescents
It helps to keep in mind some of the many positive traits of teenagers that we often tend to overlook:
- Abundant energy, drive, and vitality
- Idealism—and a sincere concern for the future of the world
- Ability to question contemporary values, philosophies, theologies, and institutions
- Courage and the willingness to take risks
- Feeling of independence
- Strong sense of fairness and dislike of intolerance
- Flexibility and adaptability to change
- Openness and honesty
- Loyalty to organizations and causes
- Sense of humor
- Optimism and positive outlook
- Ability to think seriously and deeply
- Sensitivity to the feelings of others

Adapted from Diane E. Papalia
and Sally W. Olds
Human Development

Why do so many teenagers seem frustrated and in conflict?

Because they are often torn between competing motives. In adolescence, the achievement motive often comes up against another strong human motive—the motive for affiliation, or the desire to be around other people. In other words, the desire to succeed and the desire to be popular pull in opposite directions.

Consider, for instance, what might happen on the night before an exam. Jim, wanting to do well on the test, may announce that he must not be disturbed because he plans to study. But friends phone unexpectedly with an invitation to a party, which arouses the desire to be part of the group. It is clear that only one of these motives can be satisfied. Deciding between them may create agony because anxiety and frustration accompany either choice. Opting to study risks being seen as a "bookworm" by friends—and choosing to go out risks doing poorly on the exam and encountering disdain from parents and teachers.

Many such conflicts arise routinely for adolescents. Some take the resulting frustrations in their stride and appear relatively unperturbed once they decide which way to turn. Others are unable to select an acceptable solution and resort to tears or temper tantrums. Still others may respond with varying degrees of confusion, disappointment, anger, depression, or apathy.

How can parents help teenagers be responsible yet independent?

Confidence and self-esteem are highest in democratically run families. These are families where parents encourage independent behavior, seek the active participation of children in family affairs, and offer a lot of support for their children's feelings, opinions, and activities. In such families, the reasons for rules and expectations are explained frequently. The parents are reasonable, loving, respectful, and fair—neither overly strict nor permissive. They are good models for their teenagers to identify with and imitate.

In contrast, two other kinds of parents can actually aggravate the difficulties of the adolescent years. One is autocratic parents, who insist that their word is law and that adolescents do not have the right to make decisions. Their children often show continued dependency, lack of confidence, and low self-esteem. A second is overly permissive parents, who take a completely "hands-off" position—either because they are not interested or they overestimate the wisdom of letting children "do their own thing." Teenage children of both these types of parents tend not to develop a sense of responsibility for their own actions.

Is self-motivation important in adolescence?

Yes, vitally. Adolescents need the freedom to make up their own minds. They want to know where their parents stand on issues, but they also want to come to their own conclusions. They want to be listened to and respected while still searching for answers.

Achievement motivation is often based on a factor discussed at the start of this book: *locus of control.* Do we, in general, believe that we control our own lives? Or do we live at the mercy of outside events? Youngsters with an "internal locus of control" feel their chances of success depend mainly on their own abilities and efforts. They tend to take responsibility for their own actions and try hard to reach their goals. They are careful but not timid in the risks they are willing to take. In contrast, those with an "external locus of control" are less likely to strive hard to reach their objectives. When they do succeed, they tend to attribute their achievement to lucky circumstances or to decide that what they did must have been very easy. They are also often reckless in their actions.

It is vital to help adolescents acquire an internal locus of control. The dual result is likely to be greater self-confidence and the zeal to do better in school.

What causes adolescents to lose their self-confidence?

It can be the result of consistently not getting recognition for their efforts, coming off second best in competition, being put down once too often in school or at home, or making an embarrassing mistake or two in public.

A lack of self-confidence can drain the fun out of life, turning every challenge and opportunity for success into a trauma. Self-confidence is essential to motivation and well-being, "the bedrock of the human personality," according to the famous psychoanalyst Harry Stack Sullivan.

ⁿ§ Research evidence does not permit us to say that a high self-concept will automatically lead to high achievement, but it does allow us to conclude that high achievement rarely occurs in the absence of a reasonably high self-concept.

Don E. Hamachek
Psychology in Teaching, Learning, and Growth

How can parents help boost self-confidence when it is faltering?

An important key is to play up positive qualities. Offer praise and rewards for the skills and strengths of your children rather than comparing them unfavorably with others. Your son or daughter may have quite different pluses from those of the boy or girl down the street—and they may not exactly fit your expectations. But they should be nurtured and cherished nevertheless. The result is likely to help stir their willingness to use all the potential that lies within them.

Isn't it especially hard to convince teenage girls that school achievement is important? They're so worried that boys won't like them if they get straight "A"s.

Despite continuing shifts in sex roles, this worry seems to continue among teenage girls. Rather than fearing failure, many adolescent girls harbor an underlying fear of success. Competing, being aggressive, and getting the best grade—in other words, behaving in ways that increase chances of school success—have traditionally been seen as "unfeminine" or altogether masculine. As a result, girls may shy away from such behaviors to preserve their feminine reputation.

Interesting results emerged from one study in which a sample of ninety female college students were asked to write a story in response to this cue: "After first-term finals, Anne finds herself at the top of her class." A roughly equal number of college men were given the same story, but it was about "John." Stories that "avoided success" were written by 65 percent of the women and only 9 percent of the men. In fact, three main themes emerged in the women's stories—fear of social rejection, concern about Anne's normality or femininity, and denial of the possibility that such an episode could take place. The investigator concluded that many females will use their intellectual potential fully only in noncompetitive settings. They are most likely to play down their mental capacities when competing against men.

Fortunately, the anxieties of girls over achievement are likely to lessen gradually as more and more women move into influential positions where they can serve as role models.

🎜 Boys are unsexed by failure and girls by success.
Margaret Mead

Are there many cases where an unmotivated teenager—whether boy or girl—gets "turned on" later in life?

There are many more such cases than we ever assumed.

The usual way of studying how the traits and experiences of childhood affect characteristics in a later period is to start with the grown person and try to work back. In contrast, so-called longitudinal studies *begin* with the child. Typical of this type of research is the Berkeley, California, study described at the start of the book, which probably offers the richest collection of data ever assembled on human beings over a long period.

The researchers began studying their subjects as infants—every third child born in Berkeley over an eighteen-month period beginning in January 1928. The children were weighed, measured, tested, interviewed, and observed numerous times until they passed through their fourth decade of life. Special information about them was also obtained from their parents, teachers, classmates, and themselves.

When the children in the study were teenagers, researcher Jean W. Macfarlane and her associates made predictions about them as adults—their personalities, their success in marriage and work, their ability to cope with the problems of life. The investigators were surprised by the results of their analysis after the subjects had been followed up at the age of thirty. In many cases, their anticipations turned out to be wrong.

Many of the most mature adults—integrated, competent, clear about their values, and accepting of themselves and others—were those who, earlier, had been faced with difficult situations and whose characteristic responses had seemed to compound their problems. They included chronic rebels who had been expelled from school, highly intelligent students who were nevertheless academic failures, children filled with hostility—unhappy, withdrawn, oversensitive. The behavior regarded by the investigators as disruptive to growth and maturity seemed in these cases to have led directly or indirectly to adult strength.

One of the former rebels recalled that he had desperately needed approval "even if it was from kids as maladjusted as I was." To maintain his rebel status, he said, he had had to commit all of his intelligence and stamina, a circumstance he believed contributed to his adult strength in tackling difficult problems. "I hope my children find less wasteful ways to mature," he remarked, "but who knows?"

How many teenagers fall into such a "turnaround" category?

There's no way to say—but in the Berkeley study, close to half of the subjects fell into the group for whom inadequate or crippled personalities had been predicted. Yet as adults, almost all of them were better than had been expected, and some of them far better.

One girl, when first seen, had been suspicious of the study staff and hostile toward its members. She lived with a rejecting mother and a disturbed aunt, and she hated both home and school. To escape, while still in high school, she married a boy as erratic and immature as she. They soon separated. But at thirty, with the investigators dreading the impending interview, in came a personable, well-groomed, gracious woman with two buoyant but well-mannered children. She had married again and was living a stable, contented life.

One youngster who is remembered with special pride is now the highly successful manager of a large business concern. Years ago, he had been a shy little boy without friends. Though he had dropped in from time to time to see members of the research staff, his communications were often limited to hello and good-bye. After high school, he enlisted in the Army, and since he had taken some shop courses, he was asked to help with the building and repair work at his post. First he was flattered that anyone should think he could do anything; then he was proud that he could actually do it.

After his service, he went to business school, where he got all "A"s, as compared to "C"s in high school. Now, he says the most interesting part of his job is to give people "something to do that is a little harder than what they have done or think they can do— but not something they would fail at—and then to watch them expand. Nothing is more exciting to me than to see people get confidence"—which he himself had lacked for so long.

A number of other subjects had similar experiences. They did not achieve "ego identity"—did not find themselves—until they had been forced into an opportunity, or been given one, to take on a responsible role that offered a sense of worth they had missed at home. Often these youngsters did not find this new and satisfying role until they had left both their childhood homes and their home-towns.

꿏 One wouldn't expect the ill-used sickly boy, serving beer in a German cabaret, to become the philosopher and astronomer Kepler, one of the greatest men of his time; or the young soldier, who spent his youth in battles and sieges, to be the great Descartes, one of the most original of thinkers.

> Ronald Stanley Illingworth and
> Cynthia Mary Illingworth
> *Lessons from Childhood*

Why were the predictions about these unhappy youngsters wrong in so many cases?

For one thing, the investigators gave too much weight to the troublesome, "sick" elements in a child's life—quite naturally, in view of the many studies that have traced all of our mental ills to such elements. At the same time, they gave little weight to the healthful, maturity-inducing elements.

The investigators also overestimated the durability of certain "undesirable" behaviors and attitudes shown habitually over a long period. Sometimes, to the investigators' surprise, the undesirable but long-continued patterns were converted into almost the opposite characteristics. For example, it was predicted that overdependent boys with energetic and dominant mothers would pick wives like the mothers and continue the pattern of overdependence. Instead nearly all such boys chose girls who were lacking in confidence. They thus won themselves a role as the proud male protector and giver of support, and in this role, say the investigators, their motivation thrived.

We psychologists, led by Freud himself, have been largely responsible for the tendency to "live scared." For decades we have emphasized primarily why young people lose their moorings, falter in their motivation, and break down under stress. All but ignored have been the vast number who appear to be crumbling—but who emerge unharmed, as competent, and contented adults.

CHAPTER SEVEN
ᴄᏻ Home and Family

Home. The word itself evokes strong emotions. Whether a posh suburban rambler, a midtown condo, or a rural trailer, home is the most influential force in the child's development. It is where human relationships are patterned, personalities shaped, goals and visions of life formed. It is where childhood fears are assuaged, adolescent conflicts played out. And it is largely in the home that the child's intellect is nurtured or thwarted, and the zest for knowledge ignited or cooled.

There are those who doubt whether the American home will continue for long as the cornerstone of our children's lives. For many Americans, home has become little more than a place to rest between trips. Today we seem to be ready to go just about anywhere at a moment's notice—whether it is to follow a career or an impulse. Such incessant mobility keeps many couples from growing roots in any neighborhood. Alvin Toffler, well-known chronicler of our society's future, envisions an even more mobile family in the years ahead—one based primarily on transient rather than on permanent relationships.

The home as a center of intellectual ferment appears to be threatened also by the increasing dispersion of its residents. We teach our children the ultimate goal of independence and self-sufficiency by encouraging them to leave home—the earlier the better. Meanwhile, the role of the extended family—grandparents, aunts, uncles, cousins—has weakened. Today the aged among us are shunted away at the drop of a cane to housing developments or nursing homes, thus depriving our children of both the support and the wisdom of the elderly.

Why then this chapter?

Because the doomsayers are wrong. The traditions of home and family, while threatened, are far from dead. Every generation, or so it seems, bemoans the demise of the family. Yet it survives. Indeed, traditional living patterns are far more prevalent than many suppose. Surveys indicate that 90 to 95 percent of Americans get married sooner or later. A study of 2,500 students in Boston showed that 94 percent believed that they would marry within ten years, and all but two percent of them eventually.

It is true enough, of course, that many more marriages break up today than in the past. About 2.5 million Americans appear in divorce courts each year. The divorce rate has increased eight times over since the turn of the century, and has doubled since 1965. But take note: About four out of every five divorced persons marry again, and many of them successfully. Most marriage partners, moreover, commit themselves to having children. According to the U.S. Bureau of the Census, about 90 percent of young adult women expect to become mothers. "It is the destiny of flesh and blood to be familial," writes Michael Novak.

Within the family, who is it that most influences the young?

For too long, mother has been the target of both censure and praise for all that happens to children. Whether kids turn out to be bright or dull, academic achievers or failures, creative or hyperactive—all was laid at mother's doorstep. Today we know better. Mother deserves neither all the blame nor all the credit for what her children become. She does not stand alone.

The father's role, for years regarded only as economically useful, has too long been ignored. Most experts used to believe that father contributes very little to the intellectual growth of the child. Now, however, a host of studies show that his impact has been sorely underestimated. The father's sole purpose is not just to help amass enough dollars to pay for the child's education; like the mother, he wields considerable influence on the child's accumulation of skills and knowledge, and devotion to intellectual pursuits. It is clear today that the father's inadequacy or absence can erode the child's intellectual development, and his presence can enrich it.

The child's mind, moreover, can be influenced by the entire circle of family members. The extended family, while admittedly getting thinner, persists as a major source of intellectual nourishment and stimulation for the young. When we were children, it was natural enough to find assorted family figures in our own homes, or family-like figures nearby in the homes of close friends that surrounded us. Today, in a world grown more remote, it is not easy for children to find similar resources. But despite the fact that they are becoming increasingly rare, such psychological lifelines turn out to be as enriching as ever.

Children cannot select the homes they grow up in. A newborn may be plunged into a household warmed by nurturant love between parents, or torn from the very beginning by contention and strife; blessedly free of psychological distress, or overwhelmed by depression and anxiety; without competition from other children, or already filled with siblings zealously struggling for attention in the household; supported by an extended family and community, or isolated and bereft of such precious contacts.

Each of us must help ensure that the home environment will enrich rather than erode the development of our children's minds. For the quality of family life that leaves its signature—for better or worse—from the very beginning.

What factors in the home can particularly help stimulate a child's desire to succeed in school?

There is something to be learned on this score from the results of a study of low income families. Some of the children of these families did well in school; others from precisely similar backgrounds failed.

Three factors seemed to characterize homes of children with high academic achievement. First, their parents were continuously interested in their children's school life; they kept in touch with teachers and knew precisely what was expected. Second, the parents saw school as the stairway up from the abyss of poverty, and they encouraged their children every step of the way. Finally, especially in single-parent families, there was in each child's life an adult besides the parent—a grandparent, say, or neighbor—who nurtured the child with additional encouragement and emotional support.

Isn't helping children with their homework the key?

Not the only one by any means. Opportunities to teach and inspire—to ignite the child's mind—occur naturally in the course of everyday life, and these can be more important in the long run than rote drilling on homework tasks.

Dorothy Rich, president of the Home and School Institute in Washington, D.C., is an expert in helping children find such learning opportunities. To help develop children's writing skills, for example, she suggests asking youngsters to write shopping lists and notes to relatives and friends. To sharpen math skills, they can calculate the cost of gas being pumped into the auto's tank. To help them make judgments, they can be challenged to tell why they like a certain story, someone's behavior, or a particular park. Rich does not contend that kids should go without schools—only that much depends on what goes on at home as well. It is important to keep in touch with the school in order to mesh as much as possible the activities of the classroom and the home.

⌇   Some Home Learning Exercises

The following exercises are suggested by the Home and School Institute in Washington, D.C., to help bolster the three-R skills of children from about three to seven. They can also improve the powers of observation, memory, and reasoning.

- Ask your children to find certain letters of the alphabet on the labels of cans or boxes.
- Keep folding a paper towel or napkin and ask them to identify fractions of the whole.
- Ask them to find on the store shelves the items that, together, you have written down on the shopping list.
- Cut up comic strips and have them write their own words for the balloons.
- Let them count and match objects—socks, shoes, towels.
- Ask them to look around the room for a minute and then tell you everything they saw.
- Tell them to be silent for 30 seconds and just listen. Then ask them to tell you all the things they've heard—a car, a bird, a telephone, a dog barking, a baby crying.

The choice of activities need not be entirely random. The child's teacher can often point the way toward areas of learning for which everyday practice would be helpful.

Don't some children mind when their parents stay in close contact with the school?

Some may mind—but generally speaking, the benefits far outweigh the risks. In fact, for many children, the extent of parental interest and involvement in the school program may be a surprisingly potent factor in their academic progress. It helps, for example, to become involved in the PTA, or in coaching an extracurricular activity. It is important also to listen empathetically to children's views of school, and to try to help solve their problems of adaptation in the classroom.

Physician-biochemist Irwin J. Kopin, who is now scientific director of the National Institute of Neurological and Communicative Diseases and Stroke, recalls his inward satisfaction as a child when he spied his mother approaching the Bronx school where he was a first-grader. She was bringing a bottle of hot soup to help her son through the day. The message to young Irwin was clear: School was important enough for his mother to view it as a natural extension of their home.

Parents who remain totally disengaged from the educational process may unwittingly communicate to the child that school does not carry a very high priority—that their participation is not really worth the effort. And remember—it is important to show interest in school throughout the year. If you pay attention only at report card time, it says to the child: "I'm not interested in what you're doing—only in the marks you're making." Visit the teacher when things are going great—not just when problems arise.

  Of course, parents are helpful, too. You could use them for homeroom parents, or they could run errands for teachers. Parents can do a lot of things!

Josi Davis
Fourth grade, Key Elementary
School, Washington, D.C.

What bearing does family income have on a child's intelligence and achievement?

Not as much as many have assumed. Affluence is hardly a guarantee that children will realize their potential. Wealthy parents can be remote figures, capable of providing clothes and cars in abundance, but little of themselves or their generation. Despite unlimited financial resources, family interactions in wealthy homes can be flat and perfunctory, far too superficial for children ever to gain entry into their parents' minds or to evoke their esteem.

The precious blend of intellectual nourishment and loving attention typically enjoyed by achieving youngsters is not the domain of any one social class—or race or color or religion. It is hinged instead on a communion of mind and spirit, a psychological connectedness that lies well beyond the demographer's capacity to chart.

Psychological problems that interfere with normal intellectual development often flourish in large and stylish homes—in communities filled with comfortable schools, libraries, and recreation facilities. A stream of statistics reveals that alcohol and drug use, early unwanted pregnancy, crime, and a devotion to bizarre and self-punishing religious cults are on the rise among children who emerge not from homes of poverty but from those of the middle and upper classes.

Bennett L. Leventhal, Director of the Child Psychiatric Clinic at the University of Chicago Medical School, believes that many well-to-do parents minimize the burden of being a parent. "They think that because they're doing alright, their kids will naturally do alright, too." Chicago psychiatrist Roy R. Grinker, Jr., has described his treatment of children of the "super rich." Some of these children have as much as 20 or 30 million dollars—yet, in the words of Grinker, "They are unable to extract a dime's worth of pleasure from it. They feel empty, bored, and chronically depressed."

The parents described by Grinker tend to be jaded and uncommunicative, too busy with their own pleasures to become aware of even the most obvious cries for help by their children. Yet, when their children form attachments to others, they show signs of jealousy and rage. These rich parents do not provide strong, constructive role models for their children, according to Grinker.

What these children miss—and what children at any economic level need—is that steady gleam of pride and pleasure in the eyes of parents as they observe their developing offspring.

⋙ The material success of parents can be a detriment to child-raising if it comes at the expense of time that should be spent with their children. Children can tell fairly young what their parents consider important. If they see everything comes ahead of them, there is likely to be trouble ahead.

Lee Salk

Then is it the interaction with kids that is so important for their intellectual development?

Vitally. No matter how thoroughly a home supplies the individual physical needs of its occupants, it will fail to enrich the minds of children if it provides only a sumptuous set of cubicles into which people regularly disappear in silence. To be intellectually and emotionally rewarding, homes must offer sufficient opportunities for communal living as well. The homes we remember with pleasurable nostalgia were not necessarily richly decorated or filled with endless rooms, but rather warm and accepting places, where everyone could meet and interact casually without tension.

In too many homes today, the end of dinner typically signals a race from the table and the start of private activities that mean an end of togetherness. Perhaps worse, it heralds the assembly of the family in front of a blaring TV or video game machine that block out all opportunities for exchanging information, ideas, or feelings.

In our own childhood, the hours spent in free-ranging intellectual cohabitation with adults were among the richest we knew. They occurred spontaneously, day or night, whenever family members or friends gathered, and they provided for us and our young contemporaries sturdy links to the minds of "grown-ups." Without benefit of *Mister Rogers* or *Sesame Street,* without toys-for-teaching or flashcards-for-fundamentals, life itself brought an incitement to learn. We were, you might say, the beneficiaries of a chronic enrichment program, delivered via the blessedly porous intellectual barrier separating the generations.

Because the stimulating world of our elders was always open to us, we required no cleverly wrought games to be seduced by intellectual pursuits, no solitary afternoons of TV or video game machines to ignite our imagination. Ours were unbroken chains of associations with adults who cared enough always to share themselves with their young.

The *nature* of family communications is, of course, important as well. Investigators studying the styles of parental utterances to children have developed evidence that erratic and faulty communications patterns—disjointed, ambiguous, uncertain—can impair the ability of youngsters to learn what is expected of them, to understand instructions, to think clearly, and to develop normal relations with others. Children need to feel a sense of order and logic in our communications with them.

෴ There needs to be a place where children will know that they belong, where they have an unquestioned right to be, where there will always be responsible adults to welcome them and care for them.

Margaret Mead

Quite apart from communication as such, how important is a feeling of orderliness in the household?

The human yearning for a sense of order and predictability in life begins early in childhood, and when it remains unfulfilled, the ground can be laid for the kind of anxiety that blocks the child's learning and achievement. Children's psychological well-being often depends on the presence in their lives of recurrent and dependable themes, familiar motifs that give life a comforting coherence and logic.

Young children reveal their inner need for an orderly existence in their insatiable delight with the repetitive and the familiar—songs and rhymes that accompany mother's feelings, the endless round of "peek-a-boo" games, and perhaps most clearly, in the rituals of bedtime.

Such devotion by children to rituals is symptomatic of a more pervasive need for order and regularity best fulfilled in the family context. Whether for the tribal child returning from the hunt, or the suburban preschooler on his weary, end-of-the-day bus ride, the home has traditionally served as a sanctuary of stability in a world of unknowns. Tent or tenement, duplex or high-rise, it is the one place where events can at last be anticipated, where the expected really happens, where an often chaotic universe may be made coherent and whole.

~~~ Order is heaven's first law.
        Alexander Pope

Are many homes lacking in an orderly routine?

For countless children, even the comforting routines of everyday life—eating, sleeping, waking—are absent. Nowhere are they able to find an underlying motif that offers stability or purpose to their young years. Their existence seems chaotic and open-ended, each day bringing new episodes of life disconnected from those that came yesterday or that will follow tomorrow. The result is often a loss of intellectual drive and energy.

The residue of such a disordered existence were portrayed by John Rothchild and Susan Berns Wolf in their book, *The Children of the Counterculture,* written after the authors had visited a group of diverse communities made up of young parents who were the dropouts and "hippies" of the 1960s. Already in their middle years and mothers and fathers themselves, they were now settled within urban and rural communes under the banner of new Eastern religious sects.

Rothchild and Wolf wondered how life was turning out in these communes, especially for the children. The authors were struck by the boredom, apathy, and melancholy of the children, many of whom showed signs of emotional disturbance and psychological disorganization. The cause was not difficult to find. Without schools, toys, stimulation, or direction, without a sense of order and purpose and routine in life, the children took on an aimless and rudderless quality. Nowhere in this new Utopia could one find a coherent thread in the lives of the children. They were growing up in an unstructured and aimless world, without the benefit of an overriding perception of its order or purpose.

Unhappily, the same is true for countless contemporary children. Too many homes today remain merely thoroughfares—without a unifying theme. The dimension of family life at issue here is unrelated to social class. Disordered, chaotic homes are common to rich and poor alike, to children of all races and in all places—on rural farms and in crowded city apartments, in the ghetto tenement, the high-rise, and the glistening suburban home.

What can parents do to help give life at home a sense of organized routine and direction?

There are numerous opportunities to introduce rituals—activities that can be enjoyed and appreciated by all family members as a unit. Gordon Shipman, who has written extensively on marriage and the family, has identified a number of them. Holiday and religious rituals can play an important function in many families, giving the child a sense of recurring and dependable themes in the family's existence as a solid unit. Some homes employ "strategic rituals," specific processes that are invoked to help in decision-making; one example is a family council, even including the appointment of officers, who "govern" the household. Many families convert the mealtime to a discussion ritual, an opportunity to hear each other out and share experiences of the day. And in some families, there are work rituals—tasks that are relevant to all members of the family, and which all in the family can share.

> Every family can create its own way of doing things. Today's rituals are tomorrow's memories, and a binding link among the generations.
>
> Gordon Shipman
> "Memories That Make Families Strong"

When families break up, the orderliness and routines of life are obviously destroyed. What specifically is the impact of divorce on the child's intellect?

Among the children of divorce extensively studied by Judith Wallerstein and Joan Kelly, authors of *Surviving the Breakup,* one of the most common problems observed was lowered academic achievement. Teachers also reported a high level of anxiety in more than half the children, who were often described as unusually restless. Instead of doing their work quietly, these children constantly roamed around the classroom, interfering with student activities. A number showed moderate to severe difficulty in concentrating on school work.

Many children of divorce begin to daydream more than usual, and they seem unable to handle their sadness and worry about their own future and their parents' well-being. Some display outbursts of temper, fighting, and others tend to withdraw. Such problems combine to affect academic progress, sometimes leading to significant declines in school performance.

The child's inner turmoil can be reflected in scores made on tests of intelligence. Remember that performance on IQ tests requires attention, perseverance, and concentration—the kinds of capacities that are depleted by emotional tension and stress. You would hardly expect kids whose parents have just had a knock-down-drag-out separation to be able to apply themselves with the same zeal in a testing situation as children blessed with peaceful and nurturant homes.

While untoward changes in the attitudes and behavior of kids may occur almost immediately after divorce, at times they are delayed. Some youngsters maintain a good adjustment during the acute phases of the divorce, only to deteriorate markedly later, especially if they are exposed to heightened tensions in their postdivorce families.

Always, of course, there are the kids who beat the odds. Some youngsters—especially adolescents who had always done well—actually find increased energy for school after the separation. And children from families in which the father or mother has been abusive or otherwise hurtful to the child's self-esteem frequently show a marked developmental spurt following the first year of marital separation.

❧ . . . children of divorce need special understanding and special help—for a child's heart breaks easily and is especially vulnerable to events over which it has no control. And although it often appears that children recover quickly from emotional shocks, most children simply repress those feelings that they fear and do not understand; they express them later in aberrant behavior.

W. Keith Hafer
Coping with Bereavement from Death or Divorce

What is it about family discord that leads children to encounter problems?

Researchers point to three main factors. First, all children need stable and warm family interactions as a basis for building meaningful relationships of their own outside the home; household quarrels and discord interfere with the development of such relationships. Second, family warfare gives the child an abnormal model of interpersonal behavior—and children are likely to pattern their own behavior after this model. And third, where there is marital discord, kids find it more difficult to determine how they are expected to behave; parents whose energies are drained by marital disputes are likely to provide inconsistent discipline and child-rearing approaches.

Isn't it better for the child if parents who are constantly at war do part company?

Sometimes, yes. Consider these two cases:

Tom, now eight years old, is viewed by all who know him as a difficult child. He would rather fight than play with friends, and he inspires anger rather than affection from teachers, parents, and neighbors. He has been known to steal, lies all the time, is disruptive in class, and is making no progress academically. Awash in rage and self-doubt, Tom is already branded by his teacher as a "budding delinquent."

Sandy is ten. She has lost interest in everyone and everything, is unable to find pleasure in life or even concentrate on a simple chore. The task of living has become an uphill struggle; her sleep is disturbed, her appetite failing. She seldom plays with friends, and a few weeks ago, she swallowed the contents of a full bottle of medicine in an attempt, she said later, "to stop this mean world."

Both Tom and Sandy are living in homes torn by chronic strife. Few days pass without screaming and arguments, angry confrontations, and sometimes even physical violence between mother and father. Even "quiet" days are likely to be scarred by a brooding and ominous silence.

The plight of these two children illustrates the finding that youngsters who grow up in an environment of constant parental warfare are high risks for developing mental health problems. Their predicament is an example of why several researchers believe that chronically discordant marriages are indeed more disturbing to children than divorce. These experts view divorce as the preferable alternative. In spite of all the problems associated with divorce, many children in single-parent families appear to function more adequately than children in conflict-ridden but "intact" families.

Unfortunately, however, it is not always safe to assume that the marital conflict will end with the termination of the marriage. In too many cases, animosity between parents often survives the legal divorce by many years. One study found that a third of the children of divorce continued to experience open parental discord even five years after the dissolution of the parents' marriage. Divorce is, after all, a loss without finality. Children may continue for many years to see the "departed" parent as often as several times a week.

In short, the intended effects of divorce—to relieve marital distress and reduce the developmental problems encountered by children—are not always realized. Instead unintended effects—shock, depression, anger, shame, insecurity—are generated not only by the separation but by the tensions that follow.

Five Ground Rules for Fighting around the Kids

Most parents cannot help quarreling at times, but all of us can take steps to reduce the impact on our children.

- Don't enmesh your child in your quarrels. A child is not psychologically prepared to act as your therapist or as a messenger across the conjugal trenches.
- Make sure your child doesn't feel guilty for having caused the fight.
- Don't try to hide your quarrels altogether. A frozen smile as a cover for clenched teeth never works, and kids are thrown off by emotional dishonesty. You needn't go into *all* the details, but it pays to avoid acting as if everything is OK when it really isn't.
- When the storm is over, clear the air. Let your child know that you have worked out your differences.
- Don't allow quarrels to cause dramatic shifts in your relationships with your child. Resist the temptation to take out your anger on the child or, at the other extreme, to begin acting unusually anxious and protective.

The anxieties generated in youngsters by a major disruption in their lives can compromise their receptivity to learning, their willingness to experiment with new material, their ability to concentrate, and their overall attitude toward school.

Judith Wallerstein and Joan Kelly
Surviving the Breakup

How can a child's positive adjustment to divorce best be ensured?

Psychologists John Moreland and Andrew Schwebel, in summarizing studies of the impact of divorce on children, point to five factors that help: agreement between ex-spouses on child-rearing approaches; demonstrations of positive and constructive attitudes toward each other by the divorced parents; a low level of conflict between ex-spouses; emotional maturity of the custodial parent; and frequent contact between the child and the noncustodial parent. In short, it seems crucial that both parents recognize their continued roles in their children's lives *and* that they cooperate in these roles.

What specifically makes the act of divorce so disturbing to the minds of children?

Like death, divorce is a "loss event," an occasion for bereavement and mourning. But in addition, according to Wallerstein, divorce introduces some specially difficult elements.

Loss due to death is final, and the lost person is irretrievable. The reality of death, therefore, is in some ways easier to acknowledge. Divorce carries no similar finality; it seems reasonable to the child that the loss can be repaired at any time. As a result, a child of divorce is more likely to experience—sometimes into adulthood—the persistent, gnawing sense that the loss can be undone. Keep in mind, too, that divorce is frequently preceded by several separations. Having gone through the ordeal before, the child may feel that this "final" separation may also be reversed.

Moreover, unlike death, divorce is always a voluntary decision for at least one of the partners, and the participants—including the child—are keenly aware of this fact. The stress generated for children, therefore, always carries the message that the divorce may have been avoided—and that someone is guilty for creating the family's unhappiness. Children are also aware of their feelings of anger, anguish, and vulnerability—but they know that they cannot fully express these feelings without hurting or angering one or both parents, and thus further impairing their own position.

There is, in addition, an element of self-blame present for some children—more so than in the case of death. Children of divorce often feel, in other words, that their sins of omission or commission, however minor, may have caused the divorce. "I played too noisy." "I didn't give Mom the message from Dad." "My dog was naughty." These ideas can persist for a long time, especially in the minds of young children. It is difficult to imagine a child performing with zest and with focused attention to school work when saddled with such fantasies of guilt.

Finally, the postdivorce period is unusually lonely for children. Unlike the social network that rallies for the ceremony of death and the support of the bereaved in the immediate aftermath of a parental loss, no back-up systems appear when a divorce occurs. Often friends and neighbors stay away, and grandparents take sides in the conflict.

&ঽ   I try to help Mom and Dad in every way and to do jobs when I am told and when they say take Andre and Scotty to your room. . . . I do what I am told with taking the trash to the dump and to clean furniture and when Mom and Dad are having friends over for a Sunday school class I try to stay far away. I written all this because sometimes the family just does not work out and I hope that in the future that what I wrote will straighten out things in the family.

Laura, age 8

What accounts for the differences between youngsters who do well in school after the breakup and those who do not?

One important factor appears to be the custodial parent's ability to maintain the child's routine and to protect the child from the turmoil surrounding divorce. It helps, too, if the other parent senses the child's needs and responds to them in a comforting and supportive way.

Youngsters who do poorly suffer feelings of rejection and neglect, poor self-esteem, anger, and depression. The tumultuous events following the breakup simply overtax their ability to function in school.

Contributing factors are a deterioration in the relationship between custodial parent and child, or the other parent's failure to remain interested in the child. Sometimes, of course, the child may end up living with a seriously disturbed parent—an impasse virtually designed to thwart academic progress. In short, when turmoil continues in the house after the split and children are not protected from it, learning is bound to suffer.

Are there specific indications that certain children of divorce will continue to do well in school after the split?

The Wallerstein-Kelly study found that among girls who were in preschool or the primary grades when the separation occurred, school achievement apparently depended on a strong identification with a competent mother and a solid relationship between mother and child. More important for boys was the father's interest or the presence of an involved and committed stepfather.

Among young boys who started school after the breakup, good academic work seemed to depend on the physical availability of mothers able to remain undistracted by a job outside the home. The important factor for girls of the same age seemed to be less the physical availability of mother than her economic security— that is, her freedom from worry over where the money for rent or other obligations was coming from.

A notable group of students came to the investigators' attention during a five-year follow-up—a group made up of children who actually reversed their mediocre academic history following their parents' divorce. In some cases, a tutor had put the child on the right track. Others had enjoyed the unqualified support of a loving stepparent.

Do children show the same adjustment reactions to their parents' divorce both at home and at school?

Often they do—but sometimes there are marked differences in home and school behaviors.

Wallerstein and Kelly told of Jason, a second-grader whose teacher described him as "a highly motivated child scholastically. "He wants to be on top of his class, and he is. Jason has adjusted really well to the divorce . . . he speaks equally of both his father and his mother. . . . He's entirely delightful!" Yet, at home, Jason was unruly, often threw temper tantrums, and left obscene notes for his mother's boyfriends—all manifestations of his anger over the divorce. Indeed, the following year, his school work began to deteriorate.

The investigators also took note of a number of younger children who were cooperative with their mothers, maintained a cheerful demeanor, and helped out with the household chores. It was as if they were trying to make certain that the remaining parent would not leave them. At school, however, these children fought with their peers, cried "over nothing," and clung to the teacher for support and affection.

Does age make a difference in how a child is affected by divorce?

Some, but children of all ages are vulnerable. Young children are likely to have the most trouble in the first few years following the divorce. They are more prone to blame themselves, to misperceive and exaggerate their parents' needs, and to distort the prospects of reconciliation. Youngsters in elementary school also tend to feel an intense longing for the father, who is usually the absent parent in divorce. Some adolescents are better than younger kids at gauging the responsibility for the divorce, coping with practical problems, and resolving conflicts over loyalty. But many of them encounter trouble, too. Overwhelmed by the family breakup, they become depressed, find it hard to concentrate in school or to maintain the friendships so essential to their development. A recent follow-up study shows that ten years after the divorce, many older children show a residue of problems no longer experienced by younger children.

Are girls more likely than boys to be affected by marital discord and divorce?

Quite the opposite. Boys from divorced families show a higher rate of behavior disorders and troubles getting along with both teachers and peers. They are more likely also to behave more aggressively at home. University of Virginia psychologist E. Mavis Hetherington has summarized the data succinctly: "Boys suffer more intensely and over a longer period than do girls."

Why is it that boys are more vulnerable?

One reason is that boys tend to get less support from their peers, parents, and teachers when the going gets rough. Another is that the absence of father is more stressful for boys since it is so essential for them to have a male model. Mothers still typically retain custody of children, and because children are generally less compliant toward mothers than toward fathers, they are likely to experience more confrontations and punishment. Says Hetherington: "Somehow, we think that little girls need to be nurtured through stress, while boys should be tougher and get through on their own. Well, that's a farce. Boys are very vulnerable to stress in an intact family or to conflict in a post-divorce family."

Can't older siblings and members of the extended family help the affected children and parents?

It stands to reason that if aunts, uncles, grandparents, and older brothers and sisters are available, they can help to alleviate the distressing effects of divorce on the young child. The trouble is that fewer relatives live close by nowadays, so their contributions tend to be more limited.

Can teachers help deal with the child's stress when the family is in trouble?

Some can, but they need the cooperation of the child's parents. Teachers cannot be expected to guess that the changes in a pupil's classroom behavior are the result of tensions as home. They are usually dependent on parents for information to help them appreciate the reasons for changes in a student's mood and performance. Often, too, they need parents' permission to discuss such matters with the youngsters.

Many parents feel that teachers cannot be trusted with such intimate family information, thus confirming the teachers' feelings that they should not intrude. The end result of these failures in communication is that the children receive less support than they otherwise might—support they desperately need.

Some children may, of course, gain strength by virtue of a close relationship with a specially friendly teacher. Very young children, for example, may seek out such a teacher for nurturance, and they may check frequently to make certain that the teacher approves of them and their work. When kids display such a relentless need for reassurance, it is important that the teacher discuss their vulnerability with the parents.

To a certain extent, the school itself provides a valuable structure for children at a time when their major structure, the family, is falling apart. Regardless of how they are functioning in the classroom, many children are strengthened simply because they have to engage in the school routine, are required to perform certain school tasks inside and outside the school, and encounter certain social contacts as a matter of course. On the whole, however, Wallerstein and Kelly found little evidence to suggest that the availability of the school as a support system shapes the child's eventual adjustment. For the majority of kids, the quality of parental support is a far stronger factor in the course of the child's future.

I have yet to find a teacher who believes that the correlation between declining test scores and other measures of academic performance and the dramatic increase in divorce . . . is mere coincidence. Talk with a teacher about the handicaps that children bring with them to the classroom each morning and the conversation always comes around to the effect of shattered or nonexistent families. . . . The truth is that no teacher and no school system has ever been able to compensate for the damage that parents can do to a child. And American parents are doing more damage to more children than ever before.

Jody Powell
"Educational Crisis?
Blame the Parents"

What's the verdict on single-parent families as far as the child's intellectual development and school progress are concerned?

Sobering. Most of the relevant studies have been of mother-headed families, and judged by school performance and by both achievement and intelligence tests, children growing up in such families do not do as well as those from intact families. The pattern, which appears to be more pronounced for boys, does not always surface immediately but rather emerges over the school years.

What accounts for the problems among children raised by a single parent?

A number of explanations are advanced by psychologists E. Mavis Hetherington and Ross D. Parke. The most compelling is that children living only with mother are likely to get less attention and interact less with adults than do kids in nuclear families. "There is some evidence," they write, "that many mothers in divorced families are less likely to read to their children at bedtime, prolong child-care routines in a playful way, or eat with their children." Many of these mothers are suffering from "task overload"; they are forced to deal with family tasks and responsibilities usually shared by two adults.

In addition, of course, the stimulating input of the father is missing. It is noteworthy in this connection that the lags in intellectual development of children living with their divorced mothers is similar to those shown by youngsters living in intact families—but where the father is absent a good deal of the time.

How do divorced fathers stack up as single parents?

In his book, *Fathers,* Parke points out that paternal custody, though increasing, is still a new and relatively rare phenomenon. Our understanding of its impact on kids, therefore, remains limited. But the evidence does seem to indicate that men who do win custody generally manage the tasks of child care with surprising effectiveness. Fathers, Parke points out, tend to use additional caretakers for support—babysitters, relatives, daycare centers, and friends—more so than do mothers.

ـ&ۤ In spite of their increasing numbers, fathers with custody of their children are still viewed as "brave explorers of the new sex role frontier." Consequently people often treat them differently from the way they treat divorced mothers who have custody. Fathers with custody receive more offers of help, say in the form of babysitting or dinner invitations. And they generally get more credit: "Isn't George a terrific father and he does it alone!" How often do single mothers get extra credit for managing on their own? For fathers, raising children singlehandedly is considered a special role, while for single mothers, it's expected that they should and can do it.

Ross D. Parke
Fathers

Will remarriage and the formation of a new family reduce the emotional turmoil interfering with the child's intellectual activity?

Sometimes they will—but not always by any means. Many children find it difficult to accept a parent's remarriage. Psychiatrist Carl Feinstein and clinical psychologist Arthur Bodin have cited a number of the reasons. Some children, for example, continue to hope for the reunion of their parents, and when mother and father continue to see each other—especially to discuss matters of child rearing—it lends credibility to the fantasy.

Other children are upset by the dishonesty of a parent who introduces a new companion as "only a friend" and then quickly remarries. At times, new stepparents assume a leading role in child rearing and discipline faster than the child is ready to accept, or perhaps worse, they make it clear that they have no real interest in the children because they have already gone through the experience of raising a family.

For these and other reasons, the new family unit does not automatically eliminate the child's sense of personal guilt, conflicting loyalties, or the conviction that the volume of attention and affection available has significantly decreased.

Is it unusual for stepparents to be good parents?

Not at all. More than 10 percent of American children live with a natural parent and stepparent, usually a stepfather. And the evidence is that stepparents can help children develop in a healthy fashion. The secret—as in all parenting—seems to lie in the degree of sympathy and devotion shown to the child.

The evidence suggests that children who live with a stepfather or father surrogate can perform academically just as well as children in nuclear families—and often better than children in one-parent families. Children living with stepparents turn out, on the average, to be as successful and achieving as other youngsters. They also view themselves as just as content.

The degree of acceptance of the stepparent often depends on the child's age. One large investigation found that the roughest period is adolescence. It is particularly difficult to become a stepparent to teenagers, who typically have already nurtured and established bonds elsewhere. Because they are struggling to achieve their independence, they are likely to resist building ties with a new family member. In happily remarried families, however, children generally do not experience serious problems—even when the natural fathers continue to visit their children after the mother remarries.

Especially for harassed parents adjusting to divorce, TV can become a convenient technique to occupy kids. Can TV-watching lead to learning difficulties?

Heavy watching probably can—and unfortunately, many children continue on an extremely heavy diet of television. The viewing day for most children ranges from two to six hours. Surveys find that two- to five-year-olds watch an average of thirty-one hours of TV per week—meaning more than four hours each day. By the end of high school, our kids will have spent more than 17,000 hours in front of a television set—5,000 more than in the classroom.

School children who are heavy watchers of television seem to be affected in a number of areas of school performance, notably in their reading ability. In one study, five- to eleven-year-olds were found to put much less effort into school work than did light viewers. When parents were asked to cut their first-graders' viewing time in half, the children became more reflective, spent more time reading, and actually improved on some measures of intelligence. Another study demonstrated that sixth-graders who watched less than one hour of television each day scored 7 percent higher on academic achievement tests than their classmates who watched four or more hours each day.

A Canadian research team studied children in three towns— one without television, another with only Canadian government TV, and a third with both Canadian and American commercial television. Children in the town without television had better reading skills and were more fluent verbally than children living with TV. Moreover, when television was later introduced to the TV-less town, the children's skills declined. The researchers concluded that TV, by reducing the time children spend reading, can prevent them from mastering the skills they need to become proficient readers.

Does heavy TV viewing affect the child's classroom performance?

Unquestionably, according to Joan Anderson Wilkins, a former "videoholic" now campaigning to rid families of their addiction. Television, says Wilkins, requires nothing of its viewers, and therefore children—many of whom have watched between 5,000 and 8,000 hours of television before starting kindergarten—are likely to be unprepared for the demands of the academic environment. Their years of sitting passively in front of the TV may have disrupted the development of skills necessary for learning—among them, the use of powers of the imagination, concentration, and independent persistence at tasks.

Can TV influence children's ideas about achievement?

It can and does—at least among heavy viewers, who are more likely to develop stereotyped attitudes about males as the world's movers and shakers, and females as meek subordinates. Why this occurs becomes clear when we examine closely the way television portrays the sexes. Men are more likely to be depicted as aggressive, decisive, and competent; women, in contrast, are more often characterized as warm and sociable—but occupied primarily in child care or housework.

How much TV is enough?

Experts appear to agree that younger children should watch less than older ones. Most are of the opinion that preschoolers should be limited to an hour a day at most, preferably a half hour at a time, and that the parent should try to share the experience with the child. In this way there can be interaction between the child and parent, avoiding the potentially unfortunate one-way input from TV screen to child. Elementary school children should spend no more than two hours a day watching television.

Keep in mind that from earliest childhood to age eighteen, no other daily activity with the exception of sleeping is likely so heavily to dominate a child's life. Every family, therefore, must decide on the rules designed to tame TV that best fit the household.

✍ Questions to help tell if your child is watching too much TV
- Is the TV set on constantly when your children are at home?
- Are your kids unable to launch any entertainment or play activity on their own?
- Does the child choose TV even when friends are available?
- Does the household conversation center on television programs and characters?
- Is TV becoming an escape from the real world rather than serving as a natural break in a varied diet of activities?
- Is the viewing random—rather than directed to special events and interests?

What can be done if a child watches too much TV?

There are a number of ways to help reduce the amount of time kids spend in front of the TV set. One way is to teach children to become informed television consumers. Go over the listings, select appropriate programs, watch the programs with them—and afterward discuss what you have seen together. All this takes time, of course, but it can pay off.

It is helpful also to make a list of alternative activities—taking a bicycle ride, reading a book, going for a walk or run, working on a hobby, playing a game with siblings or peers. The child can be told to choose to do something from the list before being allowed to watch television. This will not only divert attention from TV, but may form the basis for the development of a wider span of interests and experiences, some of which children may come to enjoy and to prefer over watching television.

The entire family might be forbidden to engage in random viewing—that is, simply turning on the set to catch whatever is on the tube. This rule makes it necessary to have a specific program in mind beforehand; when the intended program is over, the set can be turned off immediately. Finally, instead of watching television, read with your young children.

⋙ The parent is a very strong model for the child. If their parents are heavy [television] watchers, the children tend to be heavy watchers also.

Dorothy Singer
Yale University

Can some television watching be beneficial?

Like any other medium—books, magazines, photographs, radio, tapes—television can be turned to the service of positive educational goals. Obviously, television can be a rich source of educational information for kids. Current events programs and news telecasts, for instance, certainly have the potential for expanding a child's interests and horizons.

The potential value of television has been demonstrated by studies in which preschool children were exposed to educational TV programs emphasizing the importance of being cooperative, friendly, and helpful. Their later behavior clearly reflected what they had seen. Other studies have shown that certain TV programs can help increase cooperative play and expressiveness.

Evaluators have found that numerous youngsters who watch the educational program *Sesame Street* display improvement in a variety of cognitive skills—and the more often they watch the program each week, the greater the improvement.

Thus, in at least some cases, television evidently *can* teach children in positive ways. But keep in mind that this applies to specially crafted educational programs—not to run-of-the-mill TV fare.

⋙ . . . children learn from watching television, and what they learn depends on what they watch. The programs they see on television change their behavior. If they look at violent or aggressive programs, they tend to become more aggressive and disobedient. But if they look at prosocial programs, they will more likely become more generous, friendly, and self-controlled. Television can have beneficial effects; it is a potential force for good.

David Pearl
Television and Behavior

What about home computers? Can they help children learn?

They are not likely to turn a totally unmotivated child into a world-beater, but they do offer some unique possibilities for some children.

To begin with, computers can teach accuracy because it is impossible to "communicate" with the computer—that is, to operate it—with incorrect codes and messages. Equally important, computers provide what psychologists refer to as "immediate reinforcement;" they respond in an instant, while the student's interest is still high, letting the user know whether the response that has been made is correct or not. And finally, children can pace their learning by using programs suited to their speed, even allowing the child to fail at a task for long periods without losing patience with the child.

But what computers obviously lack is the human factor—the precious interaction between adult and child that often lies at the heart of the learning process. Says Roy Pea, of the Bank Street College of Education: "Computers are deficient in just the things people are good at—such as giving advice, encouragement, and emotional support."

Can home video games be used as teaching tools?

That is exactly what their manufacturers are touting. Millions of American children—from preschool to high school—are now playing electronic video games at home as casually as we, their parents, played marbles. Home video games are by far the fastest growing item on the toy and hobby market, with annual sales soaring into the billions of dollars. A growing portion of this market is made up of video games featured as a way to help children develop and sharpen their intellectual skills.

Manufacturers were quick to spot the possibility of merging the modern world of electronics with the traditional world of education. With the help of today's dazzling computer technology, children can now learn to run a lemonade stand business, plan and manage a sprawling farm, create a design, compose a melody, solve a murder, or handicap horses at the track.

Some child development experts view home video games as a promising avenue for expanding the intellectual horizons of children—for stimulating their minds, and helping them learn faster and better, and with more motivation. In playing these games, they believe, children may be challenged to dig deep into the wellsprings of their intelligence and creativity, and to practice such basic skills as spelling, vocabulary, and logical reasoning.

Michael J. Moone, president of Atari's Consumer Electronics Division, claims that his company is developing not just fun and games, but a technology that "is rooted in real learning concepts, and addresses the real needs and curiosities of children."

Other experts in child development and education, and many parents as well, take entirely the opposite view. They regard home video games—even those with built-in educational goals—as a potential threat to the normal development of children. They are fearful that these modern electronic toys will begin to dominate the lives of their young—walling them off from the social stimulation of friends, encouraging laziness, and keeping them from the real world of studying, learning, and homework.

Some are concerned with the violence embedded in these games. "When I hear the whine of those bombers and rat-tat-tat of those guns," one mother says, "I wonder what it is doing to my child's mind." She is not alone. Rutgers University child researcher Michael Lewis believes that electronic games—especially because they come so close to simulating reality—can encourage the wrong kind of behavior.

The truth about video games lies somewhere between these two extreme points of view. Parents need to be aware of the strengths and weaknesses of this new force in the playroom—and to make certain that the video game revolution pays off for their children in constructive ways.

⌘ No compulsory learning can remain in the soul. In teaching children, train them by a kind of game.

Plato

How can parents capitalize on the video game craze?

By matching the games in your home with the special needs and interests of your child. Each passing month brings a startling increase in the number and variety of video games available for the home. Many of them, of course, are intended just for fun. Others, however, put a premium on special skills of the young players—for example, on numerical skills, recognizing letters or words, eye-hand coordination, or reaction time. In consultation with your child's teachers, it is possible to select those video games most likely to sharpen the child's capacities in an area that needs improvement—whether vocabulary, math, visual perception, or motor coordination.

Psychologist Cecil N. Clark and academic therapist Faith T. Clark of Bethesda, Maryland, use modern computer technology as one technique to help treat children beset by learning difficulties and lagging motivation. From their wide selection of materials, they attempt to identify precisely those that match the student's needs. The results, they report, have been "stunning," even for children with long histories of failure.

It makes good sense also to choose for the home those games that incorporate subjects of special interest to the child. For some, it may be music; for others, science; for still others, the world of finance. This learning may seem too sugar coated for some parents. But keep in mind that many children can be stimulated by their electronic fun-and-games to become more immersed in a favorite subject matter, and thereby enhance a special skill or aptitude.

Don't allow video games to separate your child from the rest of the world. Like television, video games are seductive, and they can soon begin to dominate the leisure time of children. Such games, because they can so easily be played alone, tend to discourage inter-action with peers, thus keeping youngsters from important sources of social stimulation. In the view of New York family therapist Donald A. Block, "The games encourage isolation and splitting . . . and contribute little to social skills." Play with others, in con-trast, brings children into a world that is more enriching to their personalities than most parents realize. Studies show that children learn a great deal about life from the social interactions that take place while playing with peers. For the sake of healthy personality development, therefore, it makes good sense to set reasonable limits on the amount of time that children are allowed to spend alone, transfixed by the narrow world of the video screen. Certainly, young-sters who already tend to be shy and withdrawn hardly need the added impetus of solitary games to keep them from interacting with others. For such children, it is especially important to create opportunities for group play away from the video games—or for enjoying these games in the company of friends or family.

Can video games help motivate the child?

Yes, they can be used as a technique for giving children feelings of mastery and self-confidence. Many children—especially those who have experienced a history of failure—need most of all to develop a sense of self-assurance. They need to enjoy the conviction that they are capable of controlling the environment, and of accomplishing what they set out to do.

In the view of Jerry D. Chaffin, professor of special education at the University of Kansas, educational video games in the home can do just that. They often incorporate many of the attractive features that motivate children to spend long hours at video arcades. They can, for example, offer children quick and clear feedback about their performance, allowing them literally to see improvement taking place before their very eyes. Moreover, the games place no ceiling on excellence. They are so constructed that the young player remains constantly aware of still another goal within reach.

A special source of motivation lies in the opportunity these games give youngsters to win in competition with others. Many home video games can be played by children—even those as young as five years—on even terms with virtually anyone. Parents who join children in the fun often find that the competition acts as a motivational spur for their young "opponents" to excel.

Aren't girls typically left out of the world of video games?

Unfortunately, the world of video games—indeed the entire computer industry—tends to be male-oriented. The video arcade has in fact been described by researchers as "a den of teenage male culture, a place where teenage boys gather with their buddies."

Educational electronic games for the home reflect a similar bias toward male consumers. The themes so prevalent in the arcades— the physical competition of baseball, football, military combat— tend to dominate video games in the playroom as well. When you are choosing video games as a way to motivate learning, be careful, therefore to select some that appeal as much to the girls in your home as to their brothers.

Isn't there a danger that video games will close off other channels to a child's mind?

The danger certainly does exist—at least for some children. And that is why video games, however enticing they may be, should not become the sole source of the child's intellectual stimulation. Young people need to be "turned on" not only by the signals and flashes of machines, but by the thoughts and ideas of other human beings. "At its best," writes Francis Roberts, director of elementary and secondary school programs for the National Endowment of the Humanities, "education is a human process."

Numerous studies, cited earlier in the book, bear this out. They show that children, beginning from birth, profit in their intellectual development from the stimulation of language and ideas they receive from their parents and others in the family. In the years of our own childhood, long before the days of TV or fancy computer electronics, it was the give-and-take of everyday interactions in the home that brought an avalanche of learning.

Indeed a single charismatic teacher—whether inside the classroom or outside—can be more precious to the mind of the child in the long run than the most complex electronic circuitry delivering an abundance of information devoid of human inspiration. The world of electronics and computers will never eliminate the child's need for interpersonal channels of communication.

With the cost of electronic products moving downward, the popularity of video games is not likely to abate. These games seem destined to find a solid niche in the environment of our young. Used sensibly, there is no reason to keep them from being enjoyed in the home. To begin with, they can be pure fun—and children need periods for relaxing diversions as much as adults do. At their best, however, video games can succeed in merging the fanciful world of play with the practical world of learning. Accomplishing this merger, however, will take the good judgment and wisdom of parents as they survey the widening horizons of their children's electronic universe.

CHAPTER EIGHT
✌ᡈ Roadblocks to Learning

As many parents discover, the path of a child's intellectual development is not always smooth. It can be strewn with roadblocks—psychological or physical problems that impede learning and threaten to keep the child from reaching the limits of the potential within.

Among all the impediments that children face, learning disabilities are among the most difficult to understand and accept. Children with such disabilities are typically normal or above average in intelligence, yet their academic performance remains far below their ability. They can hear and see perfectly well, but they often have problems with visual and auditory perception. Some even show the same symptoms as children known to be brain-damaged—poor motor coordination, for example—yet their brains are actually not damaged in any way. They may be quite motivated to learn, but their disability prevents them from acquiring knowledge quickly or smoothly. In the end they become frustrated, and some turn aside altogether from the adventure of learning.

Learning disabilities are a significant cause of emotional distress and behavior disorders among children and adolescents, and they comprise the greatest single reason children drop out of school. Three-fourths of the youngsters who end up in juvenile detention centers suffer from a learning problem, and it is one of the most common features among children referred to psychiatric clinics because of disturbed or disturbing behavior. Many thousands of children, because they fail to read adequately, suffer years of frustration, humiliation, and loss of self-esteem. Many become withdrawn; some turn into troubled adolescents who seem bent on turning their wrath against society. Others, viewed as retarded because they cannot read, are misassigned to classes for retarded children and sometimes even to institutions.

For many children, learning would progress smoothly were it not for their underlying emotional difficulties. Because they cannot handle the frustrations and stresses in their lives, their academic performance suffers. Some may become withdrawn and depressed, while still others may face their classroom tasks with such overwhelming anxieties that their learning potential is drowned altogether. In a surprisingly large number of other cases, the child's psychological problems are not caused by stress at all. Instead the problems turn out to be physical in origin—malfunctions of the body that go undetected but that seriously hamper the operation of the mind.

The pessimism of parents whose children face roadblocks in their intellectual development is understandable enough. These children pose problems not only in how they learn but in how they interact with their environment. They can quickly cause others around them to feel frustrated and angry. We *know* they can do better, but they score startlingly low on tests, never seeming to be able to perform anywhere near their grade level.

As this book makes clear, however, the evidence suggests an optimistic outlook. Many children who do best as adults often have experienced the most difficult beginnings. Albert Einstein, whose rocky childhood was described earlier, had trouble with language skills and with numbers. Nelson Rockefeller, governor of New York and later vice president of the United States, struggled throughout his life to spell correctly and to read; when making a speech, he often set aside the manuscript out of fear that he would confuse the facts and figures in it. Woodrow Wilson was eleven years old before he learned to read. Other prominent figures who overcame disabling roadblocks in their learning as children include the renowned brain surgeon Harvey Cushing, bacteriologist Paul Ehrlich, and military hero General George S. Patton.

Such cases are joined by countless more people who are less well known, but whose histories are equally inspiring. Together, they confirm how consistently we have underestimated the resiliency of children—their capacities to overcome the seemingly insuperable obstacles in their path.

How can you tell if a child is suffering from a learning disability?

There is little agreement among educators and psychologists over the term "learning disability," and in fact, many experts in the field reject the term itself. Alan O. Ross, in his book *Learning Disability: The Unrealized Potential,* points out that it is easier to find agreement on what does *not* fall under the term. Many children encounter snags in learning but are hardly "disabled." A child regarded as having a learning disability is neither mentally retarded, physically impaired, emotionally disturbed, nor the victim of gross disadvantages in the environment. Despite normal or above-average IQ, such children simply cannot perform up to their potential, and they fall behind their peers in the classroom.

In 1975, a federal law—the Education for All Handicapped Children Act—helped define learning disability as an impairment in learning that cannot be explained, "a disorder in one or more basic psychological processes involved in understanding or in using language, spoken or written . . ." In short, children who are learning disabled are impaired in their ability to listen, think, speak, read, write, spell, or do mathematical calculations in a way that you would hardly expect given their native intellectual equipment.

Is it possible to detect children with learning disabilities long before they begin their schooling?

In extreme cases, yes. But it is especially beginning around age three that children can be "red flagged" for indications that their learning might be impeded. Testing for prekindergarten children typically includes, for example, measures of their ability to understand and answer questions, to follow instructions, to recognize and name colors, and to distinguish between concepts such as "right" and "left," or "before" and "after." Combined with other tests of perception and comprehension, such examinations are used to predict readiness for reading and other academic tasks.

How many American children are actually learning disabled?

About 7.5 million. Some say the number has drastically increased recently, but this is probably not the case. Instead, we are simply more sensitized to the problem than ever before. The disabilities have also become more noticeable because, in former years, children with such handicaps would be likely to drop out of school early. Today learning disabled children remain in school longer since, fortunately, many schools are taking constructive steps to deal with their problems.

❧ Checklist of Learning Disability Symptoms
    This list, useful for children in grades one through eight, was developed by the New York Institute for Child Development, Inc. Does your child:
- Seem very bright and articulate but cannot seem to understand reading matter?
- Move lips while reading or follow the line with a finger?
- Complain of seeing things bigger or smaller than they are?
- Frequently go out of the lines when coloring?
- Avoid sports or activities that involve catching and throwing?
- Seem uncoordinated or sloppy when running?
- Frequently walk into things or trip?
- Use one hand for some things and the other hand for other things?
- Confuse right with left?
- Go up or down stairs one step at a time?
- Get distracted easily?
- Have a short attention span?
- Seem to "tune out" at times?
- Perform the same tasks inconsistently from one day to the next?
- Get frustrated easily?

    If your answer is "yes" to a number of these questions—say five or more—you might do well to visit your pediatrician to check out whether physical problems may be affecting the child's capacity to learn. If your child's school has an LD (Learning Disability) team, request an evaluation. And if the child seems to require more extensive evaluation, inquire at colleges, universities, or hospitals in your area; many such institutions have excellent diagnostic centers.

Aren't many such children simply stubborn and unwilling to learn?

    It is precisely this belief that has frequently caused children with learning disabilities to be stigmatized. Someone, either teacher or parent, becomes convinced that they are purposely not doing well—that they are "spoiled," poorly motivated, or willfully obstructionist. But the truth is that learning difficulties are not a matter of will or choice. Children who have them simply cannot easily make their way in the usual school setting.

How can parents deal constructively with children who encounter a learning disability?

Here is a list of suggestions that most experts in the field would agree on:

- Read and talk to the child, and engage in interactions that help generate independent activities.
- Deal with the child as normal and capable, but with an impediment to learning that is temporary and correctable.
- Provide the child with calm surroundings and a structured routine.
- Don't insist on entering the child in first grade unless there is evidence of readiness, or unless the school offers special training.
- Praise and reward every success no matter how small and how slowly achieved.
- Save and display every shred of evidence that the child is progressing.
- Don't nag a child to do better in school than is possible. You cannot help learning disabled children by telling them to pay attention or by punishing them for not paying attention; such tactics may only cause a child to lose confidence and drop all interest in learning.
- Be frank but encouraging when the child asks questions about what is really wrong.
- When a child seems depressed or otherwise deeply affected by experiences in school or with peers, consider consultation with a psychologist or psychiatrist. Consultation—or a period of treatment, if necessary—may assist the parent as well as the child.
- Remember that a federal law now requires the detection and education of handicapped children—which includes youngsters affected by learning disabilities. One requirement of the law is consultation among parents, school authorities, and specialists for the purpose of drawing up an individual educational plan

for each child. You may have to push to get special programs under way in your community.

- Children who fall seriously behind the norm may need to be in a school class where there is a minimum of distraction and stimulation, and a maximum of one-on-one attention. Your school system should have or know about such resources, or you can make contact with the nearest branch of the Association for Children with Learning Disabilities (ACLD), which has 50 state affiliates and nearly 800 local chapters: 4156 Library Road, Pittsburgh, Pennsylvania 15234.

~≈§ It is vital that the child hear over and over and over again from different sources that he is intelligent, that he needs more time to learn than others, but that he will make it in the world. He needs as much information about himself as he can handle, and he needs it frequently. He may still feel dumb. But at least he knows he is not retarded and does not have any brain diseases or whatever else he may secretly dread.

Sally Smith
No Easy Answers

Does the behavior of children with learning disability always follow the same pattern?

No. For example, some may be less active than the usual child, while others are hyperactive. Some may be inconsistent, displaying a particular knowledge or skill one day and then drawing a blank the next, and some may be unable to remember more than a couple steps in a series of directions. Many are inflexible and rigid—insisting, for example, on wearing the same clothes or eating the same food for lunch every day, or being unable to change smoothly from one activity to another. Often, too, children with learning disabilities cannot accept making a mistake or they may blow up or quit altogether if a mistake is discovered in their work. The same child may be supercritical of errors made by classmates.

~≈§ Some Suggestions for Teachers of Children with Learning Disabilities

- Give directions that are short and simple, and present them in small increments.

- Keep in mind that affected children need praise or other rewards for every success, even if it has taken months of repeated practice to learn how to write one letter.
- Provide evidence that the child is progressing—for example, samples of work in a folder so that the child can compare present with past efforts in copying designs, doing arithmetic, writing letters of the alphabet, and the like.
- Use tape recorders to help those children who can say what they wish to write but cannot actually write it. Have them listen to the recording and decide if it sounds the way they wish it to. When it does, have them copy it on paper. Correct the copy for spelling or syntax; then have the students make a final copy by writing or by typing.
- If you become anxious about your ability to handle an affected child, consult with persons who have specialized in working with such youngsters.

Can a child who is beset by a learning disability develop emotional problems as well?

In some cases yes, not only from the stress and frustration generated by their learning difficulties, but because they end up feeling stigmatized.

Children with learning disabilities are often placed in special classrooms, and they become victims of scorn or derision by schoolmates or labeled as "different" by teachers. Because they often find themselves profiting little from schooling, they easily develop chronic feelings of inferiority. Some become so frustrated that they turn to antisocial and aggressive behavior. Others may withdraw and become depressed, further blocking their capacity to learn.

Are learning disabilities inherited?

A number of studies suggest that heredity may very well predispose a child to develop a learning disability. For example, these studies show similar patterns in parents and children. Moreover, in a given family, learning problems tend to afflict more than one child.

What is "dyslexia"?

An especially agonizing learning disability—the inability to read. A government report lists a number of problems that seem associated with dyslexia, including hyperactivity, difficulty with language, difficulty with knowing right from left and up from down, problems with physical coordination and balancing, and faulty memory.

A genetic factor seems to be especially marked in the case of extreme reading disabilities. One research team found that over 80 percent of children with this type of impairment had relatives suffering from the same type of problem.

⌇ Self-portrait of a Child with a Learning Disability

My name is Matt Ward. I have a learning disability. Some kids seem to be terrific at schoolwork without even trying. Me, I really work hard just to keep up. I figure that it's a job that I do because I have to. I want to be a doctor someday, so I've got to keep on top of it.

They say that the brain is like a complicated computer. If that's so, then my wires are a little crossed up. For instance, I'm right-handed on some things, and left-handed on others. And I often get mixed up over which is which.

My memory plays tricks on me, too, and causes two big school problems. One is that I have trouble remembering what letters *sound* like when they're put together. Sometimes the word "neat" seems as though it's really two words—"ne at." Sometimes I think it's "net" or "nate" as if it rhymed with "great." And sometimes I can remember that it's "neat." That slows down my reading because I know there wouldn't be a sentence that says "He was ne at in his work," so I know I have to stop and check it out again.

The other problem is that I can easily forget how a word is supposed to *look*. If I copy it from a book, I get it right. But when I'm on my own, especially in reading, I sometimes goof up. The word "great" might come out "gneat" because "r" often looks like "n" to me. You'd get stuck, too, if you were trying to read a word like "gneat."

Barbara Adams
Like It Is: Facts and Feelings about Handicaps from Kids Who Know

What about pregnancy complications? Do they lead to learning disabilities?

Some researchers claim to have found a connection between learning disability and untoward events during pregnancy or around the time of the child's birth. A study in the United Kingdom found, for instance, that among children who were failing in reading, writing, and spelling at age seven, the rate of premature births was unusually high.

But the issue is not a simple one. Mothers and children who experience such complications are much more likely to come from impoverished families, to be undernourished, and to receive inadequate prenatal care. Conceivably, these factors play a role in learning disabilities.

Is learning disability permanent?

Hardly. Given proper instruction through programs specially suited to the child's needs, the problem often disappears in time. A child with a learning disability is not permanently damaged or impaired, and many such children become achievers as adults. Although their spelling may remain poor and their reading below par, many of them go on to attain enormous success in various fields. The child learns ways to compensate—to cope and to conquer the problem.

Even children with quite serious learning disabilities can come through all right if they get the skilled and patient teaching they need. One seven-year-old boy required five years in a special program before he began to read. After another two years he was reading above grade level and was caught up in mathematics. He still has trouble spelling—but he is headed for college.

ᴥᔆ Getting through College Successfully
    The Admissions Testing Program of the College Board has published a brochure for students with special needs (Box 2891, Princeton, New Jersey 08541).
    Special editions of tests are available to students with learning disabilities as well as other disabilities. These students are given more time to take the tests, and they may use a reader or an "amanuensis" (someone who will write for them). Given individual attention to their learning needs and given approximately the same opportunities in life, young people with learning problems can do at least as well as their linguistically more facile schoolmates—judged by their later academic and occupational achievement.

What does it actually mean when a child is described as hyperactive?

"Hyperactive" is a catch-all word used to describe overly active children, many of whom get into trouble both in school and out because of their restlessness and their need to keep moving. Only some kids with learning disabilities are hyperactive, and certainly many hyperactive children show no signs of having a learning disability.

Differences in amount of motor activity appear among children from the day they are born. Some quickly reveal themselves to be restless and constantly on the move, while others can comfortably remain placid and still. The restless ones rarely complain about their overactivity. Instead they complain about teachers picking on them, other children fighting with them, parents blaming them. In other words, they tend not to recognize how their own behavior may provoke troubling responses from others. Hyperactive children are typically referred for treatment by parents or teachers because they upset others through their restless and pushy behavior.

A child who is simply very active may be trying to others, but is usually not in need of special attention. On the other hand, it has been recognized for over a century that hyperactivity can sometimes be part of a larger set of clinical symptoms that, together, do pose a problem. In these cases the child is also impulsive, distractible, excitable, aggressive toward others, and emotionally unpredictable. And not surprisingly, such a child could be the victim of learning problems as well.

Why do some children become hyperactive in the first place?

The causes of hyperactivity are unknown. Investigators have studied the possibility that it is the result of physical factors such as lack of oxygen or injury during childbirth, or neurological damage during pregnancy. Others have focused on psychological factors such as family conflict. But there is no firm answer.

When does hyperactivity first begin to be a problem?

Typically, in the elementary school years. Behaviors which were disturbing but tolerable at home are not so easily accepted in the classroom. In time academic problems increase, along with antisocial behaviors. The clinical picture varies from the child who is silly, immature, and not performing up to expected standards to the child who is always "in a sweat," aggressive, and impossible to control in a regular classroom setting.

Careful interviews with parents often reveal that the symptoms of hyperactivity were discernible from early childhood. Mothers often say that the baby seemed to be unusually active, constantly alert, and difficult to soothe. They recall irregularity in body functions—colic, sleeping and eating disturbances, and frequent crying.

None of these early symptoms alone, of course, is necessarily characteristic of hyperactive children. Once the child begins to walk, however, other problems surface—and now the high activity level and difficulties in paying attention become more noticeable. The child seems to lack any sense of control, moves from one activity to another quickly, and is totally unaffected by disciplinary measures that usually work with other children.

Parents report that, from an early age, such children always seemed to have an unusual amount of energy and less need for sleep than their siblings. They also seemed to wear out shoes, clothing, bicycles, and toys faster than other children. Parents and teachers note "fidgetiness," an inability to sit still for any length of time, a tendency to talk a great deal, and an inability to keep their hands to themselves.

Remember that many children who are very active—and, therefore, troublesome to adults at times—are not truly hyperactive. Psychiatrist Michael Rutter has described the difference: Hyperactivity can be distinguished from ordinary restlessness by its severity, its pervasiveness, its early beginnings, and its association with serious disorders of attention and concentration.

⋙ My son is 21 months old and has totally disrupted our household since he was an infant.

He is big for his age—the size his now 5-year-old sister was at 3. He pushes and shoves other kids, slaps, kicks and screams. He climbs onto kitchen counters, turns off the water heater and unscrews almost everything, even the storm door. He opens the refrigerator and climbs in.

Nothing seems to make him happy. Lately he has begun to bang his head or hit himself when he is frustrated and mad. He pulls over his highchair and anything else that isn't nailed down. There are few toys he'll play with. He's started to enjoy books, but has ripped all the pages. He loves to be outside and we try to stay out for a couple of hours every day.

We are a calm, loving family and I've tried to be more loving, talk softly and explain. I have tried every form of discipline I know, confined him to his room, made him sit in a chair, ignored his screams. I've even tried spanking him with the wooden spoon, but nothing works.

Marguerite Kelly
"Parent's Almanac: The Hyperactive Child"
(*The Washington Post*)

How does hyperactivity become apparent in the classroom?

Many hyperactive children oppose school as a way of life because it is too confining. Being forced to sit still all day within the four walls is a tough assignment even for many average restless kids who have to keep a lock on their energy and excitement. But the problem is especially severe for the child who is altogether unable to sit still.

Distractibility and a short attention span are clearly noticeable in school. The typical hyperactive child is unable to persevere with classwork and homework, and is easily distracted by outside stimuli. Such a child finds it difficult, for example, to listen to a story or to take part in games for any length of time.

The hyperactive youngster is sometimes impulsive—as shown by such behaviors as jumping around, climbing out of the seat, shouting out tactless statements, and blurting out answers without thinking questions through. There may be temper tantrums and fights over trivial matters, low frustration tolerance, and a tendency to become overexcited and more active in stimulating situations, especially in large groups of children.

Do hyperactive children ever settle down?

So many parents have by now heard about the "hyperactive child" that they naturally become alarmed when they think they detect its signs in their own children. They have read all sorts of myths in the popular press about what lifelong troubles these signs bode. It is true that there is a tendency for the most extremely hyperactive kids to end up with problems. But except for this atypical group, most hyperactive children eventually adapt reasonably well. As time passes, the problem is usually mastered. The behavior pattern labeled as hyperactivity generally gets channeled into a forceful, productive, and energetic personality style.

~~§ Three "Don'ts" for Parents of Hyperactive Children
- Don't treat hyperactive children as if they were the victims of some dread, incurable disease that spells only failure and an uncertain future.
- Don't communicate anxiety or disappointment.
- Don't go to extremes, becoming either impossibly overcontrolling or foolishly overpermissive.

What treatment is a truly hyperactive child likely to receive?

Treatment will vary depending on the special needs of a particular youngster. In some cases, the doctor or psychologist might simply recommend educational programs designed to build up the child's skills and, at the same time, the child's eroding self-concept. Sometimes, behavior modification techniques will be used—that is, techniques for methodically rewarding desirable behavior. Some children need emotional support and psychotherapy to deal with underlying psychological stress and conflict, and still others may profit from drugs that mute the worst symptoms of hyperactivity.

How effective actually are drugs in treating extremely hyperactive kids?

Three out of four improve—usually for just a limited time, however; the remainder show no change or even grow worse. There is, in other words, little consistency in the results. Researchers have come across youngsters who are getting some benefit from the drugs as long as eight years after they were first prescribed. On the other hand, one follow-up of children who had been placed on the drugs two years earlier was disappointing: Those who had continued to take them seemed on the average to be having as much trouble academically and socially as those who had dropped them.

The bottom line is this: For reasons not yet known, stimulant drugs benefit only some hyperactive children—and then mainly in conjunction with other approaches.

Do these stimulant drugs produce any side effects?

You can safely assume that virtually *any* drug will produce effects beyond those specifically intended—and stimulant drugs used to treat hyperactive children are no different. A variety of complaints have been catalogued, among them sleep disturbances, loss of appetite and nausea, irritability and crying, lethargy and depression, headaches and dizziness, tremors and nervous tics, dry mouth, and more.

Usually these side effects can be handled by adjusting the drug dose. One problem, however, has proved to be more troublesome: a suppression in the child's normal gains in height and weight during prolonged treatment. Children removed from medication during the summer months showed what researchers describe as a "rebound" effect—that is, an abnormally large weight increase. This "catch-up," however, did not entirely compensate for the retarded weight gain induced by the previous nine months of therapy. Moreover, the summer gains in height were even less satisfactory.

Experts have concluded that children should be removed from stimulant drugs over the summer months to permit at least partial compensation for the suppressed weight and height gain caused by months of treatment. Even more important, make sure a doctor closely watches the child's drug response throughout treatment.

Much has been made of the effect of food additives. Can you really help children overcome hyperactivity by controlling their diet?

The theory—originated in the early 1970s by allergist Benjamin Feingold—holds that synthetic food additives and colorings trigger behavior problems in up to one half of all hyperactive children. But researchers have found no hard evidence to support this surprisingly popular theory. Their data show that synthetic food additives simply cannot be linked to hyperactivity in large numbers of kids.

In a typical experiment, children considered hyperactive by their parents and teachers are placed into two groups. One receives the Feingold diet containing no additives, while the other receives a diet containing average amounts of additives and colorings. The results of such studies show no significant differences in behavioral changes between the two groups.

Nevertheless, some parents continue to report positive changes in their children's behavior due to the removal of additives. The bottom line seems to be that while a few children react favorably, Feingold's sweeping claims have as yet not received very much scientific support.

What happens to hyperactive kids who aren't treated, or for whom treatment fails?

It seems that, eventually, they overcome the problem—but the struggle may leave its marks. One study followed children from birth into adulthood. The researchers found that boys who were hyperactive shortly after birth continued to be so during a good part of their childhood, but eventually, in high school and college, they made just as good grades as did more placid boys. The hyperactive pattern in girls appeared to wane even earlier. In general, it appears that hyperactivity often eventually fades sometime after high school—either because the nervous system has matured or has somehow overcome the original trouble.

But there is sometimes a residual problem: Even when the symptoms of hyperactivity die down, the children's earlier bitter experiences with family, teachers, and peers may leave them with a level of self-esteem so low that emotional problems persist.

Apart from learning disabilities, don't some children face emotional roadblocks in their efforts to learn and achieve?

It is rare for children not to encounter some psychological problems at one time or another during their growing-up years. Rutter cites numerous studies showing that most children encounter passing periods of emotional turmoil and behavioral difficulties. "To a considerable extent," he writes, "these are part and parcel of growing up and are not themselves a cause for concern. Isolated 'symptoms' are extremely common and are typically of little significance."

Still, some children clearly suffer psychiatric disorders which block their normal development and require professional treatment. Such disorders are not diagnosable because of a single item of behavior but, rather, because of a pattern of symptoms which persist and impede the development of the child's intellectual potential. It is estimated that around 12 million children in the United States experience some measure of mental health problems—among them severe anxiety and depression.

Can anxiety cause failures in memory?

Memory failure is often the result of an inability to pay attention—which is typical of the anxious person. Numerous studies have shown that children's capacities for memory can be depleted by anxiety. The pervasive cloud of anxiety distracts the child, draining attention from relevant incoming information and thus blocking memory.

Is the anxious child less likely to achieve academically?

Not if the anxiety is only moderate. In fact a modest amount of anxiety over performance may help motivate learning, focus attention, and keep the mind "sharp." Young adolescents with moderate anxiety levels have been found to achieve more than students who were either very low in anxiety—with a "don't-care-at-all" attitude—or very high in anxiety.

As this finding implies, severe anxiety *is* likely to interfere with learning and depress achievement. Huge numbers of kids go to school each day feeling scared. They have stomachaches, tense muscles, headaches, and many of the other psychosomatic symptoms that tensions can generate. Their anxiety also makes them irritable and reluctant to get to school on time, and tempts them to stay home whenever they can.

Anxiety reduces the ability to cope with school tasks, particularly test-taking. Children who are scared will generally do less well on tests than they should, given their actual abilities.

Do many children suffer from test anxiety?

They most certainly do—and the impact of their anxiety on test performance tends to become greater as they grow older.

Studies show that performance declines among children who grow increasingly anxious, and that performance improves among those whose anxiety wanes. The message for parents is clear: When we generate excessive anxiety in our children as a result of our desire for them to excel and "make it," we may actually be accomplishing the opposite effect.

In the modern school, the child is tested and retested day after day. As a result, many kids feel as if they are on trial, and they develop an attitude of self-blame. Highly anxious children have little respect for themselves. They see themselves as inferior, and when things go wrong, they are inclined to assume it is all their fault. But at the same time, they tend to be hostile to others, including parents; their frustration surfaces in displays of temper.

How can parents help the anxious child?

By not creating such a high level of anxiety about failing that it affects the child's overall self-concept.

Many children harbor an extremely acute and intense fear of failure. They doubt everything about themselves, including their ability to pass a test or to perform problems correctly. The anxiety of some youngsters rises to such an intense level that it interferes with clear thinking and, ultimately leads to a withdrawal of interest in school tasks. The result is that many bright children who have a strong urge to improve their intellectual skills actually fail to do so. High levels of anxiety and doubts about their ability block their effectiveness on tests, and cause them to become profoundly discouraged.

How unusual is it for children to be anxious about going to school?

Such fear is common enough in early childhood. Most kids show reluctance or outright fear over the prospects of separating from their protectors and venturing out into the unknown. But eventually the child's anxiety is outweighed by a sense of curiosity and by anticipation of the exciting world they have heard about from older siblings and peers.

The fears of some children may be exacerbated by unpleasant experiences at school. A threatening teacher, an unfriendly group of classmates, a bullying child at the neighboring desk, embarrassment over having to go to the "john" too often, failing in a test— such experiences can cause a child to become acutely anxious each morning as the time for leavetaking approaches. But as the environment changes—or the child adapts—the anxiety pattern disappears.

Don't some children develop a serious school phobia?

Yes, but it is usually part of a larger problem in separating from home and family.

If the child who refuses to go to school is generally cheerful and lively, that would tend to rule out the possibility of a more pervasive difficulty. On the other hand, if the child is anxious when mother leaves the house, cries constantly when left with a sitter, and is reluctant to stay with neighbors or relatives, to play with friends, or to stay over at a friend's house, then the so-called "school phobia" is likely to be one element of a larger problem in overcoming anxiety over separation.

Children with a pervasive and morbid fear of school, in other words, are usually not just anxious about school itself. They are generally withdrawn and miserable, lacking in interest, uninvolved in activities, reluctant to go out with friends, or unable to concentrate on their work.

Can children suffer from depression as adults do?

They can—and they do so in numbers that are surprising even to mental health professionals.

Among all persons receiving care for depression in clinics and hospitals, nearly one-fifth are under eighteen years of age. But beyond the children suffering severe depression are the countless others whose lives are shrouded by the "blues," by feelings of disenchantment and melancholy that dull their zest and cloud their horizons. Available data probably underestimate the true scope of the problem.

Unfortunately, however, depression in the early years is easy to miss. Unlike the adult, some depressed children can remain active and capable of displaying interest in their environment even while "down." Moreover, young children are typically unaware of the meaning of depression and do not complain about it as adults do.

Does that mean that some children can be very depressed without anyone knowing about it?

Indeed they can. In fact there is a category of depression which experts have called "masked depression." The condition has now been implicated in problem behavior ranging from temper tantrums and truancy to school phobias and outright academic failure. Chronically fatigued or bored youngsters who appear unable to achieve up to their intellectual potential or who are frightened of the prospects of leaving home for school may be the victims of a previously unrecognized form of depression.

So, too, may the hyperactive child who cannot remain still for a moment, and who soon becomes a problem for the teacher and parent alike. University of California psychiatric researcher William E. Bunney is among those suggesting that hyperactivity can be an offshoot of depression. Indeed future research may reveal that some hyperactive children profit from stimulant drugs because they are effective in overcoming the underlying depression that, according to Bunney, may be the true source of their nervous agitation. Perhaps the child who fidgets endlessly is compensating for an underlying feeling of emptiness and despair. Young hypochondriacs who are overly fearful for their health and survival are often found to be depressed, as are children who chronically complain of such symptoms as nausea, headaches, or stomachaches.

Even delinquent behavior has now been shown in some cases to be related to a depressive mood. In a study of 120 teenage delinquents, one researcher found evidence of depression in almost half of the youths. It may be that even though antisocial behavior results in punishment and pain, it serves to block out the even more excruciating feelings of despair and loneliness that rumble beneath the surface of the unruly child's life.

What causes young children to become depressed?

As in adults, the most common cause is an experience of loss. Often the loss is dramatic and obvious—the death of a beloved relative, the destruction by fire of treasured possessions, the disappearance of a favorite pet. But sometimes it is more subtle. For example, the child simply loses the interest or involvement of someone important. The occasion may be a remarriage, the arrival of a new sibling, a friend's departure, or family tensions that significantly reduce the quality of love and warmth surrounding the child.

The child's sense of mourning can also arise from seemingly routine events: a string of poor grades, friendship broken, daily taunts in the playground, repeated rejection by a Little League coach. The disappointments and hurts of childhood are often considerably more bitter than parents realize. Experiences that seem trivial to us can be monumental from the perspective of a child.

~§ Children's griefs are little, certainly. But so is the child. . . . Grief is a matter of relativity; the sorrow should be estimated by its proportion to the sorrower; a gash is as painful to one as an amputation is to another.

Percy Bysshe Shelley

How can you tell whether a child is just temporarily upset or suffering a serious depression?

There is no easy answer because severe depression may produce much the same symptoms as the normal temporary "down" that most children suffer from time to time. However, in the severely depressed child, the symptoms will be intense and more persistent.

Depressed children typically lose interest in school and the capacity to perform at their usual level. They lack self-confidence, they have a low opinion of themselves and their abilities, feel defeated, lose their energy and drive, withdraw into themselves, spend more time alone, and—like adults who are depressed—lose their enthusiasm and interest in the future. Their attitudes are overwhelmingly negative and their behavior may become hostile and difficult to control.

Like adults, they may display physical symptoms—a change in eating habits marked either by loss of appetite or overeating, or a change in sleeping habits such as broken sleep, morning fatigue, or an escape into sleep by remaining in bed. Chronic physical complaints—headaches, nausea, stomachaches—may emerge with no apparent cause. Depressed kids are also often preoccupied with fears about health and survival.

How can parents best deal with the depressed child?

Here are some steps parents can take to help a child handle a troublesome "down" period:

• Be a sensitive observer. Although children often hide their true feelings, many express their despair at odd moments. A six-year-old, caught in the crisis of her mother's sudden illness, sits at her father's desk and stares into the distance; a ten-year-old, repeatedly rejected by his preoccupied father, looks up from his dinner plate and suddenly asks, "Where would a person be if he were never born?" If you are sensitive, you can learn to recognize an expression of a child's grief. If such expressions appear often enough, it is time to try to discover their source.

- Create open channels of communication. Through actions as well as words, let your child know you are available to listen. Sometimes the parent's role is merely to help children get together with someone to whom they can freely express their feelings—a neighbor, an older friend, a favorite teacher, or a close relative.

- Acknowledge your child's feelings. When children are down, it is important to accept the validity of their sadness. Children struggling with the blues should know that the adults in their lives understand how they feel. Depressed youngsters should be encouraged to be as honest as they can about their feelings, and reassured that such feelings are nothing to be ashamed of.

- Don't "psychologize" and label. Avoid suggesting, by what you say or do, that your child is a psychiatric casualty. Let the child know that feelings of loss and depression, however acute and painful, are an inevitable and acceptable part of life.

- Help your child enjoy positive feedback. It is important for the depressed child to experience the feeling of success. Encourage such a child to do something usually done well—jump rope, swim, draw, play cards, teach the dog tricks—whatever. Even little triumphs can help restore lost self-esteem. Try to withhold criticism or actions that are likely to inspire feelings of inadequacy or inferiority; the depressed child is usually full of those already.

- Create episodes of pleasure whenever possible. It often helps depressed children to find an activity that may lift their spirits— a hobby, a new and engrossing game, a sightseeing trip. Anything that offers an element of interest and excitement is likely to direct thoughts outward rather than inward. Breaking up the depressed youngster's usual routine sometimes works wonders, too. New foods or restaurants, new books, new friends, time away in a new place, even a newly rearranged room can help renew a child's interest in life.

Are depressed children suicide risks?

When depression becomes intense, a child may be so over-whelmed by feelings of despair and hopelessness that thoughts of suicide begin to surface. Children who suffer from chronic and recurring depressions are particularly vulnerable to the idea of escaping their problems through death.

At an age when they are supposed to have everything to live for, almost 5,000 teenagers and young adults each year—over a dozen a day—are so deep in despair that they commit suicide. Self-destruction ranks second only to accidents as the leading cause of death among young people. The suicide rate among fifteen- to nineteen-year-olds has doubled during the past ten years, and self-destruction is becoming increasingly common even among children as young as ten years old.

The actual number of child suicides is probably much higher than official figures indicate. Many are disguised by family members, often with the physician's cooperation, as deaths attributable to other causes. Moreover, for every young person who dies by suicide, there are many others who try unsuccessfully to kill themselves. Psychologist Calvin J. Frederick, an expert on suicidal behavior, estimates that among young people, suicide attempts outnumber actual suicides by 50 to 1.

It is unlikely that children suffering their first bout of depression will consider suicide. But youngsters who talk of suicide should be taken seriously. It's unwise to dismiss suicidal threats or to try to argue a suicidal youngster out of despondency. Be available and listen patiently. And get professional advice as soon as possible.

How to Deal with the Suicidal Child

- Take every suicidal threat seriously. Don't be afraid to ask despondent youngsters if they are really thinking about taking their lives. The mention won't plant the idea in their heads. Rather, it relieves depressed children to know that they are being taken seriously, that they are better understood than they suspected.
- Don't dismiss a suicidal threat and underestimate its importance. Never say, "Oh, forget it. You won't kill yourself. You can't really mean it. You're not the type." That kind of remark may be heard as a challenge. The suicidal youngster needs attention, not dismissal. Anyone desperate enough can be "the type."

- Don't try to analyze the child's behavior, confusing the child by interpreting various acts or emotional states during the moment of crisis. That should be done later by a professional.
- Be willing to listen. You may have heard the story before, but hear it again. Be genuinely interested, be strong, stable, and firm.
- Seek professional help.

Is it possible for a child to appear emotionally disturbed in one setting—say, in the school—and perfectly normal in another?

That is actually more common than people generally believe. Many youngsters are described by their teachers as "impossible"—unreasonably aggressive, hostile, and disruptive—yet are never so outside of school, and certainly not at home.

A child may exhibit problem behavior only in certain specific situations. For Rutter, such episodes clearly imply that disorders in children must be seen as an interaction between the child and the environment—not solely as a problem *within* the child. It is important, therefore, to pay attention to the setting in which a child becomes emotionally distressed, as well as to the child who, alone, is supposedly "the problem."

Are boys or girls more likely to encounter roadblocks in their learning?

According to the evidence, boys are more vulnerable to psychological problems throughout childhood. During the first grade, they are referred for psychological help about ten times more frequently than girls. The problems they present include an inability to concentrate or follow directions, shyness, slow learning and absenteeism. Many more boys than girls are also considered hyperactive. Boys continue during the middle childhood years to encounter greater personality and behavior problems—and, as a result, a higher rate of school failure.

How serious a problem are drugs and alcohol for kids in school?

Serious enough—but from the evidence, less so than in the recent past, at least as far as drugs are concerned.

In the late 1970s, drug use in schools reached its peak. About 15 percent of the graduating classes of elementary schools had tried marijuana, and many had experimented with LSD, angel dust and other drugs. Among high school seniors, 60 percent had tried marijuana and nearly 11 percent were daily users. In recent years, however, there has been a sharp drop in the popularity of at least some drugs among young people. The number of high school seniors who had used marijuana daily, for example, fell to 7 percent by 1981—perhaps because of a growing conviction that it was injurious to health. The percentages of those who had ever tried angel dust also went down substantially, but there has been a recent increase in the use of cocaine, Quaaludes, and amphetamines.

In the case of alcohol, however, the results of a national survey suggest that its use has remained at a high level. For example, among tenth- to twelfth-graders, 87 percent reported ever having a drink, while 81 percent reported drinking in the year prior to the survey. One in every four students drinks at least once a week, and nearly 15 percent could be classified as "heavy drinkers." Six percent of twelfth-graders drink daily.

∿§   Signs of Drug or Alcohol Use in Children
  • Abrupt change in mood or attitude
  • Sudden decline in attendance or performance at work or school
  • Sudden resistance to discipline at home or school
  • Impaired relationship with family or friends
  • Ignoring curfews
  • Unusual flare-ups of temper
  • Increased borrowing of money from parents or friends; stealing from home, school, or employer
  • Heightened secrecy about actions and possessions
  • Associating with a new group of friends, especially with those who use drugs

While these behaviors may indicate drug use, they may also reflect normal teenage growing pains. By observing your child, getting to know his or her friends, and talking to your child about problems, including drugs and alcohol, you should be able to learn whether he or she is involved.

Parents: What You Can Do about Drug Abuse
National Institute on Drug Abuse

Can marijuana affect the child's learning?

According to the National Institute on Drug Abuse, research shows that its effects may interfere with learning by producing impaired thinking, reading comprehension, and verbal and arithmetic skills. Scientists also believe that marijuana may interfere with the development of social skills and may encourage psychological escapism. Youngsters need to learn how to make decisions, to cope with failure, handle success, and shape their own beliefs and values. By providing an escape from such normal "growing pains," marijuana can prevent young people from learning to become mature, independent, and responsible.

Virtually the same verdict can be given where other substances—including alcohol—are concerned. Heavy drinking can lead to serious cognitive problems. The reason is straightforward: Alcohol destroys brain cells—which is why the perceptual skills and problem-solving abilities of heavy and consistent drinkers are weakened.

Why do young people begin drinking alcohol?

There appears to be no single reason, but rather a pattern of reasons. Drinking by youngsters is related to such factors as the perception that friends drink and expect them to do likewise; accessibility of alcohol and social settings where unsupervised drinking can take place; low levels of self-esteem; belief that drinking is a sign of maturity and adulthood; the perception that drinking in adolescence is a normal aspect of human development—"par for the course"; the perception that parents approve of youthful drinking; and rebelliousness.

≈§ If schools take the trouble to make all pupils feel they matter and have a unique contribution to make to the community, it is lessening the chances that they will endanger their own health or that of others by indulging in practices that make them feel more adult but put them very much at risk from the health point of view. Self-esteem is a very important factor in regulating basic human drives and appetites.

The Health Ministry of London, 1979

What's the theory about drugs? Why do some kids get "hooked"?

There are many theories. According to one, it all depends on the view that drug users have of themselves. After experimenting with drugs, some young people develop a belief that they are simply unable to cope without them. Continued use sets up a vicious circle. As users rely increasingly on drugs to feel in control, they repeatedly confirm their belief that they are powerless to cope on their own. Each failure to function without drugs strengthens that belief until they become addicted and are in fact unable to face life without chemical assistance.

Another theory is that young people who move into heavy drug use have trouble handling their anxieties about achievement. According to this theory, such individuals turn to drugs in the first place to find transient relief from the pressure to achieve and the fear of failure. Once the effects wear off, their anxieties return and they again seek the relief of drugs. The process continues to mushroom until experiencing the effects of the drug becomes an end in itself.

How can parents help prevent their children from falling into the trap of drug or alcohol abuse?

Strong family relationships and support help children develop the personal values and self-confidence they need to resist peer pressure to use these substances. In addition, parents should be prepared to provide accurate information. This doesn't mean becoming an expert, but it does mean having enough facts—plentifully available from the National Institute on Drug Abuse and the National Institute on Alcohol Abuse and Alcoholism, both in Rockville, Maryland—to back up your views.

Too many parents wait until their kids are heavily into drug or alcohol use before initiating a discussion. You should talk with your children *before* the problems surface. And keep in mind that much of the information youngsters have is inaccurate—and that it's up to you to set the record straight. Your discussions should not be "one-shot" events. Children need to be reminded frequently where their parents stand on the subject of the abuse of drugs or alcohol.

Can a child with a lot of early psychological problems straighten out eventually?

Thirty years ago, when we were psychology students, such reversals would have been regarded as "flukes"—as rare exceptions to the accepted rule of human development. A child's personality, we were taught, is laid down early in life, and after the first few years, the chances for significant change are slim.

Today, in contrast, evidence from many careful follow-up studies demonstrates that the ballgame of child development is *never* over. Even youngsters who seem to be careening toward lives of chronic maladjustment and failure can emerge ultimately as wholesome and productive adults.

Can there sometimes be a physical cause for a child's emotional problems?

Much more often than parents and doctors realize. Not every dramatic change in personality and behavior needs to have an emotional basis. Mental health problems—depression, anxiety, phobias, even delinquent behavior—often spring from malfunctions of the body rather than the mind.

Some physical conditions can produce the kind of changes in behavior and academic performance that send parents racing to the nearest child psychiatrist—to no avail. Despite what all of us have been taught, if a child is disturbed—hostile, withdrawn, fearful, hyperactive—it doesn't necessarily have to be the result of environmental stress. Each of us is a mix of physical and psychological forces, of blood and hormones, of emotions and attitudes. It is easy to forget that, in children as well as adults, the body and the mind do not live apart; they are elements of a single human system controlled by that miraculous computer, the brain. That's why when normal physical processes are disrupted, the child's mental health is also likely to suffer.

Can hidden physical problems affect learning?

Yes, and cases are unfortunately much more common than even mental health professionals suppose.

Consider the case of Mark Barnes, a brilliant and charming fifteen-year-old. Last year, he became chronically anxious and depressed, began staying in bed too late to attend classes, dropped all his friends, stopped eating, and belligerently thwarted his parents at every turn. The signs of emotional illness seemed so serious that Mark's parents sought treatment for him by the best child psychiatrist in town. Six months later, he was back on top of his class—and the world.

But it was not the therapy that turned Mark around. His symptoms were actually the result of a physical illness rather than psychological "hangups." Mark's psychotherapy helped him handle the stress he was under, but he regained his well-being only after he received appropriate medical treatment.

It was a chance meeting between Mark's parents and his childhood pediatrician that led to Mark's return to good health. The pediatrician ordered blood tests, and his suspicions were confirmed. The young patient was suffering the emotional fallout typical in severe cases of *mononucleosis* ("mono"), a viral blood disorder found frequently among adolescents and young adults.

Besides mono, what other hidden ailments can cause trouble?

Hypoglycemia, or abnormally low level of sugar in the blood, is a common cause of behavioral and learning problems. Because of a change in the brain's functioning, younger children may become fretful; older children may show violent outbursts or act negative or confused. Among the symptoms are weakness, depression, insomnia, drowsiness, restlessness, and inability to concentrate. Prolonged hypoglycemia can result in brain damage, so a physician's advice is essential. Fortunately, a doctor's diagnosis can readily lead to a careful dietary program—and complete recovery.

Equally severe behavior problems can arise from glandular malfunctions. An example is *hypothyroidism,* which stems from too low a level of hormone produced by the thyroid gland. For more than half a century, researchers and doctors have recognized the inevitability of mental retardation in children born with hypothyroidism unless there is adequate treatment—thyroid hormone in steadily increasing doses.

Now, however, it is clear that the condition can produce dramatic changes in behavior as well—from lethargy and language difficulties to depression and excessive eating. It can create emotional turmoil even among those who develop it late in childhood or in adolescence.

Seventeen-year-old Bill Hadley was one such victim. Bill had to travel 45 minutes on a bus to his job in a supermarket. Late one afternoon, suddenly and unaccountably, he felt that he could no longer endure the bus trip home. He felt shaky and exhausted, filled with an inexplicable dread. His panic mounting, Bill ran from the bus, hailed a cab, and went home to bed. The next morning he awoke trembling.

Bill's doctor arranged for tests, and, in every case, the results were negative—except one. Bill had hypothyroidism. The doctor prescribed an extract of the thyroid gland and advised the young man to stay home until he had lost the sharp edge of his nervousness and terror.

It was three weeks before Bill returned to work, and during that time, his doctor wisely persuaded him to see a psychiatrist for a few visits to help soothe the road back to reality. But the core of Bill's troubles—and the critical treatment—had been physical.

The opposite of Bill's condition, known as *hyperthyroidism,* occurs when the level of thyroid hormone is too high rather than too low. From a study of seventy children with this problem, Krishna Saxena, a Harvard Medical School pediatrician, and his colleagues identified a startling array of symptoms: nervousness and restlessness, difficulties with school work, crying spells, temper tantrums, irritability, lack of concentration.

Other investigators have found that some children with hyperthyroidism become extremely anxious and emotionally unstable, while others are converted into excitable, quarrelsome, and hostile creatures. Victims have occasionally even flirted with suicide—all of this not because of too much stress, but only because of excess hormone pouring out of the thyroid gland tucked away in the neck.

⮜§ Hypoglycemia: One Mother's Story

Paul seemed to have problems from the very beginning. He was always erratic, rebellious, unpredictable. Every day brought new crises. Paul's teachers found him uncontrollable. They recognized that he was exceptionally bright, but he seemed constantly to be bored and disinterested. They said he was an "underachiever," and probably always would be.

I took him to a clinical psychologist, who found that Paul's achievement scores were way above average one day and way below the next. The psychologist concluded that Paul needed therapy to cope with the "inner conflicts" that confused him and made him feel insecure.

Despite intensive treatment, Paul's behavior deteriorated over the years. Often he seemed irrational and hysterical—almost violent.

One day when he was in junior high school, while watching television, Paul suddenly started to pace up and down the room. He began to perspire and to complain of feeling cold. He lay on the couch, shivering, as though he had a high fever, and soon lapsed into what appeared to be a semiconscious state. He moaned about being in pain but couldn't explain where. He begged to be helped, all the while pleading for something to eat. When food arrived, he quickly gorged himself, and by the time the doctor came, Paul appeared miraculously to be well.

The demand for food made the doctor suspect a physical problem—and tests confirmed his hunch: The level of sugar in Paul's blood was abnormally low. All along, he had been a victim of hypoglycemia.

Can an anemic child develop psychological problems?

Indeed so. Ann is a typical example, a pale and frightened-looking twelve-year-old, who was the object of worry for years by her parents and teachers alike.

Ann was chronically depressed, disinterested, and remote. In a flat and lifeless voice, she told a child psychiatrist that she cared about no one and was interested in nothing. Her sleep was fitful and filled with nightmares, and her appetite was failing. Ann rarely played with friends, and life seemed to have no meaning for her. "I'm just nuthin" was her favorite phrase.

Ann's problem, it turned out, stemmed not primarily from sibling rivalry or family tensions, as a psychiatrist first concluded. Such troubles were indeed present, and they certainly did not help Ann. But her main problem, it turned out, was instead *iron deficiency anemia*, a readily treated blood condition resulting in the depletion of the body's iron stores. Ann's stresses at home were significantly augmented by her physical condition.

Anemic children are known to suffer from fatigue, weakness,

and poor appetite. But psychiatrist Sidney L. Werkman and his associates have found that affected children are also generally less mature, more easily frightened, and more passive. They cry more often, throw more tantrums, fight more, have more sleeping disturbances, are more often bed-wetters, and display more nervous habits like finger-sucking and nailbiting. Talks with a sympathetic child psychiatrist will undoubtedly help such children deal with their disturbed feelings, but it is a regimen of iron pills, not psychotherapy, that offers their best hope for emotional health.

Are physical factors that affect a child's behavior often overlooked?

Too many parents and teachers have been falsely persuaded that every shade of a child's behavior is filled only with deep and potent psychological meanings. The experts have taught us to recognize that unresolved stress and conflict can produce in our young painful emotional symptoms—anxiety, depression, phobias, and delinquent and even criminal behavior. True enough. But the fact is that these very same symptoms—and more—can arise from purely physical causes as well.

In seeking help for a child, therefore, it is important to start with a thorough physical exam. A knowing doctor can rule out the presence of physical problems as a cause of emotional ones. Indeed some psychiatrists—the really thorough ones—insist upon such an examination before they begin to apply their own healing arts.

CHAPTER NINE
⨕ Getting Help

Martin, a ten-year-old with average intelligence, is unable either to read or write. At school his teachers report him to be inattentive, alternatively hostile and withdrawn, and totally unmotivated to learn. At home he is likely to be found alone in his room, disinterested in other members of the family, and with no plans even to begin his homework. Martin has a history of stuttering, soiling himself, and stealing. In every grade, his teachers have regarded him as "a problem."

Marcia is also ten. Her mother describes her as "a challenge to live with." She constantly wants to know the reasons for things, and she would sometimes rather read a book than do her math homework. Marcia is inquisitive and kind, alert and cheerful, but she has her share of fears. Nights are especially difficult for her. She is frightened of the dark and insists on sleeping with a light nearby and her radio on.

From even these brief histories, it should be apparent that Martin is clearly in need of professional help, while Marcia probably is not. Yet it is Marcia's parents who have taken their child on a round of visits to the local mental health clinic because "she is such an impossible neurotic," while Martin has never been seen by a mental health worker.

Why?

The answer lies in the welter of confusion and tension that surrounds the process of seeking help.

Some parents, like Marcia's, are primed to look for psychological problems everywhere. They have been oversold on the need for professional intervention in virtually every aspect of their children's lives. Like so many other mothers and fathers, they are victims of the age of psychology and its parade of experts in child development, from Sigmund Freud himself to today's overzealous "radio psychologist." These experts have taught us that psychologicalfactors are important in shaping the child's personality, and that they must be attended to if the personality goes awry. But the message has been overstated by many professionals and overlearned by eager parents.

Even more common is the reluctance of countless parents, like Martin's, to seek help when it *is* indicated. To begin with, they are beset by a sense of shame and guilt. They are convinced that asking for help is an admission of defeat—and will mark the child and family with a taint of abnormality.

Moreover, there is a surprising amount of ignorance among otherwise well-informed parents about mental health professionals—who they are, what services they offer, and how they actually provide them. For some parents, the quest for assistance is so confusing that even when the motivation to do something constructive is there, it is aborted. One father, concerned about his daughter's chronic depression and school failures, finally gave up his search for help. "I'd heard about ten dozen kinds of 'shrinks,' but all of them were selling something different. It was just too confusing. Finally, we decided just to struggle along on our own."

This father's decision may backfire, but it is understandable. A puzzling array of tests and therapies now confront those who seek help for their children, and choosing among them becomes more difficult all the time. When reaching out for assistance, already anxious parents face two additional burdens: First they must sort through the many kinds of help available, and then they must decide on a particular one. The choices can be extremely stressful in themselves.

Parents need at least some general guidelines to assist them as potential consumers of children's mental health services. Such information can save time and money. More important, it may help preserve the future well-being and productivity of both children and their families.

How does a person actually judge when to seek professional help for a child?

Even the most seasoned psychiatrists cannot provide a clear dividing line between "abnormal" and "normal," or "sick" and "well." Certainly occasional, transient problems are not sufficient reason for initiating a course of treatment. Many children encounter difficulties in growing up, and they display various adjustment problems in their behavior—including erratic performance in school, withdrawal, disobedience, and aggressiveness. Or they may have temper tantrums, suck their thumbs, or wet their beds. Such troublesome behaviors often improve without intervention. Sometimes they represent a child's cry for attention which, when given, eliminates the difficulty.

Parents should first observe the child's problem behavior to see whether it improves, or whether instead it continues or worsens over time. It is when symptoms are either intense or prolonged and unyielding that professional help is advisable. Keep in mind that no round of testing or psychotherapy is "fun and games." Such activities are serious business, properly undertaken only for the most compelling reasons.

⋙ Some Signs That a Child Needs Help
- Undue, prolonged anxiety or fearfulness
- Acute conflicts—either internal or interpersonal
- Prolonged depression or withdrawal
- Destructive behavior and thoughts—against oneself or others
- Abrupt changes in mood and behavior
- Chronic physical illness caused by tension and stress
- Behavior that differs greatly from that of children the same age
- Difficulty with self-control
- Plummeting grades or academic failure
- Marked and prolonged discrepancy between potential and performance

How valid is the teacher's opinion that a child needs help?

School is, after all, the child's workplace, and so the teacher is often in the best position to observe children at close hand and for hours on end—the way they approach their tasks, whether they run into academic difficulties, how they relate to their peers, and in general, how they respond to stress. Parents are not always the best judges of their children's psychological well-being. Often it *is* an outsider—typically a teacher—who first notices that a child very much needs help, and who encourages parents to seek assistance.

Teachers usually refer students thought to need attention to the school psychologist—that is, a psychologist who works in the school setting and who is expert in school-related problems and issues.

What services do school psychologists typically provide?

They work in various ways in behalf of the child—with teachers, parents, school administrators, specialists such as those in reading, and with community agencies. They explore how parents and the school can work together to help youngsters handle their difficulties, and, when indicated, they help structure educational programs to help meet the unique needs of a particular child. They also help in referring for special placements those children whose severe learning or adjustment difficulties interfere with their academic progress in a regular classroom setting, or they see to it that such children receive specialized tutoring or counseling.

School psychologists are concerned with the psychological factors that are important in children's academic performance. If the scope of a youngster's problem appears to extend well beyond the academic setting, they typically make referrals to appropriate resources in the community.

Remember that the very same services provided by school psychologists can be secured from psychologists working in general practice in the community. Indeed to maintain privacy, some parents prefer to have their children diagnosed and evaluated outside the school setting.

What kinds of tests do school psychologists usually give the child who is referred to them?

To help assess the child's overall intellectual capacities, the psychologist is likely to administer an IQ test such as the Wechsler Intelligence Scale for Children described in Chapter 5. The psychologist would also want to gauge the child's real achievement level in such areas as reading, spelling, and arithmetic, and would, therefore, administer a standardized achievement test that makes it possible to identify where the child stands in various school subjects in relation to others at the same age and grade level.

To help appraise the child's emotional well-being, the school psychologist might use one or more of the many personality tests available. The method of scoring on these tests permits comparison of the individual child's responses with those made in the past by large numbers of children—including, of course, children with emotional problems such as anxiety, depression, or the tendency to act out inner conflicts. In this way, it is possible to gauge how far from the "norm" the child's test responses fall.

᳁ᷤ The skill and special contribution of the psychologist lies not in the ability to administer tests—most people can quickly master the mechanics of test administration—but in the ability to correctly interpret test findings on the basis of a knowledge of the research literature.

Michael Berger
In *Child Psychiatry: Modern Approaches,*
Michael Rutter and Lionel Hersov, eds.

With so many tests available, can the psychologist use the results to get a completely accurate picture of the child?

Tests can tell only part of the story of a child's aptitude, achievement, and personality. They were never designed to provide the sole basis for assessing a child, or for recommending steps to be taken to improve the child's academic adjustment and performance.

Think of the tests your doctor might give to help diagnose a physical problem—x-rays, blood tests, urine tests. It would be unrealistic to try to decide in every case what is ailing you—and what to do about it—from such tests alone. The doctor would also often want to see what you looked like, to hear you tell about yourself—your work, your family, what you feel like day in and day out. Sometimes it is helpful for the doctor to get information about you and your symptoms from close family members as well.

In the same way, the school psychologist needs to secure a comprehensive picture of children as they function in the school setting and, to a degree, outside.

Despite its value, can't the use of tests have unfortunate consequences for the child?

Sometimes it can. Youngsters in our society are all too quickly categorized by labels as a result of the "diagnoses" arrived at from psychological tests. School children might be branded as "retarded," for example, or "disturbed," or "delinquent." Such labels are often stigmatizing to kids, causing them to be isolated from the usual school opportunities, taunted by other children, and rejected by school staff. Worse yet, children may ultimately incorporate into their self-concepts the labels affixed to them as a result of testing, and they may begin to believe so strongly in their validity that their lives become self-fulfilling prophecies.

As part of her classic studies of children unfairly labeled by their schools, University of California sociologist Jane Mercer followed a group of children who had been placed in hospitals for the mentally retarded. Some had gone home to their parents and communities while others remained in the hospital.

What distinguished the two groups?

Mercer found that those who went back to the family had not fully accepted the negative label of "retarded," had not made it part of their being. They believed that the whole episode was a mistake, that they didn't belong in a hospital. Equally important, their families had supported their view. Parents and other family members were intent on seeing that the victim was released from the hospital and reentered the mainstream as a normal human being.

In contrast was the group who stagnated in the hospital—a group with similar IQs, comparable in most vital statistics save one: *Their* families *had* accepted the label. When Mercer and her team visited such family members, they would find them saying: "Oh, yes, it's too bad, he's mentally retarded. We know he'll have to be dependent all his life, and he won't even be able to earn a living." A self-fulfilling prophecy had in fact been realized in the lives of the victims.

◆ [Inappropriate classification] can blight the life of a child, reducing opportunity, diminishing his competence and self-esteem, alienating him from others, nurturing a meanness of spirit, and making him less a person than he could become. Nothing less than the futures of children is at stake.

Nicholas Hobbs
The Futures of Children

But isn't it beneficial to separate children with special needs into special classes?

The task for schools is to deal democratically with each child as an individual human being, not as an item in a diagnostic manual. The relevant federal law states that each child must be served in school in a "least restrictive environment."

It is true enough that if a child is seriously disabled and cannot function even with special attention in the classroom, separation into special classrooms may be indicated. But except in cases of extreme need, most children profit from being allowed to remain in the "mainstream." Mercer points out that "those having learning problems can learn a great deal from being with normal peers. After all, children who are hurting . . . are going to be dealing with normals all their lives, and they can hardly learn to do so if they are segregated during their entire childhood."

The integration into the normal classroom of children who are having difficulty can be beneficial to their peers as well.

⭕ If you have no problems, how are you going to learn to work with, to be concerned about, to be tolerant of, to be kind and loving toward children who learn slowly, or are emotionally troubled? . . . How can you learn to be a human being?

Jane Mercer
University of California

What kind of help should children get who begin to flounder academically because of emotional problems?

As described in previous chapters, many youngsters have trouble academically because of poor motivation or because of learning disabilities. But in addition, there are many who fail in school because their mental energies are being sapped by serious emotional problems. Such children are typically referred by the school psychologist for psychotherapy.

How can parents go about preparing a child for an encounter with a therapist?

Children have a right to know what to expect—what the therapist actually does, and who will be involved. By preparing youngsters beforehand, parents can ensure that they will approach the experience in a more cooperative, more reassured and trustful, and less anxious frame of mind. Edward M. Adams, author of *How to Prepare the Child for the Psychologist,* suggests the following guidelines:

- Tell the child that the therapist sees many children every year. The child is thus assured of not being singled out—or punished.
- Describe the therapist as a person who helps children. Without mentioning names, it might be useful to describe how another child was helped.
- Let the child know that the therapist will talk with the parents, and that teachers may also be contacted about school work and classroom behavior.
- Describe what the therapist does. Don't hesitate to talk about "tests," but explain that these tests are different from the kind given in the classroom and that the results will be used to make important and helpful decisions.
- Identify the people who will know the results of any evaluations that are done.
- Answer questions and clarify any misunderstandings.
- After the child's session, don't make a fuss. Some children may want to talk about their experiences, while others may remain silent.

Aren't there a variety of approaches to therapy?

Yes. The general goals of various treatments are roughly the same, though the means of improving a child's attitudes and behavior may differ. Psychoanalytically oriented treatment stresses the child's unconscious motivations and repressed emotional experiences. Behavioral therapy works toward eliminating a particular problem behavior, such as phobias, bedwetting or nail-biting. A cognitive approach is aimed at modifying the thoughts that lie behind problem behavior. And the list goes on.

Despite their differences in orientation, however, most therapists cannot be classified rigidly under one system of treatment. Experienced therapists are generally less rigidly committed to specific methods and more responsive to a particular child's needs.

But even more important than details of technique is the quality of the therapist—as a professional and as a person.

How does a person go about finding a good child therapist?

While you might trust finding someone to repair your television by random selection through the telephone book, you would not want to give your child's psyche over to the care of a counselor chosen in this way.

A good place to start searching for a child therapist is in your pediatrician's office. Pediatricians, like most physicians, often refer their patients to psychotherapists, and are likely to know who is available and reputable in the community. Others in the service professions may also be of help. Lawyers, teachers, school counselors, often stymied by the personality problems of their clients, end up suggesting therapy, and thereby accumulate knowledge of the professionals in their area.

Other parents may be even more helpful. Friends and co-workers whose children have been in treatment can be a surprisingly rich source of leads. The more investigating you do beforehand, the less likely you are to make a poor choice. If, in talking to your friends, you keep hearing the same names, you can assume you are on the right track.

Therapists fall into several different categories. How do you distinguish one from another?

The child therapist you choose is likely to come from one of three major professional groups:

Psychiatrists are medical doctors whose MD training is followed by a three-year hospital residency program in psychiatry, and licensing by the state in which they practice. To become "certified," a step required only in some areas, a psychiatrist needs two additional years of experience and must have passed a special examination. Remember: Of all mental health professionals, *only* psychiatrists may prescribe drugs.

Clinical and counseling psychologists are trained in the science of human behavior and have either a master's degree (MA or MS) or a doctorate (PhD), but no medical degree. They are trained in the use and interpretation of tests as well as therapy. Requirements for licensing and certification differ slightly from state to state, but qualifications for psychologists in private practice typically include a doctoral degree, at least two years of supervised experience, and successful completion of a national qualifying examination.

Social workers who do therapy hold a master's degree plus membership in the Academy of Certified Social Workers (ACSW). Their background also includes at least two years of clinical experience and completion of a national qualifying examination. Social workers typically are not trained in psychological testing.

Others. Much good work is also done by counselors who have been less extensively trained but who are nonetheless extraordinarily skillful in their particular areas. These include family counselors and paraprofessionals (sometimes called mental health aides), who specialize in particular problems such as alcoholism and drug abuse. You are more likely to find such mental health workers on the staff of clinics than in private practice.

How does a parent decide which particular therapist the child should see?

There are some practical steps you can take to help decide whether a particular therapist is experienced and competent enough.

To see whether or not the candidate you are considering is a seasoned professional, check on the therapist's training and experience. Begin by making certain that the therapist meets the minimal requirements of accrediting agencies. You may ask therapists about this directly or else ask them the name of the professional organization to which they belong. A call to the organization will result in a full accounting of the therapist's credentials. The library can also be helpful; check through the biographical directories of the American Psychiatric Association or the American Psychological Association for a detailed academic and work history of all practitioners in those fields.

Again, it helps to talk to parents who are consumers of child psychotherapy in your community. Focus on those who have already had the experience and are therefore likelier to be more objective than those whose children are still undergoing the process.

Parents can also arrange for a consultation with an especially prominent psychiatrist or psychologist in the community. You may not be able to afford—or even want—continued treatment for your child from such specialists, but they can help you decide what sort of therapy is needed and can assist in selecting a competent professional from the names on your list.

Is it permissible to interview a therapist beforehand?

It is foolish not to do so. When you have narrowed your choices to a few names, the best way of learning how a particular therapist works is by spending an hour in a "feeling out" interview. In making an appointment, state that you want to explore the possibilities for your child, not actually to begin treatment. Some therapists value this "courtship" process so highly that they charge for this visit only if the prospective "customer" winds up as a regular patient.

During this preliminary interview, ask as many questions as you like. How long is the treatment likely to take? What about fees and schedules? (Some therapists charge for missed appointments no matter how legitimate the excuse.) Is the therapist committed to only one system of therapy, or will the approach depend on the child? Will drugs be prescribed? Will the whole family be involved, and how often?

≈ֶ   . . . I would be utterly incensed if some stranger suddenly began to ask me personal questions, or preemptorily requested that I reproduce drawings of circles, squares, or diamonds. I would demand an explanation until I was satisfied that what I was doing was useful, harmless, and important. Does not a child, unskilled in assertive questioning, deserve the same explanation?
Edward M. Adams
"How to Prepare the Child for the Psychologist"

How much should personal feelings about a therapist enter into the decision?

Ultimately, your choice should be based on your view of the therapist's personality and how well it meshes with your child's. Public reputation and private performance do not always jibe, and the therapist who succeeds with one child may fail with another.

Although the academic credentials of therapists are important, it is their personal qualities that often determine whether or not they will be of help. The best therapist for your child may not always be the most expensive or even the most highly trained. A warm and reassuring social worker may deal much more effectively with the child's feelings of guilt than a renowned psychoanalyst.

Counselors who do not inspire a sense of trust and confidence, or who induce threatened and defensive reactions, will not likely establish a helpful relationship with the child.

How frequently is a child usually seen?

The most common schedule is one visit—usually lasting approximately an hour—per week. But the schedule can vary widely. Two or three appointments a week are not unusual, and some children are seen only once every two or three weeks. Occasionally a "when-indicated" schedule is used; parents call for an appointment whenever the situation seems to require it.

For how long?

There is no way to predict the duration of treatment. It can vary from a few visits to several years, depending on the youngster's response, the treatment approach, and the nature of the problem.

It is often difficult to decide when therapy should terminate since treatment typically leads to gradual rather than abrupt change. Children are rarely "cured," in the sense of being totally free of troubles. No one is. When therapy does terminate, the end is not necessarily abrupt. The schedule may be stretched out so the child experiences increasingly longer periods between sessions. In this way, the therapist can better gauge how the child is adjusting. And once discharged from treatment, the door is usually left open for the youngster to come back if necessary.

How much does therapy cost?

Fees of psychotherapists in private practice vary widely, starting at about $60 per session. Charges by psychologists and social workers are generally lower than psychiatrists', but you will probably not find a licensed professional with fees falling under $50 or so an hour. If you locate a therapist through a clinic, the fees are likely to be lower, often following a sliding scale based on the individual patient's income. For a listing of clinics and other mental health facilities throughout the country, write for the *Mental Health Directory*, published by the National Institute of Mental Health. Order from the Superintendent of Documents, U.S. Government Printing Office, Washington, D.C. 20402.

You should carefully check your health insurance policy to see if it provides coverage for therapeutic care. Many Americans have such coverage but don't realize it and consequently fail to benefit.

Is it par for the therapy course for parents to become part of the treatment process?

How deeply parents become involved depends on the nature of the problem and the treatment approach. For instance, family therapists would want full parental participation, whereas child psychoanalysts would be likely to work with the child individually. Some psychologists include the parent in every session with the child, others only occasionally. Still others meet with the parents separately.

Since children are not old enough to take total responsibility for their therapy, their parents must be involved. At the very least, parents have to sign release forms for school records, provide transportation, pay bills, and furnish details of the child's developmental history such as speech and motor development, eating habits, and medical background.

When parents actively participate in the treatment, they tend to learn ways to cope with their troubled youngster and improve their child-rearing skills. They also have the opportunity to discuss their feelings about the child in therapy and about their other children as well. Some parents also engage in personal therapy for themselves to supplement sessions focused on the child.

How much do parents' attitudes influence the child's therapy?

Very much. The parent can exert a positive influence on the child's treatment by being available to listen and talk, and to offer encouragement and support. On the other hand, the child's progress can be hampered when the parent openly challenges the therapist, criticizes the treatment, or makes the therapy a topic for mealtime conversations. Youngsters may also get the idea that therapy creates more difficulties than it resolves when a parent insists on hearing what happens in the sessions or dictates what should or should not be said to the therapist.

What actually happens in a child's sessions with a therapist?

The content of therapy depends on the child's age and the counselor's treatment style. Therapy may involve talking, playing, or a combination of the two.

Children under age ten often are given the opportunity to express their feelings and concerns by means of play activities—block building, story telling, drawing, or with a dollhouse or puppets. Older children can think in a more orderly fashion and have greater conceptual skills; their sessions, therefore, commonly involve more conversation or projects with specific goals and rules.

How can playing during a session be of help?

Playing is a way of getting information about the child's problems and for teaching ways to deal with them. Equally important, an emotional bond evolves between child and counselor. It is through play that children allow the therapist to get close to them and to see the world from their vantage point. Only with this perspective can the therapist hope to influence the child's psychological growth.

> Once in the child's world, the therapist finds that trucks and cars become instruments of destruction or that houses take on friendly personalities. Puppets may become people with drinking problems or dolls may clean house or go to work. Play becomes the child's manner of speech, symbolically expressing his real and imaginary worlds.
>
> Paul S. Rappoport
> "When Your Child Needs Therapy"

Are parents kept informed about the child's therapy?

Most parents naturally are eager to hear about what is taking place in their child's therapy sessions. It is frustrating to get no report of the goings-on of the treatment room.

Nevertheless, it is best not to press for details about the sessions or for progress reports from child or therapist. Parents are generally told at the outset about the practical details and general scope of the treatment, but they should expect to be somewhat left out of this momentous experience in their child's life—at least in the early phase of therapy. It takes time for children to gain trust in the therapist, and they must learn in the process that their confidences are not being betrayed.

Child therapists begin treatment at a disadvantage since children do not typically arrive for the first session on their own accord. Usually youngsters are forced into therapy—by exasperated and angry parents, teachers, the school principal, or other authorities. The therapist, being an adult in a position of power, appears to the child as "one of them" and the child tends to approach the therapy situation with suspicion, resentment, or anger. Moreover, the child tends to suspect that everything that transpires during the sessions will be reported to Mom and Dad.

Without a solid relationship between therapist and child, there can be no therapy. Therapists must pave the way for such a relationship by demonstrating loyalty, by showing they are on the child's side, and by remaining firm about the necessity for confidence between themselves and their young clients.

How then can parents tell if therapy is working?

The obvious way to tell is if the problem goes away—but this may not happen for quite a while. Meanwhile, there are a number of intermediate signs to look for. Is the child's distress decreasing? Is there an increase in patience, effort, or sense of humor? Have new, constructive behaviors developed, or self-defeating ones disappeared? Are there positive changes in attitudes, relationships, academic performance, or play patterns?

What if the therapist says drugs should be prescribed?

Before embarking on drug therapy, remember that these so-called "psychoactive" medications are extremely powerful. Make sure you know what drugs your child is getting and why. Hundreds of drugs intended to affect behavior are available today—drugs such as tranquilizers, antidepressants, or sedatives—which, used with great care, can help a child overcome a period of acute distress. You deserve to know exactly what is being prescribed, what symptoms the drug is intended to treat, and what side effects might be expected.

Children—like all patients—must be closely watched while taking medications, which can be properly administered only by experts. Though any MD (that includes psychiatrists, since they have medical degrees) may legally write a prescription for drugs, not all of them are fully aware of the latest developments in the field. So don't gamble. Be sure that those who plan to dispense drugs to your child know precisely what they are doing.

How can the "quacks" be spotted?

Most therapists are reliable professionals, but still you must be careful not to fall into the hands of the few "quacks" and "sickies" who practice therapy even though they lack adequate training and are dangerously deficient in character.

First of all, stay away from a therapist whose personality you find disturbing. Signs of unstable, impulsive, or irresponsible behavior should give you pause, as should the feeling that the therapist is aggressive, impatient or sadistic. While you ought not to expect therapists to be constantly yielding and protective, they should appear to respect you and your child and to care about the well-being of their clients.

Feel free to question treatment techniques that seem unusual or bizarre. Faith in the healer may be valuable, but don't be overly credulous. Beware of fluky practices—and if you doubt the validity of a particular technique, check it out with a local mental health association or another professional.

A further caution: Do not submit to suspiciously high fees. One of the most self-serving myths perpetrated by some therapists is that "the more you pay, the more good the treatment is likely to do." That's poppycock. Some of the greatest child clinicians work in community clinics, not for a fat fee but for the love of children. If you think you are being overcharged, discuss the matter with the therapist. If an understanding cannot be reached, consider seeking help elsewhere.

⋙ . . . not all therapists are competent, and thousands of hours are spent yearly in which two persons—a child and a "therapist"— sit together in a room, talking, playing games, building models, speaking mainly to avoid boredom, and neither having any notion of why he is there or what is happening—all in the name of psychotherapy.

Charles Shaw
When Your Child Needs Help

Are there centralized sources of information about reputable child psychotherapists?

Most communities contain a number of organizations and agencies that can help you with information about psychotherapists and psychotherapy. These include:

- The local mental health association
- Community social welfare agencies and health centers
- A nearby hospital or university medical center, or university psychology department
- The community medical society
- Community branches of the American Psychiatric Association, American Psychological Association, and the National Association of Social Workers
- The local Department of Mental Health of the American Medical Association

If you have trouble finding an agency locally, you should contact one of the following national associations:

National Mental Health Association
1021 Prince Street
Alexandria, Virginia 22314
(703) 684-7722

American Psychiatric Association
1400 K Street, N.W.
Washington, D.C. 20005
(202) 682-6000

American Psychological Association
1200 17th Street, N.W.
Washington, D.C. 20036
(202) 955-7600

National Association of Social Workers
1003 K Street, N.W., Suite 203
Washington, D.C. 20001
(202) 347-9893

American Medical Association
535 North Dearborn Street
Chicago, Illinois 60610
(312) 645-5000

Family Service Association of America
44 East 23rd Street
New York, New York 10010
(212) 674-6100

CHAPTER TEN
❧ Closing Bell: Children as Unique Individuals

"It's all in the genes. If they've got the right ones, they just can't miss."

"It's Mom. She's the key. Either she sets her kids up, or she ruins them for life."

"It's our educational system. If only we had better schools, all our children's problems would be solved."

Those statements made by adults about children are not unusual. In every age, the question of "what makes kids tick" has inspired unequivocal opinions about our young—as if the mystery of every child's development could be solved with one convincing clue, one blinding flash of adult insight.

The enigmas of human nature have not, however, yielded to such simple solutions. As this book makes clear, the characteristics of children—their motivation, achievement, intelligence, zeal for learning, responses to stress—cannot be explained in a single stroke. Nor will they ever. For each child is a unique personality, with a special pattern of attributes, and each responds to the environment in a distinct way.

Personality. That word, which we use so casually, describes one of the most complex facets of psychology. Indeed the English language has at least 18,000 words to encompass the myriad traits that comprise it. To get some idea of the variations in children's personalities, try the following exercise, adapted from *Psychology: An Introduction,* a textbook written by Jerome Kagan, Ernest Havemann, and Julius Segal.

Pick a child you know and try rating the child on one side or the other of the list of ten opposite attributes found on the next page. Those ten traits can occur in any combination. The child may fall at the left in all of them, at the right in all of them, or at the left in some and the right in others. This short list alone can actually account for an incredible variety of personalities—1,024 in all! Moreover, a child may not belong clearly at the left or at the right but somewhere in between, multiplying the possibilities even further. Keep in mind also that these ten traits are just a very tiny sample of all that exist, many others of which have been discussed throughout this book.

hard-working *or* lax
independent *or* dependent
friendly, a joiner *or* unfriendly, a loner
likes certainty *or* prefers novelty
short attention span *or* persists at tasks
high in anxiety *or* low in anxiety
grasps facts easily *or* needs time to learn
thoughtful *or* impulsive
down-to-earth *or* dreamy, impractical
talkative, eloquent *or* quiet, tongue-tied

Small wonder that grandiose generalizations about the importance of any single factor in the lives of *all* children just won't hold up. The way a particular child's mind is influenced by people and events depends on the nature of that child's makeup to begin with. Infant environment, experiences with mother, father's attitudes, teacher's personalities, family dynamics—all of these are important, as this book makes clear. But no one of them can have the identical impact on all kids. The challenge for adults is not to build a mythical "program" suitable for all children, but to adapt the best available knowledge to the special characteristics of each child.

The uniqueness of children was highlighted a few years ago in a study of the manner in which children view stressful experiences. Psychologist Kaoru Yamamoto asked fourth-, fifth-, and sixth-graders to rate twenty life events on a seven-point scale. The children's judgments differed dramatically from those we might expect. The arrival of a new baby sibling, for example, often regarded by adults as a "shocker" for youngsters, was not very highly rated. More traumatic for one child was "a poor report card," for another "being ridiculed in class," for still another "being picked last on a team."

The message for adults from such studies is clear: Each child is a unique individual, with a distinct set of perceptions, attitudes, and traits. Parents and teachers must learn to recognize and accept the child's stamp of individuality. Children show clear temperamental differences from birth, and it is obvious, therefore, that not every child can be helped to grow up in precisely the same way.

In accepting the responsibility of responding to the special needs of each child, parents are likely themselves to achieve a liberating experience. Mothers and fathers have tended to raise their kids "by the book," and they have come to believe, therefore, that any misstep along the way can spell ruin for their child. Constantly worried whether they have gotten the nuts and bolts of junior's personality screwed together quite right, they tend to see themselves as potential failures, behaving, in the words of child expert Fritz Redl, "as if a psychiatrist just flew by the window."

Such anxiety is reasonable only if you assume that all children are somehow the same—if, in effect, you deny the central fact of the science of child development: the extraordinary range of individual differences that characterize children from the moment of their birth.

The weight of the current evidence is that all children have unique strengths—even those who seem most beset by problems. We need first to be sensitive to these strengths, and then to help each child capitalize on them. This book is filled with examples of how this can be accomplished—not once and for all, but throughout the child's life. Untoward events in infancy can admittedly affect a child's capacity to learn, but not if the adults in the newborn's world work to enrich the child's environment with stimulating and motivating experiences. A caring mother's abiding presence and encouragement is clearly a source of stability and intellectual vigor, yet her absence need not have a deleterious effect on children whose fathers or other caretakers act to reinforce and reward their capabilities. The flickering sense of self-confidence in many a seemingly defeated child may be rekindled by a dedicated teacher who nurtures the child's hidden talents.

We can strengthen our young best by treating them as distinct individuals. Only in this way is it possible to rear our children with optimism—confident of helping them realize the potential each has for growing up smart and happy.

⨾ References

CHAPTER ONE

Elkind, D. *The hurried child: Growing up too fast too soon.* Reading, Mass.: Addison-Wesley, 1981.

Garmezy, N. Competence and adaptation in adult schizophrenic patients and children at risk. In *Schizophrenia: The first ten Dean Award Lectures,* ed. S. R. Dean, 163–204. New York: MSS Publications, 1973.

Honzik, M. P., and J. W. Macfarlane. Personality development and intellectual functioning from 21 months to 40 years. In *Intellectual functioning in adults: Psychological and biological influences,* ed. L. F. Jarvik, C. Eisdorfer, and J. E. Blum, 45–58. New York: Springer, 1973.

Illingworth, R. S., and C. M. Illingworth. *Lessons from childhood.* London: Livingston, 1966.

Rutter, M. Protective factors in children's responses to stress and disadvantage. In *Social competence in children: Primary prevention of psychopathology,* vol. 3, ed. M. W. Kent and J. W. Rolf. Hanover, N.H.: University Press of New England, 1979.

Segal, J. The gentle art of daydreaming. *Family Health,* March 1975, 22–25.

————. A summer dream: Let kids just do nothing. *Washington Post,* June 26, 1983, D-2.

Segal, Z. Too much, too soon. *Health,* February 1984, 64–68.

Stapleton, C., and H. Yahraes. *The importance of play.* DHHS publication no. (ADM) 80-969, 1980.

Werner, E. E., and Ruth S. Smith. *Vulnerable but invincible: A study of resilient children.* New York: McGraw-Hill, 1982.

Winn, M. *Children without childhood.* New York: Pantheon, 1983.

CHAPTER TWO

Birch, H. G. Malnutrition, learning, and intelligence. *American Journal of Public Health* 62, no. 6 (June 1972): 773–84.

Brazelton, T. B. Effect of prenatal drugs on the behavior of the neonate. *American Journal of Psychiatry* 126, no. 9 (March 1970): 1261–66.

Butler, N. R., and H. Goldstein. Smoking in pregnancy and subsequent child development. *British Medical Journal* 4 (1973): 573–75.

Collins, E., and G. Turner. Maternal effects of regular salicylate ingestion in pregnancy. *Lancet* 23 (August 1975): 335–37.

Desmond, M. M., et al. Maternal barbiturate utilization and neonatal withdrawal symptomatology. *The Journal of Pediatrics* 80, no. 2 (February 1972): 190–97.

Dubos, R. *So human an animal.* New York: Scribner, 1968.

Gots, R. E., and B. A. Gots. *Caring for your unborn child.* New York: Bantam, 1979.

Hardy, J. B., and E. D. Mellits. Does maternal smoking during pregnancy have a long-term effect on the child? *Lancet* 2 (December 23, 1972): 1332–36.

Heatherington, E. M., and R. D. Parke. *Child psychology: A contemporary viewpoint,* 2d ed. New York: McGraw-Hill, 1979.

Hill, R. M. Drugs that an unborn baby can't tolerate. *RN Magazine,* August 1977.

Hurlock, E. B. *Child development,* 6th ed. New York: McGraw-Hill, 1978.

Jones, K. L., and D. W. Smith. Recognition of the fetal alcohol syndrome in early infancy. *Lancet* 2 (1973): 999–1001.

Jones, K. L., et al. Outcome in offspring of chronic alcoholic women. *Lancet* 1 (1974): 1076–78.

Luce, G. G., and J. Segal. *Sleep.* New York: Coward-McCann, 1966.

Mirkin, B. L. *Perinatal pharmacology and therapeutics.* New York: Academic Press, 1976.

Morrison, M. *When the baby's life is so much your own.* Food and Drug Administration, DHEW publication no. (FDA) 79-1057, 1979.

Mussen, P. H., J. J. Conger, and J. Kagan. *Essentials of child development and personality.* New York: Harper & Row, 1980.

National Institute on Alcohol Abuse and Alcoholism. *Alcohol and your unborn baby.* DHEW publication no. (ADM) 78-521, 1978.

National Institute on Drug Abuse. *A woman's choice: deciding about drugs.* DHEW publication no. (ADM) 79-820, 1979.

———. *Drug dependence in pregnancy: Clinical management of mother and child.* DHEW publication no. (ADM) 79-778, 1979.

Neuberg, R. Drug dependence and pregnancy: A review of the problems and their management. *Journal of Obstetrics and Gynaecology of the British Commonwealth* 77 (December 1970): 1117–22.

Neumann, L. L. Drug abuse in pregnancy: Its effects on the fetus and newborn infant. In *Drugs and youth: The challenge today,* ed. E. Harms, 1–32. New York: Pergamon Press, 1973.

Ouellette, E., et al. Adverse effects on offspring of maternal alcohol abuse during pregnancy. *New England Journal of Medicine* 297 (1977): 528–30.

Rosen, M. G. The secret brain: Learning before birth. *Harper's,* April 1978, 46–47.

Turner, G., and E. Collins. Fetal effects of regular salicylate ingestion in pregnancy. *Lancet* 2 (August 23, 1975): 338–39.

U.S. Public Health Service. *Smoking and health: A report of the Surgeon General.* DHEW publication no. (PHS) 79-50066, 1979.

Werner, E. E., and R. S. Smith. *Vulnerable but invincible: A study of resilient children.* New York: McGraw-Hill, 1982.

Wilson, J. G. *Environment and birth defects.* New York: Academic Press, 1973.

CHAPTER THREE

Ainsworth, M. D. S., and S. M. Bell. Attachment, exploration, and separation. *Child Development* 41 (1970): 49–68.

Ainsworth, M. D. S., S. M. Bell, and D. J. Stayton. Infant-mother attachment and social development: Socialization as a product of reciprocal responsiveness to signals. In *The integration of the child into the social world,* ed. M. P. Richards. London: Cambridge University Press, 1974.

Apgar, V., and J. Beck. *Is my baby alright?* New York: Simon & Schuster, 1972.

Bower, T. G. R. The visual world of infants. *Scientific American* 215 (1966): 80–92.

Brazelton, T. B. *Infants and mothers: Differences in development.* New York: Dell, 1979.

――――. Demonstrating infants' behavior. *Children Today,* July–August 1981.

Bridger, W. N. Sensory habituation and discrimination in the human neonate. *American Journal of Psychiatry* 117 (1961): 991–96.

Brim, O. C., and J. Kagan, eds. *Constancy and change in human development.* Cambridge, Mass.: Harvard University Press, 1980.

Caputo, D. V., and W. Mandel. Consequences of low birth weight. *Developmental Psychology* 3 (1970): 363–83.

Elkind, D., and I. B. Weiner. *Development of the child.* New York: John Wiley, 1978.

Fantz, R. L. Pattern vision in newborn infants. *Science* 140 (1963): 296–97.

Fraiberg, S. *Every child's birthright.* New York: Basic Books, 1977.

Greenspan, S. P. *Parent-child bonding: The development of intimacy.* Chicago: National Committee for Prevention of Child Abuse, 1980.

Hammond, J. Hearing and response in the newborn. *Developmental Medicine and Child Neurology* 12 (1970): 3–5.

Honzik, M. P. Value and limitations of infant tests: An overview. In *Origins of intelligence,* ed. M. Lewis. New York: Plenum, 1976.

Hunt, J. McV. *Intelligence and experience.* New York: John Wiley, 1961.

Kagan, J. *The second year: The emergence of self-awareness.* Cambridge, Mass.: Harvard University Press, 1981.

Kagan, J., E. Havemann, and J. Segal. *Psychology: An introduction,* 5th ed. New York: Harcourt Brace Jovanovich, 1984.

Kagan, J., and R. E. Klein. Cross-cultural perspectives on early development. *American Psychologist* 28 (1973): 947–61.

Klaus, M. H., T. Leger, and M. A. Trause, eds. *Maternal attachment and mothering disorders: A round table.* New Brunswick, N.J.: Johnson & Johnson Baby Products, 1975.

Leventhal, A. S., and L. P. Lipsitt. Adaptation, pitch discrimination, and sound localization in the neonate. *Child Development* 47 (1976): 237–41.

Lipsitt, L. P. The study of sensory and learning processes in the newborn. *Symposium on neonatal neurology, Clinics in perinatology* 4 (1977): 163–86.

Lipsitt, L. P., T. Engen, and H. Kaye. Developmental changes in the olfactory threshold of the neonate. *Child Development* 34 (1963): 371–76.

Londerville, S., and M. Main. Security of attachment, compliance, and maternal training methods in the second year of life. *Developmental Psychology* 17 (1981): 289–99.

Luce, G. G. The physiological imprint of learning. *Mental Health Program Reports 2.* Public Health Service publication 1743, February 1968.

Maccoby, E., and S. Feldman. Mother-attachment and stranger-reactions in the third year of life. *Monographs of the Society for Research in Child Development* 37 (1972).

McCall, R. B. *Infants: The new knowledge from birth to three.* Cambridge, Mass.: Harvard University Press, 1979. (Adapted by permission. Copyright © by the McCall Children's Trust).

Mussen, P. H., J. J. Conger, and J. Kagan. *Child development and personality,* 4th ed. New York: Harper & Row, 1974.

————. *Essentials of child development and personality.* New York: Harper & Row, 1980.

Newman, B. M., and P. R. Newman. *Infancy and childhood: Development and its contexts.* New York: John Wiley, 1978.

Parke, R. D., and D. B. Sawin. Father-infant interaction in the newborn period: A reevaluation of some current myths. In *Contemporary readings in child psychology,* ed. E. M. Hetherington and R. D. Parke, 290–95. New York: McGraw-Hill, 1977.

Pines, M. Early learning. *Harper's,* April 1978, 50–51.

Pogrebin, L. C. *Growing up free: Raising your child in the 80s.* New York: McGraw-Hill, 1980.

Rutter, M. *Maternal deprivation reassessed,* 2d ed. Harmondsworth, England: Penguin, 1981.

Sroufe, L. A. Attachment and the roots of competence. *Human Development, 81/82.* Guilford, Conn.: Dushkin Publishing Group, 1981, 87–91.

CHAPTER FOUR

Adams, R. S., and B. Biddle. *Realities of teaching.* New York: Holt, 1970.

Anderson, H. H., and J. E. Brewer. Studies of teachers' classroom personalities, II: Effects of teachers' dominative and integrative contacts on children's classroom behavior. *Applied Psychology Monographs* 8 (1946).

Barker, R. G., and P. V. Gump. *Big school, small school.* Stanford: Stanford University Press, 1964.

Baumrind, D. From each according to her ability. *School Review* 80 (1972): 161–97.

Beck, J. *How to raise a brighter child.* New York: Pocket Books, 1975.

Bronfenbrenner, U. The origins of alienation. *Scientific American* 231, no. 2 (August 1974): 53–61.

Chaikin, A., E. Sigler, and V. Derlega. Non-verbal mediators of teacher expectancy effects. *Journal of Personality and Social Psychology* 30 (1974): 144–49.

Churchman, D., and K. Kristy. The guilt-salving myths that day care is better. *Washington Post,* November 16, 1980.

Covington, M. B., and R.G. Berry. *Self-worth and school learning.* New York: Holt, 1976.

Dreskin, W., and W. Dreskin. *The day care decision: What's best for you and your child.* New York: M. Evans, 1983.

Farran, D. C., and C. T. Ramey. Infant day care and attachment behaviors toward mothers and teachers. *Child Development* 48 (1977): 1112–16.

Franco, D. The child's perception of "the teacher" as compared to his perception of "the mother." *Dissertation Abstracts* 24 (1964): 3414–15.

Garmezy, N. Stressors of childhood. In *Stress, coping, and development in children,* ed. N. Garmezy and M. Rutter, 43–84. New York: McGraw-Hill, 1983.

Ginott, H. G. *Between teacher and child.* New York: Avon Books, 1975.

Groobman, D. E., J. R. Forward, and C. Peterson. Attitudes, self-esteem, and learning in formal and informal schools. *Journal of Educational Psychology* 68 (1976): 32–35.

Hall, E. Schooling in a nasty climate. *Psychology Today,* January 1982, 57–63.

Heil, L. M., and C. Washburne. Characteristics of teachers related to children's progress. *Journal of Teacher Education* 12 (1961): 401–06.

Hymes, J. L. *Three to six: Your child starts school.* Public Affairs pamphlet no. 163. New York: Public Affairs Committee, 1950.

Jacobson, A. L. Infant day care: Toward a more human environment. *Young Children* 33 (1978): 14–23.

Joffe, C. Sex role socialization and the nursery school. *Journal of Marriage and the Family* 33 (1971): 467–75.

Kagan, J., R. B. Kearsley, and P. R. Zelazo. *Infancy: Its place in human development.* Cambridge, Mass.: Harvard University Press, 1978.

Kazin, A. *A walker in the city.* New York: Harcourt Brace Jovanovich, 1951.

Kearsley, R. B., et al. Differences in separation protest between day care and home reared infants. *Pediatrics* 55 (1975): 171–75.

Keniston, K. *All our children.* New York: Harcourt Brace Jovanovich, 1977.

————. The 11-year-olds of today are the computer terminals of tomorrow. *New York Times,* February 19, 1976.

LaCrosse, E. R. *Day care for America's children.* Public Affairs pamphlet no. 470. New York: Public Affairs Committee, July 1975.

Lass, A. H., and N. L. Tasman, eds. *Going to school: An anthology of prose about teachers and students.* New York: New American Library, 1980.

Maeroff, G. I. *Don't blame the kids: The trouble with America's public schools.* New York: McGraw-Hill, 1982.

Maugham, S. *Of human bondage.* New York: Doubleday, 1915.

Miller, M. S. *Childstress: How parents and teachers can understand and answer their children's signals of stress.* New York: Doubleday, 1982.

Norman, L. E. Writers for life. *The Center Magazine.* Cited in *Going to school: An anthology of prose about teachers and students,* eds. A. H. Lass and N. L. Tasman. New York: New American Library, 1980.

Norman, M. Substitutes for mother. *Human Behavior,* February 1978.

Office of Human Development Services, Administration for Children, Youth and Families. *Day care: A statement of principles.* DHEW publication no. (OHDS) 78-31055, 1978.

Pickhardt, I. Daycare: By choice, not by chance. *Washington Post,* August 19, 1981.

Pines, M. A head start in the nursery. *Psychology Today,* September 1979, 56–68.

Quinton, D., and M. Rutter. Parenting behavior of mothers raised "in care." In *Practical lessons from longitudinal studies,* ed. A. R. Nicol. Chichester, England: John Wiley, 1983.

Rosenthal, R., and L. Jacobsen. *Pygmalion in the classroom.* New York: Holt, 1968.

Rutter, M. School effects on pupil progress: Research findings and policy applications. *Child Development* 54 (1983): 1–29.

Schlechty, P. C., and V. S. Vance. Recruitment, selection, and retention: The shape of the teaching force. *The Elementary School Journal* 83 (March 1983): 469–87.

Smith, B. *A tree grows in Brooklyn.* New York: Harper & Row, 1943.

Vance, V. S., and P. C. Schlechty. *The structure of the teaching occupation and the characteristics of teachers.* Report prepared for the National Institute of Education, Contract NIE-81-0100, 1982.

White, T. H. *In search of history.* New York: Harper & Row, 1978.

Yando, R. M., and J. Kagan. The effect of teacher tempo on the child. *Child Development* 39 (1968): 27–34.

CHAPTER FIVE

Anasatasi, A. *Psychological testing,* 5th ed. New York: Macmillan, 1982.

Belmont, L., and F. A. Marolla. Birth order, family size and intelligence. *Science* 182 (1973): 1096–1101.

Curtiss, S. *A psycholinguistic study of a modern-day "wild child."* New York: Academic Press, 1977.

Erlenmeyer-Kimling, L., and L. F. Jarvik. Genetics and intelligence. *Science* 142 (1963): 1477–79.

Glover, J. A. *A Parent's guide to intelligence testing*. Chicago: Nelson-Hall, 1979.

Goertzel, V., and M. G. Goertzel. *Cradles of eminence*. Boston: Little, Brown, 1962.

Gould, S. J. *The mismeasure of man*. New York: W. W. Norton, 1981.

Guilford, J. P. *The nature of human intelligence*. New York: McGraw-Hill, 1967.

Hamachek, D. E. *Psychology in teaching, learning, and growth*. Boston: Allyn and Bacon, 1979.

Harrell, T. W., and M. S. Harrell. Army general classification test scores for civilian occupations. *Educational and Psychological Measurement* 5 (1945): 229–39.

Heatherington, E. M., and R. D. Parke. *Child psychology: A contemporary viewpoint*. New York: McGraw-Hill, 1979.

Honzik, M. P., J. W. Macfarlane, and L. Allen. The stability of mental test performance between two and eighteen years. *Journal of Experimental Education* 17 (1948): 309–24.

James, W. *The writings of William James*. Chicago: University of Chicago Press, 1978.

Jensen, A. R. The heritability of intelligence. *Saturday Evening Post*, 1972, 9.

Kagan, J. The baby's elastic mind. *Human Nature*, January 1978, 66–73.

_____. *The growth of the child: Reflections on human development*. New York: W. W. Norton, 1979.

Kamin, L., with H. J. Eysenck. *The intelligence controversy*. New York: John Wiley, 1981.

Kimble, G. A., N. Garmezy, and E. Zigler. *Principles of general psychology*, 5th ed. New York: John Wiley, 1980.

Koluchova, J. Severe deprivation in twins. *Journal of Child Psychology and Psychiatry* 13 (1972): 107–14.

Maccoby, E. E., and C. N. Jacklin. *The psychology of sex differences*. Stanford: Stanford University Press, 1974.

MacKinnon, D. W. What makes a person creative? *Saturday Review*, February 10, 1962, 15–17.

McCall, R. B. *Infants: The new knowledge from birth to three*. Cambridge, Mass.: Harvard University Press, 1979.

Mearns, H. Every child has a gift—find it! encourage it! In *Raising kids*. New York: Berkley Books, 1981.

Meece, J. L., et al. Sex differences in math achievement: toward a model of academic choice. *Psychological Bulletin* 91 (1982): 324–48.

Moore, L. P. *Does this mean my kid's a genius?* New York: McGraw-Hill, 1981.

Murphy, G. *Human potentialities.* New York: Basic Books, 1958.

Mussen, P., J. J. Conger, and J. Kagan. *Child development and personality,* 4th ed. Harper & Row, 1974.

Newsweek. The gifted child. October 23, 1978.

Pines, M. The civilizing of Genie. *Psychology Today,* September 1981, 28.

Prather, H. *Notes to myself: My struggle to become a person.* New York: Bantam Books, 1976.

Roberts, J. L. More gifted children get classes that match their own fast pace. *Wall Street Journal,* 1982, 1.

Rutter, M. Intelligence and childhood psychiatric disorder. *British Journal of Social and Clinical Psychology* 6 (1964): 71–83.

Sameroff, A. J. Early influences on development: Fact or fancy? *Merrill Palmer Quarterly* 21 (1974): 267–94.

Scarr, S. Testing *for* children: Assessment and the many determinants of intellectual competence. *American Psychologist* 36 (1981): 1159–66.

Scarr, S., and R. A. Weinberg. IQ test performance of black children adopted by white families. *American Psychologist* 31 (October 1976): 726–39.

————. Attitudes, interests, and I.Q. *Human Nature,* April 1978, 29–36.

Skeels, H. Adult status of children with contrasting life experiences. *Monographs of the society for research in child development* 31, no. 3 (1966).

Spearman, C. *The abilities of man.* London: Macmillan, 1927.

Thurstone, L. L. *Primary mental abilities.* Psychometric Monographs no. 1. Chicago: University of Chicago Press, 1938.

————. Theories of intelligence. *Scientific Monthly,* February 1946, 101–12.

Vail, Priscilla L. The gifted child: Common sense and uncommon children. *Educating exceptional children, 79/80.* Guilford, Conn.: Dushkin Publishing Group, 1979.

Wechsler, D. Intelligence defined and undefined. *American Psychologist* 30 (1975): 135–59.

CHAPTER SIX

Argyle, M., and P. Robinson. Two origins of achievement motivation. *British Journal of Social and Clinical Psychology* 1 (1962): 107–20.

Biller, H. B. *Father, child, and sex role.* Lexington, Mass.: D. C. Heath, 1971.

Blanchard, R. W., and H. B. Biller. Father availability and academic performance among third grade boys. *Developmental Psychology* 4 (1971): 301–05.

Bronfenbrenner, U. Some familial antecedents of responsibility and leadership in adolescents. In *Leadership and interpersonal behavior,* ed. L. Petrullo and B. M. Bass, 239–72. New York: Holt, 1961.

Carlsmith, L. Effect of early father absence on scholastic aptitude. *Harvard Educational Review* 34 (1964): 3–21.

Davies, A. P. *The mind and faith of A. Powell Davies,* ed. D. W. Orville. Garden City, N.Y.: Doubleday, 1959.

Elder, G. H., Jr. Family structure and educational attainment: A cross-national analysis. *American Sociological Review* 30 (1965): 81–96.

Falbo, T. Relationship between birth category, achievement, and interpersonal orientation. *Journal of Personality and Social Psychology* 41 (1981): 121–31.

Garfinkel, D. The best "Jewish" mother in the world. *Psychology Today,* September 1983, 56–60.

Grinker, R. R. Poor little rich kid. *Psychology Today,* October 1977, 74.

Hamachek, D. E. *Psychology in teaching, learning, and growth,* 2d ed. Boston: Allyn and Bacon, 1979.

Hart, M. *Act one: An autobiography.* New York: Random House, 1976.

Hartup, W. W. Peer interaction and the development of the individual child. In *Psychopathology and Child Development,* ed. E. Schopler and R. J. Reichler, 203–18. New York: Plenum, 1976.

Hiroto, D. S. Locus of control and learned helplessness. *Journal of Experimental Psychology* 102 (1974): 187–93.

Honzik, M. P., and J. W. Macfarlane. Personality development and intellectual functioning from 21 months to 40 years. In *Intellectual functioning in adults: Psychological and biological influences,* ed. L. F. Jarvik, C. Eisdorfer, and J. E. Blum, 45–58. New York: Springer, 1973.

Illingworth, R. S., and C. M. Illingworth. *Lessons from childhood.* London: Livingston, 1966.

Kandel, D. B., and G. S. Lesser. *Youth in two worlds.* San Francisco: Jossey-Bass, 1972.

Lamb, M. E. Fathers: Forgotten contributors to child development. *Human Development* 18 (1975): 245–66.

Lamb, M. E., ed. *The role of the father in child development.* New York: John Wiley, 1976.

Macfarlane, J. W. From infancy to adulthood. *Childhood Education* 39 (1963): 336–42.

Maier, S. F., M. E. P. Seligman, and R. L. Solomon. Pavlovian fear conditioning and learned helplessness. In *Punishment and aversive behavior*, ed. B. A. Campbell and R. M. Church. New York: Appleton Century Crofts, 1969.

McClelland, D. C. *The achieving society*. Princeton: Van Nostrand, 1961.

McClelland, D. C., et al. *Talent and society*. Princeton: Van Nostrand, 1958.

Mead, M. *Blackberry winter*. New York: Morrow, 1972.

Mischel, W. How children postpone pleasure. In *Contemporary readings in child psychology*, 2d ed., ed. E. M. Hetherington and R. D. Oarke, 375–79. New York: McGraw-Hill, 1981.

Morrow, W. R., and R. C. Wilson. Family relations of bright high-achieving and underachieving high school boys. *Child Development* 32 (1961): 501–10.

Norman, R. D. The interpersonal values of achieving and nonachieving gifted children. *Journal of Psychology* 64 (1966): 49–57.

Papalia, D. E., and S. W. Olds. *Human development*, 2d ed. New York: McGraw-Hill, 1981.

Parke, R. D. *Fathers*. Cambridge, Mass.: Harvard University Press, 1981.

Quinton, D., and M. Rutter. Parenting behavior of mothers raised "in care." In *Practical lessons from longitudinal studies*, ed. A. R. Nicol. Chichester, England: John Wiley, 1983.

Saroyan, W. *The bicycle rider in Beverly Hills*. New York: Scribner, 1952.

Segal, J. Are your children too busy to dream? *Family Circle*, April 1964, 64.

———. In defense of the Jewish mother. *Washington Post*, April 2, 1978, 1–2.

———. Perseverence. *Family Circle*, March 1963, 52.

Segal, J., and H. Yahraes. *A child's journey: Forces that shape the lives of the young*. New York: McGraw-Hill, 1978.

Straus, M. A. *Behind closed doors: Violence in the American family*. New York: Doubleday, 1981.

Sutton-Smith, B., and B. G. Rosenberg. *The sibling*. New York: Holt, 1970.

Winterbottom, M. R. The relation of need for achievement to learning experience in independence and mastery. In *Motives in fantasy, action and society*, ed. J. W. Atkinson, 453–78. New York: Van Nostrand, 1958.

Yahraes, H. Physical violence in families. In *Families today: A research sampler on families and children (Vol. II)*, ed. E. Corfman. DHEW publication no. (ADM) 98-815, 1979.

CHAPTER SEVEN

Anderson, C. W. Parent-child relationships: A context for reciprocal developmental influence. *The Counseling Psychologist* 9 (1981): 35–44.

Bandura, *Aggression.* Englewood Cliffs, N.J.: Prentice-Hall, 1973.

Bane, M. J. *Here to stay.* New York: Basic Books, 1976.

Clark, K. R. Former "videoholic" campaigns to stop families from shooting up on television. *Los Angeles Times,* November 25, 1982, part XI, 6.

Erickson, R., and P. Bohannan. Stepping in: A stepfather faces real challenges. *Psychology Today,* January 1978, 52.

Eron, L. D., and L. R. Huesmann. Adolescent aggression and television. *Annals of the New York Academy of Sciences* 347 (1980): 319–31.

Fraiberg, S. *Every child's birthright: In defense of mothering.* New York: Basic Books, 1977.

Granzberg, G., and J. Steinbring. Television and the Canadian Indian. Technical Report, Department of Anthropology, University of Winnipeg, 1980.

Grinker, R. R. Poor little rich kid. *Psychology Today,* October 1977, 74.

Hafer, W. K. *Coping with bereavement from death or divorce.* Englewood Cliffs, N.J.: Prentice-Hall, 1981.

Hammond, J. Children of divorce: implications for counselors. *The School Counselor* 27 (1979): 7–14.

Hetherington, E. M., M. Cox, and R. Cox. The aftermath of divorce. In *Mother-child, father-child relations,* ed. J. H. Stevens, Jr. and M. Mathews. Washington, D.C.: National Association for the Education of Young Children, 1978.

Hetherington, E. M., and R. D. Parke. *Child psychology: A contemporary viewpoint.* New York: McGraw-Hill, 1979.

McCall, R. B., and M. Hetherington. Tracking children through the changing family. *Monitor,* May 1981, 4–5.

Mead, M. The once and future home. *Washington Post,* July 4, 1976, 1.

Moreland, J., and A. I. Schwebel. A gender role transcendent perspective on fathering. *The Counseling Psychologist* 9 (1981): 45–53.

Novak, M. The family out of favor. *Harper's,* April 1976, 37–46.

Parke, R. D. *Fathers.* Cambridge, Mass.: Harvard University Press, 1981.

Pavenstedt, E. A comparison of the child-rearing environment of upper-lower and very low-lower class families. *American Journal of Orthopsychiatry* 35 (1965): 89–98.

Pearl, D. *Television and behavior: Ten years of scientific progress and implications for the eighties. Vol. 1: Summary report.* DHHS publication no. (ADM) 82-1195, 1982.

Powell, J. Educational crisis? Blame the parent. *Washington Post,* November 12, 1983.

Rooney, R. Helping children through divorce. *McCall's,* April 1984, 42–48.

Rothchild, J., and S. Wolf. *The children of the counterculture.* New York: Doubleday, 1976.

Rubin, Z. *Liking and loving.* New York: Holt, 1973.

Segal, J. Growing up smart. *Washington Post,* March 29, 1981, 1.

Segal, J., and J. Cooper. Television, mass media, and child development. *Basic Handbook of Child Psychiatry* 4 (1979): 426–31.

Segal, J., and Z. Segal. Video tripping. *Health* 15 (April 1983): 24–30.

Shipman, G. Memories that make families strong. *Parents,* December 1977, 30.

Singer, J. L., and D. G. Singer. *Television, imagination, and aggression: A study of preschoolers.* Hillsdale, N.J.: Erlbaum, 1980.

Toffler, A. *Future shock.* New York: Random House, 1971.

U.S. Bureau of the Census. *Current population reports.* Series P-20, no. 372, 1982.

Wallerstein, J. Children of divorce: stress and developmental tasks. In *Stress, coping, and human development in children,* ed. N. Garmezy and M. Rutter. New York: McGraw-Hill, 1983.

Wallerstein, J., and J. Kelly. The effects of parental divorce: Experiences of the preschool child. *Journal of Child Psychiatry* 14 (1975): 600–16.

_____. Children and divorce: A review. *Social Work* 24 (1979): 468–75.

_____. *Surviving the breakup: How children and parents cope with divorce.* New York: Basic Books, 1980.

Wynne, L. C. Methodologic and conceptual issues in the study of schizophrenics and their families. *Journal of Psychiatric Research,* supplement 1 6 (1968): 185–99.

CHAPTER EIGHT

Adams, B. *Like it is: Facts and feelings about handicaps from kids who know.* New York: Walker, 1979.

Bawkin, H., and R. M. Bawkin. *Behavior disorders in children,* 4th ed. Philadelphia: Saunders, 1972, 462–63.

Benton, A. L., and D. Pearl. *Dyslexia: An appraisal of current knowledge.* New York: Oxford University Press, 1978.

Cantwell, D. Hyperkinetic syndrome. In *Child psychiatry: Modern approaches,* ed. M. Rutter and M. Hersov, 524–55. Oxford: Blackwell Scientific Publications, 1976.

Cruikshank, W. M. Myths and realities in learning disabilities. *Educating exceptional children, 82/83.* Guilford, Conn.: Dushkin Publishing Group, 1982, 166–72.

Farnham-Diggory, S. *Learning disabilities: A psychological perspective.* Cambridge, Mass.: Harvard University Press, 1978.

Frederick, C. Current trends in suicidal behavior in the United States. *American Journal of Psychotherapy* 32 (1978): 172–200.

Gold, S. R. The CAP control theory of drug abuse. In *Theories on drug abuse: Selected contemporary perspectives,* ed. D. J. Lettieri, M. Sayers, and H. W. Pearson, 8–11. National Institute on Drug Abuse, DHHS publication no. (ADM) 80-967, 1980.

Hersov, L. School refusal. In Rutter, M., and Hersov, L. *Child psychiatry: Modern approaches,* ed. M. Rutter and L. Hersov, 455–86. Oxford: Blackwell Scientific Publications, 1976.

Johnston, L. D., J. G. Bachman, and P. M. O'Malley. *Student drug use in America.* Rockville, Md.: National Institute on Drug Abuse, 1981.

Kelly, M. Parent's almanac: The hyperactive child. *Washington Post,* October 14, 1982, D5.

Lipton, M. *Myths and realities in biological treatments in psychiatry.* Seminar presented at Center for Advanced Study in the Behavioral Sciences, Stanford, Calif., April 23, 1980.

McKnew, D. H., Jr., L. Cytryn, and H. Yahraes. *Why isn't Johnny crying?* New York: W. W. Norton, 1983.

Misra, R. K. Achievement, anxiety, and addiction. In *Theories on drug abuse: Selected contemporary perspectives,* ed. D. J. Lettieri, M. Sayers, and H. W. Pearson, 212–14. National Institute on Drug Abuse, DHHS publication no. (ADM) 80-967, 1980.

Murphy, G. *Human potentialities.* New York: Basic Books, 1958.

National Institute on Alcohol Abuse and Alcoholism. *Facts about alcohol and alcoholism.* DHHS publication no. 81-2328, September 1981.

National Institute on Drug Abuse. *Parents: What you can do about drug abuse.* DHHS publication no. ADM 83-1267, 1978.

Petti, T. A. Depression in children: A significant disorder. *Psychosomatics* 22 (1981): 444–47.

Ross, A. O. *Learning disability: The unrealized potential.* New York: McGraw-Hill, 1977.

Rutter, M. *Helping troubled children.* Harmondsworth, England: Penguin, 1975.

Saxena, K. M., J. D. Crawford, and N. B. Talbot. Childhood thyrotoxicosis: A long-term perspective. *British Medical Journal* 2 (1964): 1153–58.

Segal, J. Children get depressed, too. *Woman's Day,* June 26, 1979, 34.

Smith, D. W., R. M. Blizzard, and L. Wilkins. The mental prognosis in hypothyroidism of infancy and childhood: A review of 128 cases. *Pediatrics* 19 (1957): 1011–22.

Smith, S. *No easy answers: teaching the learning-disabled child.* Boston: Little, Brown, 1979.

Twiford, R. *A child with a problem: A guide to the psychological disorders of children.* Englewood Cliffs, N.J.: Prentice-Hall, 1979.

Webb, T. E., and F. A. Oski. Iron deficiency anemia and scholastic achievement in young adolescents. *Journal of Pediatrics* 82 (1973): 827.

Wehrle, S. *Caring about kids: Dyslexia.* DHHS publication no. ADM 80-616, 1978.

Werkman, S. L., L. Shifman, and T. Skelly. Psychosocial correlates of iron deficiency anemia in early childhood. *Psychosomatic Medicine* 26 (March-April 1964): 125–34.

Wolf, A. W. M. *Your child's emotional health.* Public Affairs Pamphlet no. 264. New York: Public Affairs Committee, 1975.

CHAPTER NINE

Abeson, A., and J. Zettel. The end of the quiet revolution: The Education for All Handicapped Children Act of 1975. *Exceptional Children* (October 1977).

Adams, E. M. How to prepare the child for the psychologist. *Educating exceptional children, 79/80.* Guilford, Conn.: Dushkin Publishing Group, 1979, 57–58.

Axline, V. M. *Play therapy.* New York: Ballantine Books, 1969.

Barman, A., and L. Cohen. *Help for your troubled child,* Public Affairs pamphlet no. 454. New York: Public Affairs Committee, 1970.

Berger, M. Psychological testing. In Rutter, M. and Hersov, L., Eds. *Child psychiatry: Modern approaches,* ed. M. Rutter and L. Hersov. Oxford: Blackwell Scientific Publications, 1976.

Herndon, E. B. *Your child and testing.* Pueblo, Colo.: Consumer Information Center, 1981.

Hobbs, N. *The futures of children.* San Francisco: Jossey-Bass, 1975.

Mercer, J. R. Psychological assessment and the rights of children. In *The classification of children,* vol. 1, ed. N. Hobbs. San Francisco: Jossey-Bass, 1975.

Rappoport, P. S. When your child needs therapy. *Parents,* November 1981, 72.

Rutter, M. *Helping troubled children.* Harmondsworth, England: Penguin, 1975.

Shaw, C. *When your child needs help.* New York: Morrow, 1972.

Wiener, D. N. *A consumer's guide to psychotherapy.* New York: Hawthorn Books, 1975.

CHAPTER TEN

Kagan, J., E. Havemann, and J. Segal. *Psychology: An introduction,* 5th ed. New York: Harcourt Brace Jovanovich, 1984.

Yamamoto, K. Children's ratings of the stressfulness of experiences. *Developmental Psychology* 15 (1979): 581–82.

⌇ৡ Index